Confronting the Cults

Gordon R. Lewis

PRESBYTERIAN AND
REFORMED PUBLISHING COMPANY
Box 817
Phillipsburg, New Jersey 08865

To

MY PARENTS

for more than fifty years together
examples of stedfast fidelity to
the gospel

Copyright 1966

Presbyterian and Reformed Publishing Company

Library of Congress Catalog Card No. 66-26791

0-87552-323-4

Sixth printing, January 1983

PHOTOLITHOPRINTED BY CUSHING - MALLOY, INC.
ANN ARBOR, MICHIGAN, UNITED STATES OF AMERICA

PREFACE
(Second Edition)

How exciting it is to hear from people who have come to understand the gospel of God's grace and to trust in the living Christ as the Holy Spirit has used the approach of *Confronting the Cults!*

Much literature on the cults seems content to pronounce their teaching heretical and dismiss their adherents with disdain. In contrast, a distinctive objective of this is to lovingly show where cultic teaching errs and what a person must believe to receive eternal life.

The essentials of authentic faith reflected in the seven questions which are designed to help the Christian identify a missionary of the cults (pp. 6-7) are no mere private interpretation of this author. They portray (1) the great hope of Old Testament prophecy, however dimly foreshadowed at times, (2) the supreme achievement of Jesus Christ's incarnation, according to the Gospels, (3) the focal point of the Apostle's messages to non-Christians in Acts, and (4) the foundational teaching of the rest of the New Testament. The formulation of each question is based on an explicit New Testament passage.

In the attempt to write an approach useable for laymen, I may have obscured other scholarly principles upon which the approach is based. I quote the Scriptures, to the best of my ability, in accord with their grammatical, historical, and doctrinal contexts. Because of the frequent abuse of the Bible in the cults, one of the most helpful studies for those ministering to them is the science of biblical interpretation. Several books on hermeneutics (the science of scriptural interpretation) are available (B. Ramm, *Protestant Biblical Hermeneutics,* Baker Book House; R. C. Sproul, *Knowing Scripture,* InterVarsity Press; N. T. Sterrett, *How to Understand Your Bible,* InterVarsity Press).

Confronting the Cults is representative of my entire system of apologetics. It seeks to defend the Christian faith against the cultists' conflicting claims. Alleged revelations by the cults are examined in the light of Scripture and by a way of knowing (epistemology) developed at length in my *Testing Christianity's Truth-Claims: Approaches to*

Christian Apologetics (Moody Press). For example, a test of truth which philosophers call the coherence criterion is here applied to the Mormons' additional revelations. This test requires that the teachings be logically consistent and factually accurate. The Mormon "revelations" come woefully short on both standards and hence cannot be true (pp. 45-48). In conflicting interpretations of Scripture, the same criterion applies. We must accept that interpretation as true which consistently accounts for the greatest amount of the grammatical, historical, and doctrinal evidence on the subject. Arguments and interpretations in accord with these standard principles (as my apologetics text shows) cannot be dismissed as purely subjective opinion.

This revision of *Confronting the Cults* differs from the first edition in that it contains updated statistics and minor revisions and corrections.

GORDON R. LEWIS
September 14, 1978

PREFACE

Confronting the Cults attempts an approach which is at once thoughtful, usable, and challenging.

Responsible distinctions between cultic perversions and genuine Christianity require careful thought. Only a thorough investigation of the New Testament can reveal what explicit teachings, if any, must be believed in order to receive eternal life. This genuinely Christian faith may be clearly contrasted to others by putting these Scriptural truths in the form of seven questions. Anticipated answers to them are found in the cult's most influential publications. Reflecting upon these standard replies, the Christian studies relevant Scripture to help, not hurt people influenced by the cults.

This Biblical approach to the cults may be used in several different ways. The seven leading questions not only enable any Christian to recognize counterfeit Christianity. They also suggest ways in which Christians may take the initiative in discussions with neighbors, friends or callers from the cults and direct them to the heart of the gospel. The major divisions within each chapter are marked by one of these Scriptural questions. A most profitable doctrinal use of the book would compare and contrast the teachings of these major cults on one or more of the fundamental issues.

Beyond this, the work seeks to present a multiple challenge. It calls Christians to develop an attitude toward the cultists that is conducive of understanding, fairness and meaningful communication. It challenges Christians to learn from the cults the secrets of their effectiveness in our twentieth century world. It constitutes a summons to all who may be "playing church" to dedicate themselves to confronting the cults with the one gospel of Jesus Christ — the Lord of all.

The author wishes to express his gratitude to the Reverend Edward L. Hayes, Associate Professor of Christian Education and Dean, Conservative Baptist Theological Seminary, for preparing the sections entitled, "Suggestions for Teachers."

The Biblical citations, unless otherwise indicated, in chapters I to V are from the King James version; in chapter VI from *The Berkeley Version* (Grand Rapids, Michigan: Zondervan Publishing House, 1959); and in chapter VII from the *New American Standard Bible* (La Habra, California: Foundations Press, Publisher for the Lockman Foundation, 1963).

CONTENTS

THE AUTHOR

Gordon R. Lewis has been professor of systematic theology and Christian philosophy at Conservative Baptist Theological Seminary, Denver, Colorado, since 1958. Previously, he taught at Baptist Bible Seminary, Johnson City, New York, and served as a visiting professor of theology at Union Biblical Seminary, Yavatmal, Maharashtra, India (1973). He held the pastorate of People's Baptist Church, Hamilton Park, Delaware, and several interim pastorates. Lewis also served as president of the newly-organized Evangelical Philosophical Society in 1978.

Lewis has published articles in several Christian periodicals and scholarly journals and is the author of five books: *Confronting the Cults* (1966), *Decide for Yourself: A Workbook on Contemporary Challenges to Christian Faith* (1974), *What Everyone Should Know About Transcendental Meditation* (1974), and *Testing Christianity's Truth-Claims* (1976).

Professor Lewis studied at Baptist Bible Seminary and Cornell University, earning degrees at Gordon College (A.B.), Faith Theological Seminary (M.Div.), and Syracuse University (M.A. and Ph.D. in philosophy).

1

The Bible, The Christian, and
The Cults

It is safe to say without fear of successful contradiction that confrontation with the cults will be more frequent in the future than in the past. Increasing numbers of your relatives, friends, associates and neighbors will join the cults. Repeatedly you will be the target of cult propaganda via literature, radio, and television. At your door you will face persistent representatives of the cults. They are with us *en masse*, and they are here for a long time to come. For a number of reasons it is safe to make such a prediction.

Intensification of cult activity is foreshadowed by their phenomenal growth since 1900. At the dawn of the twentieth century the cults were indistinguishable as a tiny atom, but exploding like atomic bombs the cults have mushroomed upon the American religious horizon. Since 1900 the Mormons have skyrocketed from an insignificant 250,000 members to 3,966,000. The Unity School of Christianity claimed but 3,000 in 1900, but now mails its devotional booklet, *Daily Word,* to 2,000,000. Estimates place the Christian Scientists at 48,000 in 1900; they now have 3,500 churches in 57 countries. The Jehovah's Witnesses, who had but 35,000 adherents in 1900, now list 554,018 active American "ministers."[1] Fallout from these and other explosive cults will continue to concern Christians in the future.

Is not increase of counterfeit Christianity to be expected toward the end of the age? The prophecies of Christ and Paul may well apply to the cults. When Jesus was asked for signs of the end of the age and His return to earth, He spoke not only of wars, rumors of wars, famines, pestilences, and earthquakes; He also declared "many shall come in my name saying, I am Christ, and shall deceive many . . . many false prophets shall arise" (Mt. 24:5,11). Paul wrote, "Now the Spirit speaketh expressly that in the latter times some shall depart from the faith, giving heed to seducing spirits and doctrines of demons" (I Tim. 4:1). Paul also said, "the time will come when they will not endure sound doctrine, but after their own lusts shall they heap to themselves teachers having itching ears; and they shall turn away their ears from the truth and shall be turned into fables (II Tim. 4:3-4). According to Scripture, then, we have reason to expect multiplying cult memberships.

You will be increasingly faced with the cults, we predict, because of their number. Mormonism, Unity, Christian Science, Jehovah's Witnesses, and Spiritualism are among the most influential, but there are many others. You will hear from cults like Theosophy, New Thought, Divine Science, Rosicrucianism, Moral Rearmament, Swedenborgianism, Destiny of America (Anglo-Israelism), The Kingdoms of Father Divine, Christadelphianism, the Dukhobors, Fountain of the World, I Am, Psychiana, and the snake handling Holiness Branch of the Church of God in Tennessee and Kentucky.

Furthermore, the cults are here to stay because of their present global power. A Baptist missionary to South America affirmed that he had more opposition from the cults than from Roman Catholicism. A Philippine pastor considers the greatest threat to evangelicalism in his country to be a newly formed cult. What is true in South America and the Philippines seems to be universal. Evangelist Billy Graham sums it up: "I have traveled to many of our mission fields; I have talked with our missionaries and mission leaders. I know that the problem of cults is not exaggerated there or in the United States. This is a real challenge."[2]

As their history foreshadows, as the Bible predicts, as their number portends, and as their universal impact assures, you will confront the cults tomorrow. With Dr. Carl F. H. Henry we conclude, "On the basis of past performance, it is safe to prognosticate that within the next decade, all things remaining constant, the cults will intensify their propaganda and their 'sheep stealing' activities three to four times their present rate."[3] This being the case, Christians can no longer ignore the cults or dismiss them with a smirk. Rather, wise Christians must seek mature understanding of the cults in order to meet their challenge.

What Is a Cult?

The term cult here designates a religious group which claims authorization by Christ and the Bible but neglects or distorts the gospel, the central message of the Savior and the Scripture.

First, a cult is a religious movement. As such it ought not be confused with an essentially non-religious enterprise. The confusion of the non-religious with the religious is illustrated in the following letter to a popular newspaper columnist.

> DEAR ABBY: Our daughter is 19 and away at school. She writes that she is going with a man who teaches Judo. We are good Christians. Are we wrong for wanting her to go with people of her own faith?   KHV
>
> DEAR MRS. K.H.V.: Judo is short for Jujitsu — the art of self-defense without weapons. Better check the man's spiritual weapons.

Second, a cult claims the support of Christ and the Bible. Religions of the world which make no such claims are not Christian cults. Hindus, Buddhists, Muslims, and Shintoists quote neither Scripture nor Christ in an authoritative manner. They may note similarities to Christianity but do not base their teachings upon a Biblical rule of faith and practice. Leaders of the cults, on the other hand, claim to follow Christ and may quote Scripture voluminously.

Third, a cult nevertheless misses the heart of Christianity. What, then, is central in Christianity? The gospel is central because Christian life is founded upon it. The gospel proclaims the good news of Christ's personal Lordship and atoning work in fulfillment of Scriptural prediction. Paul succinctly summarizes the gospel in I Corinthians 15:3-4, "Christ died for our sins according to the Scriptures." Upon this message life is established. Hearing this good news a sinner trusts Christ Himself and finds spiritual life in union with Him (Eph. 1:13). Furthermore, according to Christ and the apostles, the Old Testament focuses upon this same gospel (Lk. 24:25-27,44-47; Acts 10:43), and so does the New Testament when understood according to sound principles of interpretation. Confirming this conclusion is the fact that the great doctrinal affirmations through the centuries of church history exalt Christ crucified for sinners and risen from the dead. Whoever fails to give pre-eminence to the gospel has missed the heart of Christianity.

But how, you say, can people accept the Bible and omit its central emphasis? The answer is at least twofold: (1) they adopt an additional authority alongside the Bible, or (2) they give prominence to a secondary tenet in place of the core of the Christian faith. In the first instance authority lies in the Bible plus Mary Baker Eddy's *Science and Health with Key to the Scriptures,* or the Bible plus *The Book of Mormon,* or the Bible plus alleged communications from the spirits of dead persons. Usually this other authority takes precedence over the Biblical in practice if not in theory. That is why Theodore G. Taggert can say that "Cults owe their origin more immediately to seers or prophets who claim to have received special revelations. These revelations are of such character as to supplant the Bible and introduce elements which are in conflict with the commonly accepted Christian tradition."[4]

Second, although a cult may not set aside Scripture for another source of authority, it nevertheless distorts the central message of inscripturated revelation. Upon the discovery of what is thought to be a truer or deeper understanding of the Bible or early Christianity, a group will "lose sight of the right distinction between fundamentals and non-fundamentals,"[5] separate from historic Christianity (usually with a bitter attack upon it), and form a distinct organization. Bernard Ramm explains,

> A cult is a religious group which places a secondary need in the position of a primary need. Any group which puts its emphasis on health, or mental hygiene, or some religio-political program is cultic. The chief enemies of man are sin and death (I Cor. 15), and the divine remedy is Jesus Christ crucified and risen from the dead. This is the first witness of the Bible (II Tim. 3:15). If the cultists heard the Holy Spirit they would hear this message. The fact that they do not so speak indicates that they do not hear the voice of the Spirit, which in turn means that they have an improper principle of religious authority.[6]

A cult, then, is any religious movement which claims the backing of Christ or the Bible, but distorts the central message of Christianity by (1) an additional revelation, and (2) by displacing a fundamental tenet of the faith with a secondary matter.[7] (Judo does not qualify!)

Identifying Cults

It is one thing to define "cult" connotatively and another to identify specific groups denoted by the term. Adherents of the cults sincerely claim to be devoted followers of Christ. The cults have Sunday Schools, church services, radio programs, telecasts, revival services, prophetic conferences, Bible correspondence schools, attractive magazines, books, tracts, miracle working power, mission societies, and challenging youth activities. Counterfeits always look genuine.

But the appearance of many marks of Christianity does not guarantee the validity of their claims. Jesus Christ, in the Sermon on the Mount, warned "Beware of false prophets which come to you in sheep's clothing but are inwardly ravening wolves" (Mt. 7:15). Paul had to alert the New Testament Christians to false apostles and deceitful workers who transformed themselves into apostles of Christ (II Cor. 11:13-15).

Neither is the quotation of Scripture in itself certification of orthodoxy, for it is possible to wrest the Scriptures to one's own destruction (II Pet. 3:16) or handle the word of God deceitfully (II Cor. 4:2). Nor is miraculous power proof in itself that a group must be of God. Difficult as it may be to persuade a healthy disciple of Mary Baker Eddy that Christian Science is cultic, the evidence of healing alone cannot demonstrate the authenticity of the religion. According to the Bible the Egyptians were able to duplicate plagues brought to pass by the power of God through Moses (Ex. 7:11-12, 22; 8:7). Other passages teach the power of Satan and his hosts to perform miracles (II Thess. 2:9; Rev. 13:13; 16:14; 19:20). Our Lord acknowledged that false Christs and false prophets would "shew great signs and wonders" (Mt. 24:24) and He foretold the judgment day when "Many will say to me . . . Lord, Lord, have we not prophesied in thy name? and in thy name have cast out devils? and in thy name done many wonderful works? And then will I profess unto them, I never knew you; Depart from me, ye that work iniquity" (Mt. 7:22-23).

How, then, can anyone know whom to believe? If an active program in the name of Christ replete with Scripture quotation and miraculous power does not guarantee the orthodoxy of a group, what can? Allegiance to the heart of Biblical revelation! The crucial tests of Christian integrity center in the Christian gospel. The following questions are designed to assist any Christian in distinguishing missionaries of the cults of the gospel. They can be asked of anyone who calls at your door.

(1) Do you base your teachings on revelations or sacred writings other than the Bible?

If your caller answers "No, we have but one final standard for all we believe," he holds the orthodox position at this point. If he acknowledges revelation other than the Bible, you immediately recognize a cultic position on authority.

(2) Is your primary task preaching the gospel?

If your visitor shows hesitancy here, or if he does not, it is well to clarify the Biblical meaning of gospel by reference to I Corinthians 15:3-4. Is his main business proclaiming this gospel? There is no other (Gal. 1:8-9).

(3) Do you believe that Jesus is the Messiah, the Christ, the anointed one of God who has come in the flesh (I Jn. 4:1-3)? Is Jesus of Nazareth the eternal Word of God become flesh (Jn. 1:1,14)?

Denial of the Lordship of Christ is the spirit of anti-Christ and II John 9 declares "Whosoever transgresseth and abideth not in the doctrine of Christ, hath not God. He that abideth in the doctrine of Christ, he hath both the Father and the Son."

(4) Do you believe that Christ's shed blood is the only basis for the forgiveness of your sins?

The Scriptures explicitly state that our trust must be in Christ's blood. "Being justified freely by his grace through the redemption that is in Christ Jesus: whom God hath set forth to be a propitiation through faith in his blood" (Rom. 3:24-25).

(5) Do you believe that Jesus rose from the dead?

The Scripture says, "if thou shalt confess with thy mouth the Lord Jesus and believe in thine heart that God hath raised him from the dead, thou shalt be saved" (Rom. 10:9-10).

(6) Are you personally trusting Jesus Christ as your own redeemer and Lord?

A person may have correct answers to all five previous questions but lack personal commitment to the living Lord of whom the gospel speaks. Indications of service for a great cause are not enough. The gospel summons every man to turn from self, sin, and Satan to trust his risen Redeemer.

(7) Do you depend upon some achievements of your own for your salvation, or is your trust exclusively in the grace of God?

Many who say they believe Christ also put confidence in some human attainments to merit justification. This belies their alleged faith. The whole books of Romans and Galatians assert that such have missed the only gospel. Ephesians 2:8-9 declares that salvation is the gift of God's grace, not of works lest any man should boast.

This sevenfold attempt to distinguish the heart of Christianity from cultic perversions is made, not to ridicule any person or organization, but lovingly to show deceived people the nucleus of revealed truth. The specific points are emphasized because they are made explicit in the Bible itself. It is the Bible which says we must recognize no other gospel, acknowledge that Jesus is the Christ, have faith in His blood, believe that He was raised from the dead, trust Him and not depend on our own works. What the Bible explicitly requires of the nature of faith and its objects, Christians demand. Christians must recognize as cultic all who displace these plainly revealed truths for something else, however commendable a less central matter may be.

These seven questions serve not only to identify a cult but to guide Christians in evangelizing cultists. With that positive goal in view the interrogations outline subsequent studies of individual cults. Centering the discussions upon essentials, these queries also facilitate comparative investigations of cultic teaching on the respective subjects.

Why Cults Thrive

"Whatever the doctrinal differences," Christians are tempted to say, "the cults must have something or they would not grow so fast! What can we learn from the amazing development of the cults?" Here are some of the instructive reasons for growth of the cults.

(1) Instead of emphasizing preaching and worship, the cults stress teaching and training every member to become a missionary of the movement. They are primarily concerned not to entertain their

members emotionally each week, but to send them into the world seven days a week as aggressive and productive representatives.

(2) Every member is expected to do door to door visitation. The Jehovah's Witnesses have a regular schedule of a stipulated number of hours a week. Mormon young people are expected to give a year or two of their lives at their own expense to missionary activity.

(3) Prospective members are given home Bible classes. Such repeated visits overcome barriers and meet personal needs. Often they produce lasting converts not only from the home but also from the neighborhood in which they are held.

(4) Attractive cult literature is available to propagandists in massive quantities at most economical rates. Jehovah's Witnesses publish *Awake*, a 30-page paper every two weeks in 23 languages and 3,250,000 copies. Also semi-monthly is their *Watchtower Magazine* which comes out in 61 languages and 3,800,000 copies. The highly regarded *Christian Science Monitor* includes its daily tract in support of the movement, and Christian Science Reading Rooms loaded with literature dot every major city.

(5) New prospects are gained from radio and TV broadcasts which present such exceptional features as the Mormon Choir and Temple organ.

(6) Many thousands of people beyond their own memberships are taught cultic doctrine through correspondence courses. Meanwhile evangelical churches often cannot stimulate their own people to serious Bible study. Capitalizing upon "mail-order religion" the Unity School of Christianity has skyrocketed to a following second only to Mormonism.

(7) The support of academic institutions is increasingly evident among the cults. In Utah Mormons claim one of the finest educational systems America can boast. The Seventh-day Adventists, if classified as a cult, also establish their own schools to train children from the beginning in their distinctive beliefs.

(8) Of course it takes sacrificial giving for extensive buildings, radio and TV programming, vast quantities of literature, and academic overhead! Tithing has played a major part in the phenomenal growth of Mormonism and Seventh-day Adventists. Their yearly per capita incomes tower far above those of non-tithing groups. Is

it not strange that those obliged by law to give a tenth do more than those who glory in inexhaustible grace?

(9) Furthermore the many activities of the cults are beamed to universal human needs. Mormons implement a social concern with concrete programs so they can boast that none of their families is ever in need. The impression may be given that standard churches are unconcerned Pharisees who pass the needy by, while the cults demonstrate good Samaritan compassion.

(10) Concern for health accompanied by promised cures proves to be an effective combination for Christian Science and other healing cults.

(11) Add to all this the fact that the cults provide their followers with a simple code of life instead of a complex maze of exhortations. They know what is expected of them and the realistic demands can be met.

The Christian Attitude Toward Cults

It has been common for Christians to ignore the cults and smile as if they were relatively insignificant and unworthy of consideration. As the cults surge ahead this "head in the sand" attitude becomes less comfortable. The church suffers heavy losses year after year because of the outright attack upon it by the cults. Aware of the sustained impact of the cults upon Christendom, no faithful steward of the gospel of Christ can remain unconcerned. What elements should compose the Christian attitude to the cults?

(1) Let us approach the cults, German scholar Heinz Horst Shrey proposes, not with polemic or argument, but with penitence. Christians ought not seek to convert the cults, but to convert themselves. This, Shrey argues, is the only honest attitude for the church to assume.[8] While we cannot agree that this is the only perspective from which to view the cults, we admit truth in the position. Christians must confess that often they have been impassive to the economically and socially needy, the suffering, the sorrowing, the unsaved. The enthusiasm and the sacrifice of the cults shame us. Their educational vision and their extensive use of modern methods of propagandizing the masses have left many of us far behind. More diligent in calling and giving, they reveal elements of truth and life

we have neglected. As Horton Davies acknowledges, "The challenge of the sects is . . . best interpreted constructively as a summons to reformation. . . . the Church of Christ has nothing to fear from the zeal and competition of the sects. She has, however, everything to fear from her own missionary apathy and lethargy."[9] Stirred by a new sense of our own negligence most surely we ought to repent and turn from our wicked ways.

(2) Conceding all the values actually found in the cults, their grievous distortions of the gospel call for an answer. To penitence we must add defense of the faith (apologetic). Aggressors have attacked Christianity at its heart. We who have been entrusted with the gospel cannot stand idly by as even well-meaning people wrest the Scriptures to their own destruction. Men must know that at the hands of the cults they receive not the message of reconciliation, but cleverly contrived counterfeits. People have a right to know that the Bible is more worthy of their faith than the alleged revelations of the cults. People have a right to hear that Jesus Christ is more than a spiritualistic medium, a Christian Science practitioner, or an archangel. People have a right to learn why we believe Jesus is the eternal Word of God who became flesh to give his life a ransom for many. People have a right to discover, after all they may have been taught to the contrary, that Jesus rose from the dead for their justification. Let every Christian be "set for the defense of the gospel" (Phil. 1:17) and "ready always to give an answer to every man that asketh . . . a reason of the hope that is in [him] with meekness and fear" (I Pet. 3:15).

(3) Many Christians seem satisfied with a refutation of cultic doctrine and condemnation of the movements. But Christians are responsible to evangelize deceived people in the cults. Are not we like Paul debtors to all men (Rom. 1:14)? Do we not owe proclamation of the gospel to the religious as well as the unreligious? Even today Christians ought to pay their debts!

Is the attempt to evangelize members of the cults a waste of time? Not if the gospel is still the power of God unto salvation to everyone that believeth (Rom. 1:16)! There may be heretics in the cults, but even they deserve two admonitions before turning attention to others (Tit. 3:10). Among the cultists there may also be apostates — people who have formerly sworn allegiance to Christ as revealed in Scripture and who have deliberately and permanently rejected the witness of the Holy Spirit to the Savior. We cannot be absolutely sure that these conditions have been fulfilled even with extensive knowledge of an individual. However, the bulk of present-day cultists have grown up in their movements never having made any other commitment. They are as deserving of the gospel as Jews, Hindus, Muslims, Buddhists, Confucianists, or Shintoists.

Are members of the cults too difficult to win to Christ? They are for mere men, but not for the Holy Spirit. Paul assured Timothy that God will give repentance and recovery out of the snare of the devil to some who are taken captive by Satan at his will (II Tim. 2:25-6). Does this not include members and even leaders of the cults? If the Lord can transform Muslims, is a Jehovah's Witness too hard for Him? He who changed fanatical Saul into missionary Paul does not quake at the sight of a cultist.

But God has chosen to reach cultists as others through human instruments. "How shall they hear without a preacher" (Rom. 10: 14)? A vast and needy mission field lies at our doorstep; the world of the cults is white unto harvest. Christians ought to be faithful in witnessing. Christians will avoid foolish and unlearned questions, but they dare not fail to ask the eternally important questions listed above. They will help direct people away from false gospels to the gospel of Christ.

Christians will not win adherents of the cults or anyone else by condemnation and castigation. Manifesting all the fruit of the Spirit— love, joy, peace, longsuffering, gentleness, kindness, meekness, and self-control, seek to lead people influenced by cultic teaching to Christ. Remember, but for the grace of God you might have been brought up in a cult. Treat people in the cults with as much respect as you would like to receive. "The weapons of our warfare are not carnal, but mighty through God to the pulling down of strongholds" (II Cor. 10:4). "The servant of the Lord must not strive; but be gentle unto all men, apt to teach, patient, in meekness instructing those that oppose themselves" (II Tim. 2:24-25). In these words Paul beautifully summarizes the general attitude which should characterize Christians confronting adherents of the cults.

In conclusion we may say, "The veritable tidal wave of strange cults that is now swirling alarmingly across the world" is one of the greatest challenges to orthodox Christianity today. That is the judg-ment of Philip Edgecumbe Hughes who includes with theological relativism, the ecumenical movement, and reunion with Rome, "The cultic hordes." In his address to the International Association for Reformed Faith and Action at its August congress in Cambridge the chairman added,

> If this satanic assault on the unique gospel is to be repelled it will only be, humanly speaking, as a result of penetrating study of the teachings and practices of the cults and a counter-attack in depth, not merely exposing their spurious and deceitful pretensions, but piercing their armour with the Sword of the Spirit, which is the Word of God, and by God's grace reclaiming through the trumpet call of the genuine gospel many who have been deluded by their falsehoods.[10]

Until now the church has been confronted by the cults; it is high time that the cults are confronted by the church! — by the members of your church! — by the reader himself!

A loving approach to cultists may be thought contradictory to 2 John 9-11: If anyone does not bring the teaching of Christ's true deity and humanity, do not take him into your house or welcome him. Since itinerate teachers were not given salaries, but hospitality, to put them up was to support them in their non-Christian cause. The principle here is not to share or support their deceptive work (verse 11). Christians ought not to give money or goods to cultists. However, compassionately and patiently seeking to help them understand and receive the gospel in no way aids or abets their cause.

FOOTNOTES

1. Figures taken from the 1965 *World Almanac*. Cf. Harold Lindsel, "Are the Cults Outpacing Our Churches?" *Christianity Today*, V (Dec. 19, 1960), 3-5; and Walter R. Martin, "Symposium on Modern Cults" *Religious Research Digest*, I (January, 1961), 41-44.

2. Cited by Walter R. Martin, *Religious Research Digest*, I (January, 1961), 28.

3. *Christianity Today*, V (December 19, 1960), 21.

4. Theodore G. Taggert, "Sect and Cult," *Twentieth Century Encyclopedia of Religious Knowledge* (Grand Rapids: Baker Book House, 1955), II, 1009. Cf. Dr. William Warren Sweet's definition of a cult as a religious group which looks for its basic authority outside Christian tradition. He wrote, "Generally cults accept Christianity, but only as a halfway station on the road to greater 'truth,' and profess to have new and additional authority beyond Christianity." Quoted by Thomas F. Zimmerman, "Where Is the 'Third Force' Going?" *Christianity Today*, IV (Aug. 1, 1960), 15.

5. J. L. Neve, *Churches and Sects of Christendom* (Blair, Nebraska: Lutheran Publishing House, 1944), p. 32.

6. Bernard Ramm, *Pattern of Authority* (Grand Rapids: Eerdmans, 1957), 35-6.

7. While sociological factors are present in connection with groups of Christians, Christianity is not primarily a sociological phenomenon. On this view the most significant differences between Christianity and the cults are doctrinal rather than economical. Since Troeltsch it has been popular to emphasize the poverty of the cults in contrast to the wealth of the established churches. This is done by Horton Davies in *The Challenge of the Sects* (Philadelphia: Westminster Press, 1961) and Elmer T. Clark, *The Small Sects in America* (revised ed.; New York: Abingdon Press, 1959). Clark writes, "In the background of nearly all sects there is a strong economic influence. These groups originate mainly among the religiously neglected poor, who find the conventional religion of their day unsuited to their social and psychological needs" (p. 16). Nevertheless Clark admits, "The sects themselves do not recognize the economic factor in their history. . . . In the sectarian mind the causes of divergence are theological" (p. 18). What ever importance unconscious economical factors may have had, the chief issues in the minds of cultists themselves are differences in teaching. From the perspective of Biblical Christianity as well, priority belongs not to the economic but the doctrinal factors.

8. Cited by G. C. Berkouer, "Review of Current Religious Thought, *Christianity Today*, IV (March 14, 1960), 39.

9. Horton Davies, *op. cit.*, p. 29.

10. *Christianity Today*, V (Sept. 11, 1961), 20.

FOR FURTHER STUDY

JOHN H. GERSTNER, *The Theology of the Major Sects* (Grand Rapids, Michigan: Baker Book House, 1956). A doctrinal discussion by a Presbyterian professor of church history and government, Pittsburgh Theological Seminary. Seventh-day Adventism, Jehovah's Witnesses, Mormonism, Liberalism, New Thought, Christian Science, Spiritualism, Theosophy, and Faith Healing are dealt with.

ANTHONY A. HOEKEMA, *The Four Major Cults* (Grand Rapids, Michigan: Wm. B. Eerdmans Publishing Company, 1963). A scholarly, thorough examination of doctrines taught by Latter-day Saints, Jehovah's Witnesses, Christian Scientists, and Seventh-day Adventists. To the marks of a cult employed in the present book, this theologian adds a group's claim to be the exclusive community of the saved, and to play a central role in eschatology.

WALTER R. MARTIN, *The Kingdom of the Cults* (Grand Rapids, Michigan: Zondervan Publishing House, 1965). The major works of an evangelical Baptist who has specialized in cult apologetics. Adopting a very broad definition of a cult, Martin includes movements within the world's religions such as the Black Muslims and Zen Buddhism.

J. K. VAN BAALEN, *The Chaos of the Cults* (4th rev. ed., Grand Rapids, Michigan: Wm. B. Eerdmans Publishing Company, 1962). A poular statement by a Christian Reformed pastor of the history and doctrines of many groups.

SUGGESTIONS FOR TEACHERS

1. Arouse interest in the study of cults by using the chart and showing comparative growth rates of leading cults in the United States.

2. Involve the group in a discussion of the definition of the word "cult." Use such questions as the following to help the group arrive at a definition:

   > How does a cult differ from world religions like Buddhism or Hinduism?
   > How does a cult deviate from orthodox Christianity?

3. Use a chalkboard to present the seven pointed questions which test a cult in the light of orthodox Christianity.

4. Draw out, through group discussion, reasons for the rapid growth of cults when presenting the material under "Why Cults Thrive."

5. Conclude with the "Christian Attitude Toward Cults." Use questions which probe the thinking of the group. What alternatives are there? What course of action is open to the Christian church in dealing with the problem of the cults?

6. To arouse expectancy for the rest of the series and to meet individual needs, distribute a 5 x 6 card to each member of the group and ask for the following information:

   (1) What cults have been most aggressive in your experience?

   (2) What questions do you have concerning cults which you would like answered in this course?

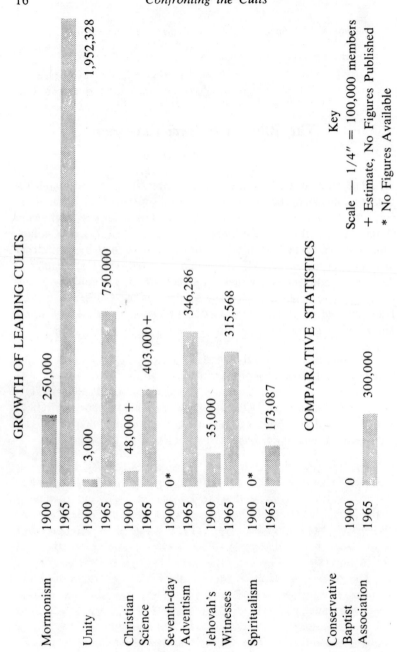

GROWTH OF LEADING CULTS

Mormonism	1900	250,000
	1965	1,952,328
Unity	1900	3,000
	1965	750,000
Christian Science	1900	48,000 +
	1965	403,000 +
Seventh-day Adventism	1900	0*
	1965	346,286
Jehovah's Witnesses	1900	35,000
	1965	315,568
Spiritualism	1900	0*
	1965	173,087

COMPARATIVE STATISTICS

Conservative Baptist Association	1900	0
	1965	300,000

Key

Scale — 1/4" = 100,000 members

+ Estimate, No Figures Published

* No Figures Available

2

The Bible, The Christian, and Jehovah's Witnesses

The faith of a Jehovah's Witness spans all time. Although the modern movement began in 1884 when Charles Taze Russell incorporated the Watchtower Bible and Tract Society, Jehovah's Witnesses trace their valiant predecessors back to Abel, son of Adam. This sense of oneness with heroes of the past strengthens confidence in a utopian future. A. H. Macmillan, for sixty years a member of the New World Society, writes, "I'm not afraid, for being with this religious movement has made me fearless of the future. . . . Now I do know where I am going. I am confident too that I know where the world is going."[1]

As to the present, Jehovah's Witnesses feel themselves a vital part of a great international cause. Each member is an active "minister" with a worldwide mission. Therefore he sacrificially devotes full or part-time service to the cause. Undaunted by repeated rebuffs at door after door, thousands of such dedicated missionaries canvass the world and distribute unbelievable amounts of literature.

In 1961, starting at Yankee Stadium in New York City, the Witnesses staged a chain of thirteen gigantic six-day assemblies, seven in North America, and six in Europe. A registered attendance of more than 400,000 persons heard A. H. Knorr's address entitled "When All Nations Unite under God's Kingdom." The president of the Watchtower Bible and Tract Society argued that "the only true unifying force today is not the United Nations but the established kingdom of Jehovah God."[2] More enthusiastic than ever, the faithful leave such rallies to denounce the satanic nature of all governments, the idolatry of saluting flags, the evil of military service for a human government, the apostasy of Christendom, and the sin of receiving blood transfusions. In the teaching of Jehovah's Witnesses,

Christians face not a few simple doctrines, but a challenging philosophy of the past, present, and future with ramifications for every sphere of life.

However, a Christian need not become an expert in all the interesting political, legal, and medical aspects of Jehovah's Witness teaching and activity. But he can, and must confront Jehovah's Witnesses with the true gospel! That is also far more important than arguing with those who may not be born-again about the identity of the 144,000 mentioned in Revelation, or about details of the millennium. In order to direct discussion to the central Biblical message a Christian may ask his Jehovah's Witness friends and callers seven leading questions. He will want to know the characteristic answers he may expect, and how he may reply in such a way as to benefit, not hurt, those he loves for Christ's sake. The remainder of this study seeks to provide a Christian with this important information.

In any discussion of religious ideas much confusion is avoided if the various parties have a common source and standard of truth. For those who measure all religions by the Biblical rule, it is sufficient to show that a view is in accord with the straightedge of Scripture. Will this be sufficient for a Jehovah's Witness? Why not ask him the first leading question? "Do you base your teachings on revelations other than the Bible?"

Jehovah's Witnesses will answer with an emphatic "No!" Unlike many other cults, the Witnesses do not subscribe to another inspired book in addition to Scripture. According to their typically anonymous writers in *What Has Religion Done for Mankind?* "There can be no question about it: the Holy Scriptures of the Bible are the standard by which to judge all religions."[3] The same measuring stick of religious truth is emphasized in *Let God Be True.*

> To let God be found true means to let God have the say as to what is the truth that sets men free. It means to accept His word, the Bible, as the truth. Hence, in this book, our appeal is to the Bible for truth. Our obligation is to back up what is said herein by quotations from the Bible for proof of truthfulness and reliability.[4]

Absolutely convinced of their own complete faithfulness to the Scriptures, the Witnesses question the Biblical allegiance of all others. "Do not take the word of some religious clergyman for it," they warn, "but search the inspired written record for yourself."[5] Ministers of all denominations — Protestants as well as Catholic — are said to distort the Bible by making it fit their traditional ideas. Thus Christians and Jehovah's Witnesses do not differ on the supreme authority of Scripture. Although there is a provisional value in the heritage of sound churches, in the final analysis any church tradition must stand under the judgment of the written Word of God.

But precisely what is the written Word to which the Jehovah's Witnesses give unqualified assent? It is their *New World Translation!* Making a mistake similar to that of the Roman Catholics who exalted the Latin Vulgate above the Greek and Hebrew texts, the Jehovah's Witnesses now seem to follow their translation whatever the evidence to the contrary. But of course everyone else who has ever looked at the evidence is said to be biased! So every other translation has been corrupted by human tradition. The "Preface" to the *New World Translation of the Christian Greek Scriptures* says,

> Religious traditions hoary with age, have been taken for granted and gone unchallenged and uninvestigated. These have been interwoven into the translations to color the thought. In support of a preferred religious view, an inconsistency and unreasonablenesss have been insinuated into the teachings of the inspired writings.

Of all the hundreds of translations in the history of the Christian church, we are called upon to believe that just one escaped bias! However, the circumstances surrounding the Jehovah's Witness version effectively dispose of this brash claim. Christians can point out that its translators stand in a definite tradition, and not an enviable one at that. In spite of the Witnesses' attempts to deny the fact, their present views are unduly influenced by "Pastor" Charles Taze Russell. In a chapter entitled "The Bible as a Divine Revelation Viewed in the Light of Reason," founder Russell wrote, "Let us examine the character of the writings claimed as inspired, to see whether their teachings correspond with the character we have *reasonably* imputed to God."[6] A later synonym for what seemed reasonable to Russell was "sanctified common sense."[7] Just how this allegedly sanctified common sense can be so superior to the Spirit-illumined Christian scholarship is not explained. Apparently "Pastor" Russell enjoyed an uncommon amount of "common sense" for without the benefit of knowledge of Greek and Hebrew[8] he boasted, "And be it known that no other system of theology even claims, or has ever attempted to harmonize in itself *every* statement of the Bible, yet nothing short of this can we claim for these views." His is a plan that "rejects not one, but harmonizes every part and item" of God's Word.[9]

The presumption which seems all too evident at the beginning of the Watchtower Society remains in evidence today. William J. Schnell has pointed out that F. W. Franz testified under oath before a court in 1954 that he and N. H. Knorr were the heads of the secret *New World* translation committee of seven and that they, not the committee, had the last word.[10] Can we expect to believe that the busy president and vice-president of a vast worldwide organization were less influenced by human tradition in their translation than numbers of scholars whose lives were dedicated to language study? Not seven, but forty-seven translators from varied denominational backgrounds checked each other's work in producing the King James version. Not seven, but seventy scholars worked to remove bias from the *New English Bible*. Is it likely that the smaller group with fewer safeguards succeeded so exceptionally when others under more favorable conditions are supposed to have failed?

Furthermore, the *New World Translation* itself reveals a lack of fidelity to the Greek New Testament. Princeton Seminary's Professor of New Testament Language and Literature, Bruce M. Metzger, in his article, "Jehovah's Witnesses and Jesus Christ,"[11] discloses some of the serious blunders. The *New World* translation of John 1:1, "the Word was a god," as Metzger says, is "a frightful mistranslation." In Colossians 1:15-17 and Revelation 3:14, he observes, there is "a bold twisting that falsifies what Paul originally wrote." Furthermore, Metzger finds that the Jehovah's Witness translators gave Philippians 2:6 "a characteristic twist" and "garbled the meaning of the original" in Titus 2:13 and II Peter 1:1.

And Metzger is not alone in his estimate of the *New World* version. Pastor Ray C. Stedman adds Philippians 1:21 and Matthew 27:50 to the list of improper translations and concludes that the *New World* Bible is as deadly as a poisoned well.[12] An attempt to be much more kindly to the Watchtower Bible and Tract Society's version is made by Steven T. Byington in a review of it published by *The Christian Century*. Nevertheless Byington criticizes the repeated use of "torture stake" for "cross," of "Jehovah" for "Lord," loose treatments of conjunctions, overtranslations of incidental implications, and "the unwise typographical trick" of capitalizing some second person pronouns.[13] Much more severe is the conclusion of cult specialist Walter R. Martin. After adding Philippians 1:22-23 and Matthew 24:3 to the previously noted mistranslations, Martin feels justified in regarding the *New World* translators as "blind leaders of the blind" (Mt. 15:14) who "wrest the scriptures to their own destruction" (II Pet. 3:16) and "turn the grace of God into lasciviousness, denying our only Master and Lord Jesus Christ" (Jude 4).[14]

While we may commend the Witnesses for their motivation to be strictly faithful to the Bible itself, we must question their success in achieving this goal. In view of the judgments of competent Greek scholars we conclude that they are not sold out to the Bible alone, as they may have imagined. It is to be hoped then, that independently of their own translation they may hear the gospel. If, instead, they tenaciously maintain the superiority of the *New World Translation*, it is not wise to labor the point. Just as you might use the Douay version with a Roman Catholic, so you can employ a *New World Translation* in presenting the gospel to Jehovah's Witnesses.

The Gospel

A second question that may be used of the Lord to help cultists see that they are missing the bullseye of Biblical revelation relates to the importance of the gospel. Ask anyone who comes to your door, "Is your main business proclaiming the gospel of Christ?

Jehovah's Witnesses will hardly reply with an unhesitating affirmative. In their scheme the gospel takes second place to the vindication of Jehovah's supremacy in the coming millennial kingdom. That was the emphasis of Russell, whose books were published under the series title, *Millennial Dawn*. That distinctive explains why their meeting places are not called churches, but kingdom halls. And that is why George D. McKinney can write,

The purpose of the church in the world is not to convert the world. The purpose, primarily, is this: "To preach the Triumphant Kingdom message throughout all the world as a witness to all nations." This witnessing for Jehovah is so designed to acquaint the inhabitants of the earth with God's divine plan so that in the great awakening (the resurrection) these will not be ignorant of God's purposes.[15]

Witnesses to Jehovah's supremacy, however, are hardly to be equated with heralds of Christ's gospel. Disregarding the disciples' great commission (Mt. 28:19-20), the Witnesses assume the Is-raelite's mission (Isa. 43:10-12; 44:8). In the midst of rampant idolatry the Jews were to be Jehovah's witnesses. They were to advise idol worshipers that beside Jehovah there is no God. Having tragi-cally failed to perform this calling, they were chastened by the experience of captivity in foreign lands. Even under those circum-stances they were unfaithful to their task. Later Paul had to write that the name of God was "blasphemed among the Gentiles" because of them (Rom. 2:24).

The first century ancestors of Jehovah's Witnesses, significantly enough, were avowed enemies of Jesus Christ. They sought to kill Him because He called God His Father "making himself equal with God" (Jn. 5:17-18). When Jesus said, "Before Abraham was, I am" they tried to stone Him for blasphemy (Jn. 8:58). A third stoning was attempted when He declared, "I and the Father are one" (Jn. 10:30). Although the Romans implemented the crucifix-ion, the first century Jehovah's witnesses charged, "We have a law, and by our law he ought to die, because he made himself the son of God" (Jn. 19:7). And when they heard of the resurrection, the earlier Jehovah's witnesses gave the soldier a bribe for lying to the effect that His body was stolen while they slept (Mt. 28:11-15). After Christ's ascension to heaven they added to their crimes the stoning of Stephen for testifying concerning Jesus Christ (Acts 7: 54-60).[16]

Ever since Christ's resurrection the major task of Christians has been faithfulness as Jesus' witnesses. Our Lord said, ". . . ye shall be witnesses unto me both in Jerusalem, and in all Judea, and in Samaria and unto the uttermost parts of the earth" (Acts 1:8). Jesus also said that when the Holy Spirit comes "that one will bear witness about me and you in turn are to bear witness (Jn. 15:26-27 NWT). To the witness of Christ to Himself, and that of the apostles and the Holy Spirit, we may add that of the prophets. "To him all the prophets bear witness that everyone putting faith in him gets forgiveness of sins through his name" (Acts 1:43 NWT). And God the Father Himself also witnesses to Christ:

> This is the witness God gives, the fact that he has borne witness concerning his Son. . . . The person not having faith in God has made him a liar, because he has not turned his faith to the witness given, that God gave us everlasting life, and this life is in his Son. He that has the Son has this life; he that does not have the Son of God does not have this life (I Jn. 5:9-12 NWT).

That the main mission of the church is witnessing to the incarnate, crucified, and risen Christ is the testimony of all the prophets, apostles, Christ, the Holy Spirit, and Jehovah God Himself. In spite of all this evidence Jehovah's Witnesses major in a message of Jehovah's vindication. Consequently they bypass the heart of the Biblical good news. They desperately need the gospel of God's redeeming love for those who miss the mark. As they call at your door or distribute literature on the street corner, they constitute as challenging a mission field as do Muslims or Jews.

Christ

In paying your spiritual debt (Rom. 1:14) to Jehovah's Witnesses you will testify more specifically to the Person of Jesus Christ, the God-man, your living Lord. Initiating the discussion in Biblical terminology you may ask a Jehovah's Witness, "Do you believe that Jesus is the Christ, the eternal Word of God who has come in the flesh?"

If the Jehovah's Witness overlooks "eternal" he may answer in the affirmative. But to understand his meaning you must press for further clarification. Does he mean that Jesus was truly God? He will reply, "No," and "Yes." No, Witnesses say, Jesus was not Jehovah God, not the one true God. On the other hand, Witnesses will say, Yes, He was "a god" as Satan was said to be a god of this world.

Do the Witnesses not believe that Jesus existed prior to His birth in Bethlehem? They do. But even in that pre-earthly state Jesus was not true deity. Rather, before coming to earth He was the first created being, the archangel Michael, the chief representative of God. C. T. Russell explains,

As he was the highest of all Jehovah's creation, so also he was the first, the direct creation of God, the "only begotten," and then he, as Jehovah's power, and in his name, created all things, — angels, principalities and powers, as well as the earthly creation.[17]

However exalted, the first created being is not an eternal member of the Godhead; he had a beginning. The doctrine of the Trinity is disallowed. "Jehovah's Witnesses believe that Jehovah God and Christ Jesus are two distinct persons and are not combined with a so-called Holy Ghost in one godhead called a trinity."[18] Clearly, then, before Bethlehem Jesus was not God and the confession that Jesus was "a god" does not mean actual deity. The Witnesses are as monotheistic as the Jews. Jesus is not the eternal Word who "was God" (Jn. 1:1).

What then do Jehovah's Witnesses believe concerning Jesus as He appeared in human flesh on earth? Did the Word become incarnate and dwell among us? "Jesus' birth on earth was not an incarnation. . . . He emptied himself of all things heavenly and spiritual . . . he was born a man. He was not clothed with flesh over an invisible spirit person, but he *was* flesh."[19] Although the Witnesses accept the doctrine of the virgin birth, they maintain that Jesus was merely human until baptized at the age of thirty. Then "God begot Jesus to be his spiritual Son . . . instead of a human son. . . . By being thus anointed with the spirit Jesus became the Messiah, . . . the Anointed."[20] When Jesus died, His human existence ended; it was annihilated. Then the spirit creature, Michael, took up his existence again in an even higher exaltation.

For the Witnesses, Jesus, before and after His earthly existence, was the highest spiritual creature, and during his life on earth was a perfect man; Jesus was never truly God. The Bible, they say, does not teach the deity of Christ.

The fact is that nowhere does the Bible teach the equality of the Son with the Father, but it teaches the very opposite; it shows the Son to be in subjection and hence inferior to the Father. Thus we are told of the Son's inferior position before he came to earth, in that he was not ambitious to be equal with God, his Father (Phil. 2:6 RSV). And while on earth he continually called attention to his Father's superiority by stating that he could do nothing of his own initiative; that only his Father is good and that "the Father is greater than I" (John 14:28 RSV). Writing long after Jesus' ascension into heaven, the apostle Paul shows that God is the head of Christ and that throughout eternity the Son will be in subjection to his Father, Jehovah God (I Cor. 11:3; 15:28).[21]

In order to help people influenced by such a challenging Jehovah's Witness argument, a Christian must focus clearly upon the issues and wisely employ relevant Scripture. The problem is not whether Jesus was a perfect man; both groups affirm that. Neither is the question whether Jesus was distinct from the Father in his pre-earthly state; both groups assert that. Rather, the difference is whether Jesus was not also eternally one in essence with the Father and the Spirit.

Around A.D. 400 Aurelius Augustine helpfully observed that the Scriptures concerning Christ may be classified in three groups.[22] There are those passages which teach the inferiority of Christ because He voluntarily became incarnate, was born as a baby, grew as a child, hungered, thirsted, grew tired, slept soundly, and suffered every temptation common to man. In this truly human condition the Father was greater than He, and He constantly sought the leading of the Father. (See Jn. 14:28; Lk. 2:40; Mk. 13:32; Jn. 5:19; Jn. 8:42; Jn. 16:28.)

A second group of texts affirms that Jesus, before the foundation of the world, was distinct from the Father. He was distinguishable as a word from the speaker of the word (Jn. 1:1); as a uniquely begotten son from His father (Jn. 1:14); as one who had priority not in time, but in rank, over all created things (Col. 1:15; Rev. 3:14); as the shining is distinguishable from the sun, and as a perfect image is distinguishable from that which it portrays (Heb. 1:3). In view of such passages the doctrine of the Trinity states that the Father and Son are eternally distinct as persons. In this respect the Bible regularly recognizes an order, placing the Father first, the Son second, and the Holy Spirit third.

But a third group of Scriptures teaches that the Father and Son are not two separate beings or Gods, but rather one essence and spiritual substance. In this respect the Son is equally God. This unity of the Godhead is not burst asunder by the threefold eternal distinctions or by the incarnation of the Son. Rather, as the doctrine of the Trinity explains, the Godhead is one in respect to essence, three in respect to personal distinctions, and three in respect to roles in the creative and redemptive programs. Only trinitarianism does justice to all three types of references. Jehovah's Witness teaching may be true to passages on Christ's humanity, and in some measure to those asserting his distinctness from the Father. But it utterly fails to account for the extensive evidence that Christ is in fact deity. A Christian who cannot present this evidence is ill-prepared to help Jehovah's Witnesses.

Contrary to the claim of Jehovah's Witnesses, then, the Bible while not neglecting Jesus' humanity, and distinctness from the Father, also teaches His essential deity. In John 1 the "Word" who became flesh (v. 14) and who was eternally "with God" (v. 1) is also declared to be God (v.1). In the *New World Translation*, however, Jehovah's Witnesses change the end of verse one so that it reads, "the Word was a god." The small "g" is required, they argue, because the Greek word for God (*theos*, from which we get "theology") is not preceded by a definite article, "the" (*ho*). When this argument is presented, any Christian as interested as Jehovah's Witness "laymen" can point out three things. First, "It overlooks entirely an established rule of Greek grammar which necessitates the rendering, '. . . and the Word was God.' . . . 'A definite predicate nominative has the article when it follows the verb; it does not have the article when it precedes the verb. . . .' "[23] In the last clause of John 1:1 the predicate nominative "God" precedes the verb "was." The order of the Greek text is "God was the Word." That order emphasizes Christ's deity, and explains the absence of the definite article. Since English word order differs from Greek, the phrase is translated, "the Word was God."

In the second place any Christian can point out to Jehovah's Witnesses that the word for "God" (*theos*) without the definite article ("the") is often used for Jehovah God. He may show this to a Witness in the *New World Translation* itself. That version translates *theos* without the article by "God," with a capital "G" in John 1:6, 12, 13; 3:2, 21! Third, any Christian can show a Jehovah's Witness the fact that some passages do designate Jesus as "the" God, using the definite article (*ho*) with "God" (*theos*). According to Matthew 1:23 the birth of Jesus fulfilled the prophetic announcement that the virgin born son should be called Immanuel, "which means when translated, 'With us is God.' " Note the capital "G" which, according to the *New World* translators, denotes Jehovah

God, *the* God (*ho theos*)! Again, when skeptical Thomas was finally overwhelmed with the evidence that Jesus had risen from the dead, he cried out, "My Master and my God" (Jn. 20:28). The Jehovah's Witnesses' own translation employs a capital "G." Their Scriptures unmistakably call Jesus Jehovah God, *the* God (*ho theos*). Furthermore, the same version represents Jesus as accepting the worship of Thomas and commending all who share his faith. "Jesus said to him: Because you have seen me have you believed? Happy are those who do not see and yet believe" (v. 29 NWT).

In many other passages the deity of Christ is taught in the Bible. Romans 9:5 is so punctuated by the *New World* translators that it does not support the deity of Jesus, but as B. B. Warfield argues, it is of Christ the passage says, "Who is in his essential being (*ho on*) none other than God over all blessed forever."[24] Philippians 2:6 does not teach that Jesus despised even seeking equality with God, but asserts that he bore the form or very essence of God and did not think His equality with God a thing to be retained.[25] In Hebrews 1:8 Jesus, who is higher than the angels, is called God (*ho theos*). "Unto the Son He saith, Thy throne O God is for ever and ever." However the Witnesses rephrase the verse, they can hardly avoid the link with Psalm 45:6-7 where it is Jehovah's throne which is eternal. Accordingly Jesus is identified with Jehovah's power in a way in which no angelic creature is. In his first epistle, the apostle John, having spoken of Christ, asserts, "He (literally 'this one,' a masculine personal pronoun agreeing with the preceding 'Christ') is the true God and eternal life" (I Jn. 5:20).

While not explicitly asserting that Jesus is God, several other passages imply as much by calling Jesus "God our Savior" (I Tim. 1:1; 2:3; 4:10; Tit. 1:3; 2:10; 3:4). In other verses the terms "Jesus" and "God" are so grammatically related as to teach their essential unity. Although ignored by the *New World* translators, this Greek structure was detected and formulated by Granville Sharp as long ago as A.D. 1798. Sharp's rule applies when two nouns of the same case connected by the Greek copulative (*kai* meaning "and") have an article preceding the first noun and no article before the second noun. In such a construction the second noun always refers to the same thing or event as the first. In this manner II Thessalonians 1:12 speaks of the grace of our God and Lord Jesus Christ, Titus 2:13 refers to the appearing of our great God and Lord Jesus

Christ; and II Peter 1:1 alludes to the righteousness of our God and Savior Jesus Christ. In each of these passages Jesus is identified with God.

Furthermore Jesus' unity with Jehovah is taught when Old Testament references to Jehovah are quoted of Christ without qualification in the New Testament. For example, according to Isaiah 6:1ff. the prophet in his temple vision saw Jehovah of hosts high and lifted up. But John explains that Isaiah saw Jesus' glory and spoke of Him (Jn. 12:41). Whereas Psalm 102:25-27 proclaims the immutability of Jehovah, Hebrews 1:10-12 applies the same passage to the changlessness of Christ. Joel 2:32 invites anyone to call upon the name of Jehovah for salvation while Romans 10:13 urges all to call upon the name of the Lord (Jesus Christ, cf. vv. 9-10). Clearly the inspired New Testament writers perceived an underlying unity between Jesus and Jehovah.

If further evidence for Christ's deity is called for, observe that divine attributes are ascribed to Him. Christ is eternal (Jn. 1:1; 17:5; Micah 5:2; Heb. 1:11), omnipresent (Jn. 3:13; Mt. 18:20; 28:20; Eph. 1:23), omniscient (Jn. 1:48; 2:25; 6:64; 16:30; 21:17; Col. 2:3), omnipotent (Mt. 28:18; Heb. 1:3), and sinless (Jn. 8:46; I Pet. 1:19).

Noteworthy also is the fact that divine works are attributed to Christ: creation (Jn. 1:3; Col. 1:16), preservation (Col. 1:17), providence (Heb. 1:3), forgiveness (Mk. 2:5-11; Lk. 5:20-24), and judgment (Jn. 5:22; James 4:12).

And one of the most remarkable phenomena of history is this, that Jews conditioned by centuries of traditional commitment to the first commandment worshiped Christ. None but God must be worshiped! When Cornelius fell at Peter's feet, the apostle responded as Christ never did, "Stand up; I myself also am a man" (Acts 10:25-6). Paul and Barnabas, hearing that the men of Lystra regarded them as gods, rent their clothes, and ran among the people crying out, "We also are men of like passions with you" (Acts 14:11-15). Overwhelmed by the things shown him by an angel of God, the apostle John fell down to worship him. But the angel said, "Be careful! Do not do that! All I am is a fellow slave of you and of your brothers who are prophets and who are observing the words of this scroll. Worship God" (Rev. 22:9 NWT).

If Jesus were not God, as the apostles and angels He would have renounced any form of worship. But Christ accepted and encouraged worship! After Peter walked on the water and was rescued by Christ, "those in the boat did obeisance to him saying: 'You are really God's Son' " (Mt. 14:33). Jesus informed His disciples that the Father had committed all judgment to the Son "in order that all may honor the Son just as they honor the Father. He that does not honor the Son does not honor the Father who sent him" (Jn. 5:23 NWT). Jesus also said, "Do not let your hearts be troubled. Exercise faith in God, exercise faith also in me. . . . He that has seen me has seen the Father also. . . . Do you not believe that I am in union with the Father and the Father is in union with me?" (Jn. 14:1,9,10 NWT). The Father has given Christ a name above every other "so that in the name of Jesus every knee should bend of those in heaven and those on earth and those under the ground, and every tongue should openly confess that Jesus Christ is Lord to the Glory of God the Father" (Phil. 2:10-11, quoting Isa. 45:23, "unto me [Jehovah] every knee shall bow"). Every created being must worship Christ — even the highest angelic being. When Christ comes into the world the Father says, "And let all God's angels worship him" (Heb. 1:6 NWT).

If Jesus Christ were not God then worship of Him would be idolatrous "worship and service of the creature rather than the Creator" (Rom. 1:25)! But since Jesus Christ is God, Jehovah's Witnesses are endangering their eternal destiny — "If you do not believe that I am he, you will die in your sins" (Jn. 8:24 NWT).

Redemption (Ransom)

Do Jehovah's Witnesses believe that Jesus died for their sins? Christians may ask individuals influenced by their teachings, "Do you believe that Christ's shed blood is the only basis for the forgiveness of your sins?"

In evaluating their reply it is important to distinguish between two types of sin: (1) that which was passed to the race by Adam, and (2) that which an individual himself commits. In short, they say that the work of Christ delivers believers from the first, but not the second. How does Christ's ransom relate to Adamic sin? Three effects of Adam's disobedience fell upon the race: the inevitability of death, the imperfect conditions of life in a cursed world, and the guilt inherited by all members of the race (Rom. 5:16,18). No human being is capable of setting himself or others free from these conditions. In compassion and love Jehovah provided for this. He asked Michael to exchange his spiritual existence for a human one, live a perfect life, and die to ransom the guilty. On the merit of Jesus' poured out life the inherited guilt of all men is removed and Edenic perfection will one day be restored in a deathless millennium.[26]

Although all men are absolved and released from the penalty of Adam's sin, Christ's ransom does not give or guarantee everlasting life or blessing to any man; but it does guarantee to every man another opportunity or trial for life everlasting.[27] All that Christ's atoning work secures for men now is "the blessing of a new trial."[28] The circumstances of this trial are "more favorable" than those of Adam's because we have experiential knowledge of evil as well as good, but the terms or conditions of our trial are "the same as in the Adamic trial."[29] What are these terms for an individual? "His own wilful obedience or wilful disobedience will decide whether he may or may not have life everlasting."[30] "Pastor" Russell further explains

> Some have been blinded in part, and some completely, by the god of this world, and they must be recovered from blindness as well as from death, that they *each for himself*, may have a *full* chance to prove, by obedience or disobedience, their worthiness or unworthiness of life everlasting. Then those who prove themselves unworthy of life will die again — the second death. . . . The death which comes as a result of individual, wilful apostasy is final. This sin hath never forgiveness, and its penalty, the second death is *everlasting* — not everlasting dying, but everlasting death — a death unbroken by a resurrection.[31]

The atonement of Christ unaccompanied by human works is an inadequate basis for eternal life. Men are "at-one-ment" with God as a result of Christ's ransom only as Adam was before his sin. What then must a man do to pass the test Adam failed? Throughout his life he must maintain "integrity," or he will be annihilated forever. Integrity is defined in *The Watchtower* as "completeness, moral innocence, perfection, simplicity."[32] Apparently the faithful need some encouragement to do the impossible, for the same article adds, "Perseverance in keeping integrity will pay off shortly to all now in the New World society."[33]

Christians will not minimize the importance of a perfect standard, but will ask whether perfection is a condition of justification in God's sight. Commendable as it may be to list the Ten Commandments and their interpretation in the Sermon on the Mount, who is sufficient for these things? Has the most faithful Jehovah's Witness kept the first and great commandment? Has he always loved God with his whole being? And has the most faithful Witness kept the second? Has he always loved his neighbor as himself (Mt. 22:37-40)? The fact is, "There is not a righteous man, not even one" (Rom. 3:10 NWT). By attempting to keep integrity, or by works of the law, "no flesh will be declared righteous before him, for by law is the accurate knowledge of sin" (Rom. 3:30 NWT).

How then can a sinful man appear righteous in the sight of God? The Scriptures say "it is as a free gift that they are being declared righteous by his undeserved kindness through the release by the ransom paid by Christ Jesus. God set him forth as an offering for propitiation through faith in his blood" (Rom. 3:24-25 NWT). On the basis of Christ's atonement alone (1) we are pardoned from all our sin, and (2) we are declared as righteous as Jesus Christ.

Where do the Scriptures teach complete pardon? "Those in union with Christ Jesus have (present tense) no condemnation" (Rom. 8:1 NWT). "He that exercises faith in him is not to be judged" (Jn. 3:18 NWT). The believer "does not come into judgment but has passed over from death to life" (Jn. 5:24 NWT). "By means of him (Christ) we have the release by ransom through the blood of that one, yes, the forgiveness of our trespasses, according to the riches of his undeserved kindness" (Eph. 1:7). According to the Bible, a believer's sins are completely forgiven; he can never be condemned for them.

Where then does the Bible ascribe complete righteousness to those who receive Christ? Perfect righteousness is an attribute of God alone. All human attempts to keep integrity fall short of God's glory (Rom. 3:23 NWT). "But now apart from law God's righteousness has been made manifest . . . yes, God's righteousness through

faith in Jesus Christ" (Rom. 3:21-22 NWT). Christ's shed blood
was required "that he might be righteous even when declaring
righteous the man that has faith in Jesus" (Rom. 3:26 NWT). But
Jehovah's Witnesses do not realize that they can experience as
David did "the happiness of the man to whom God counts righteousness apart from works: Happy are those whose lawless deeds have
been forgiven and whose sins have been covered; happy is the man
whose sin Jehovah will by no means take into account" (Rom. 4:
6-8 NWT). The Christian's prayer for Jehovah's Witnesses is identical with that of Paul for his Jewish brothers — "for their salvation."
Paul continues, "I bear them witness that they have a zeal for God;
but not according to accurate knowledge; for, because of not knowing
the righteousness of God but seeking to establish their own, they did
not subject themselves to the righteousness of God. For Christ is
the accomplished end of the Law, so that everyone exercising faith
may have righteousness" (Rom. 10:1-4 NWT). Not those who try
to maintain integrity, but those who accept Christ's atonement are
reckoned perfectly righteous in God's sight. Needless to say, the
Bible nowhere conditions this perfect righteousness upon association
with the New World Society!

The Resurrection of Christ

Another question relating to the culmination of Christ's life
may help a cultist to see the true foundation of Christianity. Ask,
"Do you believe that Jesus Christ rose from the dead?" If the response is affirmative, request an explanation. What is meant by
"resurrection"?

According to Jehovah's Witnesses the resurrection of Jesus
does not mean that the body which was crucified and buried lived
again. Their major proof text reads, "Jehovah God raised him from
the dead, not as a human Son, but as a mighty immortal spirit Son
. . . 'He being put to death in the flesh, but being made alive in
the spirit' " (I Pet. 3:18 NWT).[34] Before becoming a man He was
a spirit being; now, after the decease of the human being, the spirit
being exists again. "Pastor" Russel plainly said, "The man Jesus
is dead, forever dead."[35] What happened to the body of our Lord?
Russell replies

Our Lord's human body was . . . supernaturally removed from the tomb; because had it remained there it would have been an insurmountable obstacle to the faith of the disciples. . . . We know nothing about what became of it, except that it did not decay or corrupt (Acts 2:27,31). Whether it was dissolved into gases or whether it is still preserved somewhere as the grand memorial of God's love . . . no one knows.[36]

How then does the ingenious "Pastor" explain the resurrection appearances of Christ to the disciples? How could "an invisible spirit creature" be visible? When desiring to appear Christ "instantly created and assumed such a body of flesh and such clothing as He saw fit for the purpose intended." When the appearance was ended the same supernatural power "dissolved" them.[38] More recent Witnesses call the appearances "materializations."[39]

The central issue between Christian concepts of the resurrection and those of the Witnesses is not whether there were appearances of Christ after His death, but whether there is a continuing identity of the body in which He died and in which He subsequently appeared. "Many Christians have the idea," Russell writes, "that our Lord's glorious spiritual body is the very same body that was crucified and laid away in Joseph's tomb: they expect, when they see the Lord in glory, to identify him by the scars he received on Calvary. *This is a great mistake.*"[40]

Are Christians mistaken in asserting an identity between the crucified and risen Christ? Some tend to agree that they are. Is the resurrection body very different from the natural body. According to I Corinthians 15 the body raised from the dead is immortal, incorruptible, honorable, powerful, spiritual, heavenly, and supernatural. The resurrection body is as different from the temporal body as full-grown grain from the seed that is planted (I Cor. 15:37). All this is true. At the same time, however, there is a continuing identity between the seed that is sown and the grain that develops. This need not imply that identical particles compose the tiny seed and the high stalks. The cells of human bodies change at least every seven years, but their organic identity is uninterrupted. Is not such an organic identity traceable in the crucified and risen Lord?

In both pre- and post-crucifixion states, Christ's body was visible, tangible, and audible. He could eat with his disciples. Uniquely distinctive was "the print of the nails" (Jn. 20:25,27 NWT).

In magnifying the differences between the natural and spiritual bodies we must not overlook the similarities. "It is the Lord!" cried the disciples (Jn. 21:7). The resurrection body is not qualitatively different in every respect. Because of its organic continuity with the former body the resurrection body was the chief sign Jesus gave to Jews who questioned His authority. Jesus said, "Break down *this* temple, and in three days I will raise *it* up. . . . But he was talking about the temple of his body" (Jn. 2:20-21 NWT). The apostle John commented, "When . . . he was raised up from the dead, his disciples called to mind that he used to say this, and they believed the scripture and the saying that Jesus said" (Jn. 2:22 NWT).

The sole text which seems, at first, to support the Jehovah's Witness denial of the identity of the crucified and resurrected bodies is I Peter 3:18. Does this passage teach that Jesus' humanity was destroyed and that He became a spirit creature? It says He was "put to death in the flesh," and "made alive in the spirit" (NWT). Two possible interpretations of this verse are consistent with the rest of Scripture on the subject. First, the Greek prepositional phrase "*in* the Spirit" frequently means "*by* the Spirit." On this translation Peter refers to the Holy Spirit's agency in raising the dead. His point is similar to that of Romans 8:11 where Paul speaks of "the spirit (Spirit) of him that raised up Jesus from the dead."

A second possible interpretation of I Peter 3:18 suggests that it, like I Corinthians 15, emphasizes the differences between the fleshly body and the spiritual body without denying their continuity. The Savior conclusively demonstrated that in His resurrected state He was not merely a spirit creature. When His disciples imagined they saw a spirit (materialized before them?) Jesus said,

> See my hands and my feet, that it is I myself: feel me and see, be-
> cause a spirit does not have flesh and bones just as you behold that
> I have. And as he said this he showed them his hands and his feet.
> But while they were still not believing for sheer joy and were wonder-
> ing, he said to them: Do you have something here to eat? And they
> handed him a piece of broiled fish, and he took it and ate it before
> their eyes (Lk. 24:39-43 NWT).

When Christians assert that the resurrected Christ was not merely a spirit creature (angel) they are not mistaken; they simply repeat a truth from the lips of their Lord.

Neither are Christians mistaken in expecting to see this same (organically continuous) resurrection body when Christ appears in His glory. In that body He visibly ascended into heaven and He "will come thus in the same manner as you have beheld him going into heaven" (Acts 1:11 NWT). The identity of the coming one with the crucified Christ is repeatedly emphasized. It is He "that loves us and loosed us from our sins by means of his own blood" (Rev. 1:5 NWT). "Look! he is coming with the clouds and every eye will see him, and those who pierced him" (Rev. 1:7 NWT). The "print of the nails" is a most appropriate sign not only for those who crucified Him, but for those who praise Him throughout eternity. "You are worthy to take the scroll and open its seals, because you were slaughtered and with your blood you bought persons for God out of every tongue and people and nation" (Rev. 5:9 NWT). "The lamb that was slaughtered is worthy to receive the power and riches and wisdom and strength and honor and glory and blessing" (Rev. 5:12 NWT). It is not the Christians who are mistaken in identifying the crucified and eternally exalted Lord; those who think they will eternally praise a spirit creature who did not bleed and die for their sins "are of all men most to be pitied"! If the Jesus who died is not raised up from the dead, their preaching "is certainly in vain," their "faith is in vain," and they are still in their sins (I Cor. 15:12-19). "You will be saved," the Scriptures plainly state, upon the condition that you "exercise faith in your heart that God raised him up from the dead" (Rom. 10:9 NWT).

Personal Trust

Christians, concerned not merely to win arguments, but persons, will desire to help Jehovah's Witnesses exercise faith in Christ. Since faith is an individual matter, we ask, "Are you personally trusting Jesus Christ as your redeemer and Lord?" The Scripture says, "None that rests his faith on him will be disappointed" (Rom. 10:11 NWT).

Everyone who rests his faith on a human organization (even though called God's organization) will be disappointed. The ultimate object of Christian faith is not a Christian church nor a New World Society; it is Jesus Christ Himself. We cannot help but wonder how many Witnesses like William J. Schnell have restless hearts void of personal communion with the living Christ. After thirty years as a Witness Schnell testifies,

> A believer in the Lord Jesus Christ, I entered this religious movement in my youth, labored and planned to expand it, then realized gradually that efficient service to the society was replacing my fellowship with Christ. Too late, I discovered that I had become an obedient robot in the control of an organizational monster — the Watch Tower Society, self-appointed "God's Organization" for bringing in the "New World Society".[41]

It is little wonder that a Christian's simple testimony is often so effective. One who experiences the witness of the Holy Spirit, and assurance of sonship with God as a joint-heir to all the riches of grace, has much to offer strangers to fellowship with God. Every Christian can tell Jehovah's Witnesses about the glorious liberty of God's children. How tragic then to slam the door in the face of one outwardly a strong organization man, but inwardly bereft of the very essence of spiritual life — communion with God! Having given his own personal testimony of life in Christ, the Christian will invite a Jehovah's Witness to trust Christ too — the Christ who was God (Jn. 1:14). Of that Christ John 1:12 (NWT) says, ". . . as many as did receive him, to them he gave authority to become God's children, because they were exercising faith in his name." Since Jesus Christ is God, "None that rests his faith on him will be disappointed."

Faith Alone

A Jehovah's Witness is quite unlikely to admit that he does not believe on Christ. However, he will undoubtedly feel that faith is not enough. It may be of help to ask forthrightly, "Do you depend upon some achievements of your own to contribute to justification, or is it only by God's grace through faith?"

The *New World Translation* of Ephesians 2:8-10 explicitly states that salvation is not of works, but that those who are saved by faith are enabled by God to produce the fruit of new life in good works.

> By this undeserved kindness, indeed, you have been saved through faith; and this not owing to you, it is God's gift. No, it is not owing to works, in order that no man should have grounds for boasting. For we are a product of his work and were created in union with Christ Jesus for good works which God prepared in advance for us to walk in them.

This salvation is not merely from Adamic guilt, but also from all sin and condemnation. A sinner is righteous in the sight of God not because of anything he does, but because Christ's righteousness is shared with all who believe. The whole book of Galatians affirms this, but verse 16 of chapter 2 sums it up.

> A man is declared righteous, not due to works of the law, but only through faith toward Christ Jesus, even we have put our faith in Christ Jesus, that we may be declared righteous due to faith toward Christ and not due to works of law, because due to works of law no flesh shall be declared righteous.

In spite of the clarity and force of this truth in the Bible, Jehovah's Witnesses live in fear of losing their justification before God on the basis of their works. At any time they may be excommunicated from the Society. They are thereby excluded from preservation through the battle of Armageddon and from the kingdom of Jehovah. Picture the complete despair endured by a man like William J. Schnell.

> My full time service, of which I had been so proud, consisted of twenty-one eventful years. . . . During all this time I had faithfully made the required reports to the Society. I had certainly bought out a lot of time for the Society's use from my individual life. This record, according to my superiors, was to be my evidence that I was saved and could not be destroyed in Armageddon. Well, it was wiped out in one night! . . . I felt as one left standing in a barren wilderness, I realized with shock that all these years I had been building upon sand. Now the storms had come, and my religion edifice had come crashing down.[42]

How much better it had been if Christians twenty years before that sad experience had effectively witnessed to Mr. Schnell when he knocked at their door! It would have been better yet if concerned Christians canvassing his area had called at Mr. Schnell's home and wisely confronted him with the gospel. It is "the power of God unto salvation to everyone that believeth, to the Jew first, and also to the Greek" (Rom. 1:16).

There remains little reason to doubt that Jehovah's Witnesses, with all their devotion to Bible study, have missed the heart of Christianity. The gospel is not their primary message. They deny that Jesus is the eternal Word of God, that His atonement is the only basis for their redemption, and that He rose from the dead. There is little emphasis on personal communion with the risen Christ, and salvation is not an undeserved gift from God, but a merit badge for sin-tainted human endeavor. Their zeal for God is without knowledge (Rom. 10:1-4). The Christian's prayer to God for Jehovah's Witnesses is that they might be saved. Debtors to Greeks and barbarians, the wise and the unwise, Christians must be ready with all the wisdom, grace, and power in them to preach the gospel to Jehovah's Witnesses also. (Rom. 1:14-16).

FOR FURTHER STUDY

WALTER R. MARTIN and NORMAN H. KLANN, *Jehovah of the Watchtower* (Grand Rapids: Zondervan Publishing House, Enlarged edition, 221 pp. The best full discusion of the history, doctrines, and practices of Jehovah's Witnesses by evangelical Christians.

BRUCE M. METZGER, *The Jehovah's Witnesses and Jesus Christ: A Biblical and Theological Appraisal.* A scholarly pamphlet available from the Theological Book Agency, Princeton, New Jersey. It was originally published in *Theology Today*, April, 1953, 20 pp.

W. J. SCHNELL, *Thirty Years a Watchtower Slave* (Grand Rapids: Baker Book House, 1956), 207 pp. An account of experiences on the inside of the movement by one who left the organization.

PHILIP ELLIOTT, *"Jehovah's Witnesses" in the First and Twentieth Centuries* (Stirling, Scotland: Stirling Tract Enterprise, second revised edition, n.d.), 24 pp. A pamphlet written in an objective and considerate spirit with a unique Scriptural approach. Recommended for a return gift to your Jehovah's Witness callers.

GEORGE D. McKINNEY, *The Theology of Jehovah's Witnesses* (Grand Rapids: Zondervan Publishing House, 1962), 130 pp. A statement of the movement's views organized in the usual order of doctrines in systematic theology. Although objective research, there is inadequate evaluation from a Biblical viewpoint.

FOOTNOTES

1. A. H. Macmillan, *Faith on the March* (Englewood Cliffs, New Jersey: Prentice-Hall, Inc., 1957), pp. 4-5.
2. *The Watchtower*, October 1, 1961, p. 599.
3. *What Has Religion Done for Mankind?* (Brooklyn: Watchtower Bible and Tract Society, Inc., 1951), p. 32.
4. *Let God Be True* (revised; Brooklyn: Watchtower Bible and Tract Society, 1952), p. 9.
5. *What Has Religion Done for Mankind?* p. 56.
6. *Studies in the Scriptures* (Brooklyn: Watchtower Bible and Tract Society, 1886), I, 41.
7. *Ibid.*, p. 349.
8. W. Martin and N. Klann, *Jehovah of the Watchtower* (revised; Grand Rapids: Zondervan Publishing House, 1956), p. 20. Martin quotes the court record of Russell's perjury in claiming and disclaiming knowledge of Greek.
9. *Studies in the Scriptures*, I, 348-49.
10. *The Converted Jehovah's Witness Expositor*, Vol. I, No. 3; cited by William A. Springstead, "Hermeneutics of Jehovah's Witnesses," *The Discerner* III (Apr. June, 1961) 10.

11. Bruce M. Metzger, "The Jehovah's Witnesses and Jesus Christ," *Theology Today*, X (April, 1953), 74-80. Reprinted in pamphlet form by The Theological Book Agency, Princeton, New Jersey.

12. Ray C. Stedman, "Poisoned Water," *Religious Research Digest*, April-June, 1960, p. 30.

13. Steven T. Byington, "Review of NWT," *The Christian Century*, Nov. 1, 1950, p. 1295.

14. Martin and Klann, *op. cit.*, p. 161.

15. George D. McKinney, *The Theology of Jehovah's Witnesses* (Grand Rapids: Zondervan Publishing House, 1962), pp. 83-84.

16. For a more extensive comparison of Jehovah's Witnesses with the Jews see Philip Elliott, *Jehovah's Witnesses: In the First and Twentieth Centuries* (Stirling, Scotland: Stirling Tract Enterprise, n.d.), pp 1-24.

17. *Studies in the Scriptures*, V, 84.

18. M. G. Henschel, "Who Are the Jehovah's Witnesses?" *A Guide to the Religions of America*, ed. Leo G. Rosten (New York: Simon and Schuster, 1955), p. 59.

19. *What has Religion Done for Mankind?* p. 231.

20. *Let God Be True*, p. 38.

21. "Creeds — Gems of Truth or Chips of Error?" *Awake!* March 22, 1957, p. 6.

22. Augustine, "On the Trinity" (De Trinitate) II, 1, 3; *The Nicene and Post-Nicene Fathers* ed., Philip Schaff (Grand Rapids: Eerdmans Publishing Company, 1956), p. 38.

23. Bruce M. Metzger, *op. cit.*, p. 75.

24. B. B. Warfield, *The Lord of Glory* (reprint; Grand Rapids: Zondervan Publishing House), p. 250.

25. J. H. Thayer, *A Greek Lexicon of the New Testament* (New York: American Book Company, 1889), p. 418.

26. *Let God Be True*, pp. 112-121.

27. *Studies in the Scriptures* I, 150.

28. *Ibid.*, p. 151.   29. *Ibid.* 31. *Ibid.*, p. 152. 32. *Ibid.*, p. 158.

32. "Judge, O Jehovah!" *The Watchtower*, August 15, 1956, p. 490.

33. *Ibid.*, p. 496

34. *Let God Be True*, p. 40.

35. *Studies in the Scriptures* V, 454.

36. *Ibid.*, II, p. 129.

37. *Let God Be True*, p. 138.

38. *Studies in the Scriptures* II, 127.

39. *Let God Be True*, p. 40.

40. *Studies in the Scriptures* II 128-129.

41. W. J. Schnell, "Thirty Years a Watchtower Slave," *Power*, Feb. 16, 1958, p. 2.

42. W. J. Schnell, *Thirty Years a Watchtower Slave* (Grand Rapids: Baker Book House, 1956), p. 196.

SUGGESTIONS FOR TEACHERS

Good teaching is marked by clarity of purpose. Review the content of this study and attempt to synthesize it in your own mind. This material may best be divided into two sections for two teaching sessions. Put into a few words a statement of objectives for classroom presentation. *Confronting the Cults* differs from some other works on the subject in that its purpose is not primarily negative — refuting false doctrine, but positive — winning cultists to Christ.

1. Use the lead questions throughout the series to form the major divisions of the teachings sessions. Illustrate the value of the questions in keeping discussion centered on the gospel by moving quickly back to them from irrelevant issues.

2. Anticipate replies Christians may expect to these questions from Jehovah's Witnesses. Evaluate Jehovah's Witness position and give specific guidance in answering erroneous beliefs.

3. Build confidence for effective personal witness by helping your group formulate possible approaches and answers. Use simple role playing situations to involve the group in learning the major doctrines of Jehovah's Witnesses. After the material has been studied, allow several people to take the position of the cultist in confronting the believer. Let others assume the role of a believer. Simulate a conversation. Try various ways of presenting the truth in the face of error.

4. Secure a copy of the *New World Translation of the Christian Greek Scriptures* (or of the whole Bible) published by the Watchtower Bible and Tract Society, Inc., Brooklyn, New York. Interested class members also may wish a copy to mark for use in witnessing to members of this cult. All passages mistranslated could be marked in one way, and all passages for leading them to Christ in another way. Every verse employed in this study could thus be designated.

5. Challenge your group to a painstaking study of John 1:1 as presented here from the Greek. Christians ought not be less diligent than those they seek to help. If Jehovah's Witnesses are concerned enough to determine the structure of John 1:1 as it was originally written, is that too much for members of the Christian church?

SAMPLE LESSON PLAN

SESSION 1

Aim

To guide the class to a knowledge of Jehovah's Witness teaching on divine authority, the gospel, and Christ.

To help the class develop skills of witnessing through the use of questions and proper handling of Scripture.

Approach

Lead a discussion on reasons for the appeal of Jehovah's Witness teachings.

Outline

    I.   Divine authority — revelation
        Question: "Do you base your teachings on revelations other than the Bible?"

    II. The Gospel
        Question: "Is your main business the proclamation of the Gospel of Jesus Christ?"

    III. The Doctrine of Christ
        Question: "Do you believe that Jesus is the Christ, the eternal Word of God who has come in the flesh?"

    IV. Conclusion and summation

SESSION 2

Aim

To guide the class to a knowledge of what Jehovah's Witnesses believe about redemption, the resurrection, and personal faith.

To help the class members develop skill in handling the Scriptures as they contact Jehovah's Witnesses.

Approach

Review briefly the three key questions of the previous session.

Outline

    I.   Redemption
        Question: "Do you believe that Jesus died for your sins?"

    II. The Resurrection of Christ
        Question: "Do you believe that Jesus Christ arose from the dead bodily?"

    III. Personal faith
        Question: "Are you personally trusting Jesus Christ as your redeemer and Lord?"
        Question: "Do you depend upon some achievements of your own to contribute to justification, or is it only by God's grace through faith?"

    IV. Conclusion and summation

3

The Bible, The Christian, and
Latter-day Saints

Mormonism is America's fastest growing cult. Since 1900 Latter-day Saint membership has mushroomed from 250,000[1] to 1,952,328.[2] And most remarkably, during the last four years its missionary force has doubled! In 1959, 5,499 Mormon volunteers won some 7,019 converts; in 1962, 10,961 missionaries reaped 30,940 converts. As of March, 1963, there were 11,838 aggressive representatives who already had topped the total of converts for 1962, recording 39,894.[3]

What explains this unusual development? Most prominent of all the factors is the host of unsalaried young people who give a year or two of their lives for the cause. These fresh recruits every year impress millions of people. When their term of service is completed they return to various occupations with an unforgettable experience and a permanent ability to speak for their faith.

In the second place, every layman helps to spark the Mormon advance by unparalleled participation in the work.

> There is no paid or professional ministry. Thirty-two general officers and the presidents of missions are given living allowances. Add to this a few specialists and a staff of clerks who give their full working time to the church. These constitute all who may be classified as paid personnel. The great bulk of the work and responsibility is carried by the rank and file who receive no financial remuneration; who in fact, contribute generously not only of their time and talent, but of their means as well.[4]

A third factor contributing to Mormonism's success story is the efficient organization of its membership. Gordon B. Hinkley explains, "Everyone in the Church who is active and old enough to do something, generally has a responsibility. In fact, he may have several. And usually the greatest enthusiasm for the cause is found among those who do the most."[5]

Fourth, each member is trained to perform his duties. "Education in all its implications, is . . . a concern of the Church. Accordingly, it has used its resources liberally in fostering schools. Moreover, it has constantly urged its youth to higher achievement and usefulness through education."[6] One study indicates that Utah leads the nation in the extent of adult education.[7] Four years after President Wilkinson took over the campus of Brigham Young University (1950) top Mormon leaders gathered to dedicate twenty-two modern buildings. Three years after that they returned to dedicate twelve more.[8] In 1958 "labor missionaries" completed a multimillion dollar Hawaiian college of twenty buildings on a 100-acre campus overlooking the Pacific.[9]

Mormonism spreads, for another thing, because its prosperity is appealing. Tithing, industry, and frugality have produced a powerful religious empire.

> Unique among religions, the Mormon church efficiently runs a sugar company, grain mills and elevators, a department store, banks, newspapers, a radio and television station, a hotel and luxurious new hotel-motel, ranches, feed lots and farms to name just a few enterprises. . . . It raises peanuts in Texas, grapefruit in Arizona, prizewinning dairy stock in New Jersey and beef cattle in Florida, Georgia and Canada.[10]

As a result, no Mormon need fear extreme poverty. Built into his religion is a social security program.

> Mormonism is a self-reliant society which distributes the bounty of all its people to any member in need. Mormons do not believe in government doles. There is freedom from want in a chain of farms, storehouses, and granaries that keep on hand — together with what is stored by each family — enough food and clothing to supply *every* Mormon for a full year.[11]

Mormon prosperity is demonstrated also in extensive construction. A 38-story denominational building is going up in Salt Lake City and another skyscraper is rising on Manhattan's Fifth Avenue. Churches are going up so rapidly that on the average Latter-day Saints dedicate a building a day.[12]

In the last place the amazing growth of Mormonism must be attributed in some measure to its attractive teaching. Alleging a continuing revelation and priesthood, the Latter-day Saints appeal to many who want visible sources of divine authority. Eschewing the complicated doctrines of the Trinity and imputed righteousness, they exalt the simple and "reasonable" and join those who repudiate the notoriously offensive doctrines of predestination and eternal punishment. They emphasize, as does the *Book of Mormon*, "Men are that they might have joy" (II Nephi 2:25).

It is the doctrine of the Church of Jesus Christ of Latter-day Saints which primarily concerns evangelical Christians. Knowing that one's eternal life depends upon his acceptance of the gospel message, Christians ask whether Mormons believe that truth. With all their joys of prosperity and success, have they found the highest satisfaction of all — the joy of those "whose transgression is forgiven, whose sin is covered" (Ps. 32:1)? In order to help any who may not share the saving grace of God, we ask the following seven questions. May it please the Holy Spirit to grant many who have not enjoyed it, the "full assurance" of divine pardon (Col. 2:2).

1. *Authority*

In any discussion of religion, if the parties involved accept different sources of authoritative teaching, agreement will be unlikely. To determine whether this may be the case with a Mormon friend, ask this pointed question: "Do you base your beliefs on revelations or sacred writings other than the Bible?"

Mormons acknowledge the divine authority, not only of the Bible, but also of the *Book of Mormon, The Doctrine and Covenants, The Pearl of Great Price*, and continuous revelation in the official teaching of the President of the church. Following founder Joseph Smith's "Articles of Faith (8,9) they say, "We believe the Bible to be the word of God as far as it is translated correctly; we also believe the *Book of Mormon* to be the word of God. We believe all that God has revealed, and all that He does now reveal and we believe that He will yet reveal many great and important things pertaining to the Kingdom of God." Where do Mormons look for these future revelations?

So long as the Lord has any communication to make to the children of men, or any instructions to impart to His Church, He will make such communication through the legally appointed channel of the Priesthood; He will never go outside of it, as long, at least, as the Church of Jesus Christ of Latter-day Saints exists in its present form on the earth.[13]

Because of their doctrine of continuous revelation Latter-day Saints have strong words for Christians who insist that the Bible is the sufficient and only infallible rule of faith and practice. Smith, in the *Book of Mormon*, calls such Christians "Gentiles" and fools,"

Many of the Gentiles shall say: A Bible! A Bible! We have got a Bible, and there cannot be any more Bible, But thus saith the Lord God: . . . Thou fool, that shall say: A Bible, we have got a Bible, and we need no more Bible . . . Wherefore murmur ye, because that ye shall receive more of my word? . . . Because that ye have a Bible ye need not suppose that it contains all my words; neither need ye suppose that I have not caused more to be written" (II Nephi 29:3-10).

Are people unchristian and foolish for questioning the supposed divine authority of Mormon revelations? To the contrary, there are good reasons for concluding Mormons have been misled in adding other books to the Biblical revelation.

For one thing, Mormons are not alone in claiming continued revelation. Christian Scientists add Mary Baker Eddy's *Science and Health with Key to the Scriptures* to the Bible; the Muslims have their *Koran*; and Spiritualists think their repeated seances produce messages from the other world. No one can be expected to accept all these purported revelations without consideration. And why should we be favorably disposed toward Latter-day Saint revelations? Because the Church has grown rapidly? So did Islam and Christian Science. Are all other churches apostate and Mormons alone the source of divine ministry in these latter days? But according to Jehovah's Witnesses Mormons as well as others are part of the great apostasy and Witnesses alone constitute God's organization. In view of such contradictory and pretentious claims, Mormons will pardon us if we examine their alleged revelations more closely.

The issue is not whether the sacred writings of the Church of Jesus Christ of Latter-day Saints are popular or unpopular, but whether they are true or false. How then can we test the truth of an alleged revelation? We may ask: (1) if it is self-consistent, and (2) if it is in accord with available evidence. A mother checks the consistency of her child's story and then compares it with what she knows of the facts of the case. A judge hearing the explanation of a suspect examines it for its consistency in itself and its correlation with all the relevant evidence. Similarly, a person confronted by an alleged revelation tests its consistency and its conformity with all significant data. What God says is never contradictory; He cannot deny Himself (II Tim. 2:13). It is utterly impossible for God to lie (Tit. 1:2; Heb. 6:18; Num. 23:19). Therefore God's truth will not misrepresent historical truth. Mormons who risk so much on the validity of their alleged revelations should not fear this twofold test. First, are the Latter-day Saint scriptures logically consistent?

Difficult indeed is the task of one who tries to harmonize the teaching of Mormon revelations on any given subject. Polygamy, for example, is both commanded and condemned. According to one attempt to interpret this matter with some consistency the Mormons say polygamy as a lustful practice is condemned, but in their religion it is not lustful because many Mormon men had died and it was necessary to repopulate "Zion." But it was on July 12, 1843, in Nauvoo, Illinois, that Joseph Smith received the "revelation" concerning polygamy. The arduous journey to Utah had not yet taken its toll! Others will suggest that the contradiction is harmonized if we realize the "eternal covenant" with its attendant polygamy still stands. President Wilford Woodruff in 1890 under pressure of the United States Government, received a "revelation" to discontinue not the eternal covenant but the practice of polygamy. However, the covenant makes the practice eternal when it says, "If ye abide not in that covenant then are ye damned" (*Doctrines and Covenants* 132). It is difficult to see how even a later revelation could change such an emphatic eternal covenant.

But no alleged revelation can correct the contradiction in the polygamy passages regarding the wives of David and Solomon. The *Book of Mormon* decries "wicked practices, such as like unto David of old desiring many wives and concubines, and also Solomon, his son" (Jacob 1:15). Again, "Behold David and Solomon truly had many wives and concubines, which thing was abominable before me, saith the Lord" (Jacob 2:24). Contrast the latter "revelation" seeking to support polygamy by reference to the cases of David and Solomon. "David also received many wives and concubines, and also Solomon, . . . and David's wives and concubines were given unto him of me, by the hand of Nathan . . . and in none of these things did he sin against me save in the case of Uriah and his wife" (*Doctrines and Covenants* 132). Can a conscientious Mormon believe the plurality of David and Solomon's wives both a gift of God without sin as the *Doctrines and Covenants* teaches and a wicked and abominable practice in the sight of God as the *Book of Mormon* teaches. If a Mormon practices polygamy he will be condemned by one of his sacred writings; if he does not practice polygamy he will "be damned" by the other.

Mormon revelations are equally contradictory with respect to the question of whether there is one God or many. The *Book of Mormon* knows nothing of many Gods, but teaches the unity of Father, Son, and Holy Spirit in typical Trinitarian terminology. Smith wrote, "they are one God" (Mosiah 15:4). He refers to "Christ the Son, and God the Father, and the Holy Spirit, which is one Eternal God" (Alma 11:44). The redeemed, the *Book of Mormon* says, will sing praises around the throne "unto the Father, and unto the Son, and unto the Holy Ghost, which are one God" (Mormon 7:7). And on Smith's word this is "the only and true doctrine of the Father, and of the Son, and of the Holy Ghost, which is one God, without end" (II Nephi 31:21). When Zeezrom talked with Amulek, a man who said nothing contrary to the Spirit of the Lord, Zeezrom asked, "Is there more than one God?" Amulek answered, "No" (Alma 11:28-9).

In marked contrast to all this evidence of the oneness of the Godhead in the *Book of Mormon*, is the teaching of other Mormon revelations. Apparently Smith's ideas changed, not only on polygamy, but also on theology. He writes of "a time to come in the which, nothing shall be withheld, whether there be one God or many gods, *they* shall be manifest" (*D & C* 121:32). When it came time to create the world, the Gods had an argument.

> The Lord said, who shall I send? And one answered like unto the Son of Man, Here am I, send me. And another answered and said, Here am I, send me. And the Lord said, I will send the first. And the second was angry, and kept not his first estate, and at that day, many followed after him (*Pearl of Great Price*, Abraham, p. 41).

There follows the creation story with the name for God changed to Gods. The Gods said, ordered, organized, prepared, etc., "And the Gods said among themselves, On the seventh time we will end our work which we have counseled; and we will rest on the seventh time from all our work. . . . And thus were their decisions at the time that they counseled among themselves to form the heavens and the earth" (Abraham, p. 44). Shall a Mormon accept these later "revelations" of many Gods or the only true doctrine of the one God in the *Book of Mormon*? Latter-day Saints may try to explain the unity of Gods as one of thought and purpose, but that can hardly have been the intent of Joseph Smith's earlier statements. The inconsistency of their sacred writings remains.

The Mormons, if they believe their scriptures, must believe that all things were created and some things were not created! "The elements are eternal," according to *Doctrines and Covenants* (93:33). Consequently Talmadge argues, God "certainly did not create, in the sense of bringing into primal existence, the ultimate elements of the materials of which the earth consists."[14] On the other hand, the *Book of Mormon* teaches "he hath created all things, both the heavens and the earth, and all things that in them are, both things to act and things to be acted upon" (II Nephi 2:14). If a more emphatic statement is needed, Smith also says, "Yea, he is the very Eternal Father of heaven and of earth, and all things which in them are; he is the beginning and the end, the first and the last" (Alma 11:39). Now if all things, whether active or passive, owe their existence to God, not even the physical elements missed being created. How can a Mormon believe that the elements are both eternal and created?

The Mormon scriptures also contradict the Bible. God the Father, according to *Doctrines and Covenants*, has "a body of flesh and bones as tangible as man's (130:22b). But John 4:24 teaches, "God is spirit," and Jesus said, ". . . a spirit hath not flesh and bones as ye see me have" (Lk. 24:39). The Mormon scriptures teach that God is visible; the Bible teaches God is invisible (I Tim. 1:17; 6:16). Can a Mormon believe that God is a visible body and that God is an invisible Spirit?

A last instance of contradiction occurs in connection with the birthplace of Christ. Although the Bible reports Christ's birth in Bethlehem (Micah 5:2; Mt. 2:1,5), the *Book of Mormon* "predicts"

Jesus will be born in Jerusalem (Alma 7:9,10). Mormons attempt to explain this discrepancy by alleging that Jerusalem was once a state which included Bethlehem. But evidence for this is non-existent. They are two distinct cities five miles apart. Christ could not possibly have been born in both. One or the other of these accounts is not true. A Latter-day Saint cannot logically accept both.

Talmadge claims Mormon writings are free from contradiction, admitting the validity of this test.[15] But his claim does not stand examination. No one can believe at the same time that polygamy is eternally approved and not proper now, that there is but one God and there are many Gods, that God the Father is flesh and bones and invisible spirit, that God did not create the elements of nature but created everything there is, and that Jesus was born in both Jerusalem and Bethlehem. Even on a theory of continuous revelation God cannot deny Himself. Both Christians and Mormons agree that the Bible originates with God. But who can believe writings which contradict themselves and the Bible come from God?

Mormon claims, if true, would necessarily accord with the relevant facts as well as the law of contradiction. The Book of Mormon provides abundant opportunity for factual examination. It purports to present the history of two great civilizations in South and North America from about 600 B.C. to A.D. 421. At the command of God two Jewish brothers, Nephi and Laman, sailed with their families from Jerusalem in a home-made boat and landed in South America around 590 B.C. In spite of continued "revelations" from God the descendants warred with each other as they travelled northward. The dark skinned Lamanites who survived gave birth to many of the American Indians. Before the Nephites were wiped out one of their leaders by the name of Mormon buried plates inscribed with the history of these peoples in "reformed Egyptian hieroglyphics." The records remained in the hill Cumorah near Palmyra, New York, until Joseph Smith "dug them up" and "translated" them in 1830.

Is this story true? Several difficulties with it are noted by the impartial government sponsored Smithsonian Institution's Bureau of American Ethnology in Washington, D. C. Since Mormon missionaries often allege support from this source, inquiries are frequent. A mimeographed "Statement Regarding the Book of Mormon" says

"Smithsonian archeologists see no connection between the archeology of the New World and the subject matter of the Book (of Mormon)." The same "statement" adds the specific points which follow.

Although anthropologically a race stemming from Jews in Palestine would have the characteristics of Mediterranean Caucasoid, "The physical type of the American Indian is basically Mongoloid." Instead of travelling by boat, about 600 B.C., "It is believed that the ancestors of the present Indians came into the New World — probably over a land bridge known to have existed in the Bering Strait region during the last Ice Age — in a continuing series of migrations beginning about 30,000 years ago."

Rather than bringing a culture from the old world, "Extensive archaeological researches in southern Mexico and Central America clearly indicate that the civilizations of these regions developed locally from simple beginnings without the aid of outside stimulus."

Were the first Easterners to reach America Jews? "Present evidence indicates that the first people to reach America from the East were Norsemen who arrived in the northeastern part of North America around 1000 A.D."

And what about a language called "reformed Egyptian hieroglyphics"? We know of no authentic cases of ancient Egyptian or Hebrew writing having been found in the New World. Reports of findings of Egyptian influence in the Mexican and Central American area have been published in newspapers and magazines from time to time, but thus far no reputable Egyptologist has been able to discover any relationship between remains and those in Egypt.[16]

In view of these conclusions the Smithsonian Institution can hardly be alleged by overly enthusiastic young missionaries to have employed the Book of Mormon in its scientific research. Scientific knowledge may still be very limited, it is true. We do not know what may be discovered in future investigations. But present knowledge indicates that the Mormon story is false in every detail.

In arguing for the validity of the "reformed Egyptian" language Mormons will adduce the testimony of two linguists in New York City about 1830. The only two contemporaries qualified to identify the language are featured in the *Pearl of Great Price* and an excerpt from it published in the popular pamphlet, "Joseph Smith Tells His Own Story."[17] According to these sources, Martin Harris, a friend of Smith's, took a copy of some of the plates and their translation to Dr. Mitchell and Professor Anthon in New York City. Columbia University's professor Anthon said the translated plates were Egyptian correctly translated, and gave Harris a certificate to that effect, but when he heard how the plates were discovered tore up the certificate. Harris then left and "went to Dr. Mitchell, who sanctioned what Professor Anthon had said respecting both the characters and the translation."[18]

This account is exploded by none other than Professor Anthon himself. In a letter addressed to Mr. E. D. Howe, Painesville, Ohio, February 17, 1834, Anthon wrote with italicized emphasis, "The whole story about my having pronounced the Mormonite inscription to be 'reformed Egyptian hieroglyphics' *is perfectly false.*" He stated that a simple farmer had called on him with a note from Dr. Mitchell "requesting me to decipher, if possible, a paper which . . . Dr. Mitchell confessed he had been unable to understand." Thus Dr. Mitchell's alleged testimony is negated. Anthon further emphasized:

> *This paper was in fact a singular scrawl. It consisted of crooked characters disposed in columns and had evidently been prepared by some person who had before him at the time a book containing various alphabets. Greek and Hebrew letters, crosses, and flourishes, Roman letters inverted or placed sideways, were arranged in perpendicular columns, and the whole ended in a rude delineation of a circle, divided into various compartments, decked with strange marks, and evidently copied after the Mexican Calendar given by Humboldt, but copied in such a way as not to betray the source whence it was derived. . . . the paper contained anything else but "Egyptian hieroglyphics."*[19]

Other aspects of Smith's tale do not square with facts. The manner in which he "translated" these most unusual characters is incredible. David Whitmer, at whose home much of the work was done, included an explanation in his sermon, "An Address to All Believers in Christ."

> I will now give you a description of the manner in which the Book of Mormon was translated. Joseph Smith would put the seer stone into a hat, and put his face in the hat, drawing it closely around his face to exclude the light; and in the darkness the spiritual light would shine. A piece of something resembling parchment would appear, and on that appeared writing. One character at a time would appear, and under it was the interpretation in English. Brother Joseph would read off the English to Oliver Cowdery, who was his principal scribe, and

when it was written down and repeated to Brother Joseph to see if it was correct, then it would disappear and another character with the interpretation would appear. Thus the Book of Mormon was translated by the gift and power of God, and not by any power of man.[20]

As a result of this allegedly supernatural activity Smith said, "I told the brethren that the Book of Mormon was the most correct of any book on earth, and the keystone of our religion, and a man would get nearer to God by abiding by its precepts than by any other book."[21] Strange that this "most correct" book in later editions suffered extensive alteration by men not supernaturally endowed. In the first 25 pages there were more than 500 changes,[22] and in the whole book more than 2,800 not counting punctuation.[23]

If Smith's work was done independently from the plates as claimed, it is impossible to account for extensive sections lifted right out of the King James translation. The golden plates were, according to no less an authority than Joseph Smith, buried from A.D. 420 until he dug them up. The alleged writers of the plates could have had no contact with a translation of the Bible made in A.D. 1611. Nevertheless the Book of Mormon plagiarizes at least twenty-seven thousand words from the King James translation.[24] And some of these represent readings in all probability not in the inspired original (I Jn. 5:7; III Nephi 11:27,36) and not the best rendering of what does stand in the original.[25] Furthermore some of the "predictions" of Christ's first coming supposed to be given hundreds of years in advance show obvious dependence upon King James expressions.

In spite of all this, Mormons will produce the testimony of eleven witnesses who saw the plates Smith is said to have translated. They are presented in two groups. The three witnesses, Oliver Cowdery, David Whitmer, and Martin Harris, signed a statement to the effect that they saw the engraved plates. An angel came down from heaven and laid them before their eyes and God's voice declared that the work was true. Eight witnesses are also highly publicized, largely Whitmers and Smiths: "Christian Whitmer, Jacob Whitmer, Peter Whitmer, Jr., John Whitmer, Hiram Page, Joseph Smith, Sen., Hyrum Smith, and Samuel Smith. These say Joseph Smith showed them plates having the appearance of gold and curious engravings. "For we have seen and hefted, and know of a surety, that the said Smith has got the plates of which we have spoken."[26]

How valuable is all this testimony? Not one of these people was qualified to recognize another language. If they literally saw plates with "curious" markings and "hefted" them, this is of no scholarly significance. And in what way did they "see" them? Prior to their view of the plates, Smith gave the three witnesses this "revelation":

> Behold, I say unto you, that you must rely upon my word, which if you do with full purpose of heart, you shall have a view of the plates, and also of the breastplate, the sword of Laban, the Urim and Thummin. . . . And it is by your faith that you shall obtain a view of them . . . And ye shall testify that you have seen them even as my servant Joseph Smith, Jun., has seen them; for it is by my power that he has seen them, and it is because he had faith. (*Doctrines and Covenants* 17:1,2,5).

A prominent citizen of Palmyra asked Martin Harris, "Did you see the plates with your natural eyes, just as you see this pencil case in my hand? Now say yes or no." Harris answered, "Why, I did not see them as I do that pencil case, I saw them with the eye of faith. I saw them just as distinctly as I see anything around me — though at the time they were covered over with a cloth."[27] David Whitmer explained, "Suppose that you had a friend whose character was such that you knew it impossible that he could lie; then, if he described a city to you which you had never seen, could you not, by the eye of faith see the city just as he described it?"[28] Here is admission from one who should know, that we have not eleven literal witnesses, but just one, Joseph Smith. If people are looking for confirmation of Smith's story, they do not have it in the testimony of such "witnesses." They apparently took Smith's word for the very existence of plates. But he too saw them by faith as the passage from *Doctrines and Covenants* (17:5) declares. In all probability, then, there actually were no literally visible gold plates at all! And when the faith of these witnesses waned, eight of the eleven defected from the Church of Jesus Christ of Latter-day Saints.[29]

Where then did Smith obtain his ideas? One major source was the Bible. Not only did he quote whole chapters and sections, but he also seems to have imitated many of its stories. A second source may have been Solomon Spaulding's historical novel, *The Manuscript Found*. Mormons often disparage any idea of dependence on another book, *The Manuscript Story*. In so doing they fail to answer such students of Mormonism as E. D. Howe, Pomeroy Tucker, William A. Linn, James D. Bales, and Walter R. Martin. One such scholar, J. H. Beadle concludes, "The true theory no doubt is, that the writing of Spaulding (*The Manuscript Found*) was taken by Smith, Rigdon, Cowdery and others, as the suggestion and idea of their work; but it was greatly modified and interpolated by them."[30] A third source is a distant relative of Joseph Smith's father, Rev. Ethan Smith, who visited the family in 1822 and again in 1825. The Congregational minister thought the American Indians were descendants of the lost tribes of Israel, and sought the help of Joseph in finding Indian relics in the hill Cumorah. Joseph had access to his *View of the Hebrews*.[31] Also in circulation were James Adair's *History of the American Indians*, published in 1775, and Abbe Clavigero's *History of Mexico*, printed in 1787.[32] Add to these materials the apt imagination of Joseph Smith, a "peek stone adict" known for hunting buried treasure,[33] and the elements of the *Book of Mormon* seem adequately explained without any revelations.

The story of its supernatural origin fails to fit the facts; instead, the facts confirm the book's fallibility. It contains many anachronisms and blunders. Laban wielded a sword made of "the most precious steel" before 592 B.C.[34] (I Nephi 4:9). Although compasses are thought to have originated around A.D. 1000,[34] Nephi sailed across the ocean with the aid of a compass around 600 B.C. (I Nephi 18:12). The earliest French developed from Latin about A.D. 700,[35] but Jacob, before A.D. 421 concludes his book, by bidding his brethren "adieu" (Jacob 7:27, dated 544 B.C. and A.D. 421). Walter R. Martin concludes that the *Book of Mormon* "betrays a great lack of information and background on the subject of world history and the history of the Jewish people."[36]

But what about the prophecies of the *Book of Mormon* and the *Doctrines and Covenants*? Latter-day Saints often claim that these prove the supernatural origin of the book. And some of Smith's prophecies have come to pass. In 1844 he predicted Christ would not return to earth in the next forty years. Smith said his own name would be held for good and evil among all nations. Such prophecies, however, are not of sufficient detail and significance of themselves to prove supernatural knowledge. Others were based upon discernible trends, such as that of the Civil War, predicted December 25, 1832 (*Doctrines and Covenants* 87). At the time

Smith made the prophecy the nation expected war. On July 14, 1832, Congress passed a tariff act which South Carolina, threatening to secede, declared null and void. President Jackson sent the nation's troops and warships to Charleston. Governor Hayne vowed to defend his state's sovereignty or die "beneath its ruins."[37] Joseph Smith was not alone in predicting civil war at that dark Christmas season. Are all who did recipients of "revelation"? Furthermore, included in Smith's prediction was the assertion, ". . . then war shall be poured out upon all nations." This does not fit the facts; the Civil War did not develop into a world war.

Fifty-eight prophecies of Joseph Smith examined in detail by G. T. Harrison failed to come to pass. The former third generation Mormon concludes:

> A baseball player who did not have a higher rating as a ball player than Joseph Smith's average as a true prophet, could not even play on the cinderlot team. He would not even be able to catch a ball. After studied calculation we find his rating as a prophet to be: No hits. No runs. 58 errors.[36]

Now, even Mormon scientists acknowledge that the *Book of Mormon* story has yet to be shown to fit the facts. When Mormon missionaries say that more things have been proven true by archeology in the *Book of Mormon* than in the Bible, they may be refuted by professors of Brigham Young University, Provo, Utah. Members of the University Archeological Society writing in the Society's *Newsletter* are emphatic. "The statement that the Book of Mormon has already been proved by archeology is misleading. . . . That such an idea could exist indicates the ignorance of our people with regard to what is going on in the historical and anthropological sciences."[39] Joseph E. Vincent admits:

> Many times, Mormon missionaries have told their investigators that such late-period ruins as Monte Alban (periods III-V), Yagul, and Mitla were built by the Nephites and that the archeologists would confirm this. Both claims are untrue. However, the earliest periods of the area, Monte Alban I and II, although as yet little known, are of Pre-classic (i.e., Book of Mormon period) date. One may think of these earlier peoples as Jaredites or Nephites, but if so it must be on the basis of faith, not archeology, for so far there is no explicit evidence that the Book of Mormon peoples occupied this area (Oaxaca, in the Isthmus of Tehuantepec area of Mexico).[40]

In addition these scholars acknowledge that not one city mentioned in the *Book of Mormon* has been identified, and that Mormon missionaries have made unsupportable claims to the effect that non-Mormon archeologists have used the book in their research.[41]

It seems well within the bounds of evidence to conclude, then, that the Latter-day Saint scriptures are not only inconsistent, but unsupported by known facts. There is no evidence of the alleged races, ocean voyage, arrival in the new world, transplantation of culture, engraved plates, reformed Egyptian hieroglyphics, or any possibility to translate a foreign language on the part of the "translator." Evidence does show adequate sources of the material, and its human and erroneous character in spite of numerous corrections since the first edition.

Any mother finding her child involved in such contradictions and falsehoods as these would conclude he did not speak the truth. A judge who caught a suspect in several inconsistencies and fabrications would doubt that he told the whole truth and nothing but the truth. It is difficult to see how any other conclusion is justified with respect to the sacred writings of Mormonism.

Latter-day Saints may still insist that Joseph Smith claimed to be a prophet. Suppose we grant the possibility of prophets in the twentieth century. How would we distinguish a true prophet from a false one? We would follow the counsel given the ancient Israelites who cried out, "How shall we know the word which the Lord hath not spoken?" (Deut. 18:21). Two tests were given; the first is doctrinal. Any alleged prophet's teaching about God must be consistent with revelation to that point. Even though the self-acclaimed prophet is able to perform signs and wonders, if he says, "Let us go after other gods which thou hast not known, and let us serve them; thou shalt not hearken unto the words of that prophet, or that dreamer of dreams" (Deut. 13:2-3). Whoever directs people to another god, however wonderful his works, is not a true prophet of God. Joseph Smith's flesh-and-bones god is not the God of the Bible or Christianity. Can he be a true prophet?

The second test of a true prophet requires that every predictive sign must come to pass. Suppose a self-appointed prophet teaches the truth concerning God. Is that a sufficient guarantee of his authenticity? The Scriptures say, "When a prophet speaketh in the name of the Lord, if the thing follow not nor come to pass, that is the thing which the Lord hath not spoken, but the prophet hath spoken it presumptuously: thou shalt not be afraid of him" (Deut. 18:21-22). Whoever predicts things which fail to take place is not a true prophet of God. Joseph Smith's predictions, in numerous cases, failed to come to pass. Can he be a true prophet? May God use this evidence to deliver many sincere people from enslavement to counterfeit "revelation." Mormons who refuse to follow this evidence where it leads, nevertheless, affirm belief in the Bible, and on that basis the remaining questions can be discussed.

2. *The Gospel*

A Christian may well ask a Latter-day Saint, "Is your main business the preaching of the gospel?" Mormons may well answer, "Indeed, it is. Our Church is built upon the gospel." Others remain in an "awful state of blindness" because "the plain and most precious parts of the gospel of the Lamb . . . have been kept back by that abominable church" (I Nephi 13:32). It is precisely to restore the gospel lost in an apostate church that the Church of Jesus Christ of Latter-day Saints has been raised up. It fulfills the prediction, "I will bring forth unto them, in mine own power, much of my gospel, which shall be plain and precious, saith the Lamb" (I Nephi 13:34). Churches remain Christ's church, the Lord is quoted as saying, only "if it so be that they are built upon my gospel" (3 Nephi 27:8).

Is the present Church of Jesus Christ of Latter-day Saints now giving pre-eminence to the gospel? Because of the complexity of the program, that commendable original intention may not in fact be achieved. One or more of Mormonism's other facets which arise from varied sources may usurp the primary place of the gospel. From Roman Catholicism comes the emphasis upon a hierarchy headed not by a pope but a president who expresses present day revelations from God to man. The Campbellites suggested the concept of baptismal regeneration which leads to fascination with baptism for the dead. Judaism is reflected in a prominent priesthood and preoccupation with legalistic works. Smith's and Young's experiences in Masonry provided ideas of secret symbolism and temple ceremonies. The notion of polygamy and blood atonement (by men

now), as well as of a modern prophet, come from Islam. Mohammed
so impressed Joseph Smith that he designated himself "the modern
Mohammed." And the Rosicrucian doctrine that men are gods in
embryo sparked Smith's theory that "As man is, God once was, as
God is, man may become."[42]

Among these multiple interests the gospel may easily take
second place. That may have happened in an article by LeRoy
E. Cowles entitled, "Church of Jesus Christ of Latter-day Saints."
After only one sentence about Christ's atonement, the former
president of the University of Utah discusses Mormon history, organization, administration, education, temples, missions, giving, and
welfare.[43] On the other hand, apostle Richard Evans, in "What is
a Mormon?" emphasizes that Joseph Smith "was commissioned of
God to effect a 'restoration' of the Gospel of Jesus Christ and to
open a new Gospel 'dispensation'." Although the gospel of Jesus
Christ was proclaimed in the heavens before the world was, Evans
explains, a last restoration occurred in the early nineteenth century
beginning "the dispensation of the fullness of times."[44] In theory,
if not always in practice, Mormonism intends to give pre-eminence
to the restored gospel.

Christians have a question, however. Is the Mormon message
in fact the Biblical gospel? The popular pictorial book, *The Mormon
Story*, claims it is.

> The old but newly revealed Gospel of Jesus Christ that Joseph Smith
> was to share with his fellow men was the same as had been given to
> the "Jews" and "Gentiles" in Palestine and also to the ancient inhabi-
> tants (Nephites) in the Americas nearly 2000 years ago by Jesus
> Christ himself in person.[45]

Can Mormons make good this claim? They must or be discredited!
Their own Biblical authority insists "though we (apostles) or an
angel from heaven (Moroni) preach any other gospel unto you than
that which we have preached to you, let him be accursed" (Gal. 1:8).
For the sake of their own souls Mormons must honestly face this
destiny-determining issue. Have they believed the one true gospel?
The remaining questions of this study will serve to formulate an
answer to this fundamental consideration.

3. *Christ*

At the heart of the Biblical gospel is the doctrine of the deity and incarnation of Jesus Christ. Suppose you ask a Mormon if he believes these truths. Make your question specific: "Do you believe that Jesus is the Christ (the anointed Messiah) who was God (Jn. 1:1) and became flesh (Jn. 1:14)?" What reply is a Mormon likely to give?

One of the most influential Mormon authors, James E. Talmadge, answers emphatically:

> No one professing a belief in Christianity can consistently accept the Holy Scriptures as genuine and deny the preexistence of Christ, or doubt that before the birth of the Holy One as Mary's babe in Bethlehem of Judea, He had lived with the Father as an unembodied spirit, the Firstborn of the Father's children. . . . Christ while a man among men repeatedly affirmed the fact of His antemortal life that he came forth from the Father, and would return to the Father on the completion of His mission in mortality.[46]

But however emphatically Christ's pre-existence is asserted, Mormons do not teach His deity in a Trinitarian sense. Christ is not the Son of God as orthodox Christians have understood the Scripture, but a "spirit-child of God" as all human beings are supposed to have been prior to their birth. Mormon terminology is clarified by Lowell L. Bennion's chart of "Stages and Opportunities in Man's Eternal Life."[47]

When God, "the most intelligent" of the eternal intelligences, decided to clothe the others with spiritual form, Christ was the first-begotten. Christ was not eternally the Father's Son; He was not eternally pre-eminent. He "was the Firstborn Spirit Child, and from that day forward he has had, in all things, the pre-eminence."[48] Clearly then, Mormons do not teach that Christ was essentially one with the Father, or that He was God. And they are willing to alter Scripture which teaches Christ's actual deity. Their treatment of John 1:1 is similar to that of Jehovah's Witnesses. Senator Wallace F. Bennett in his book, *Why I Am A Mormon*, with the doctrinal "imprimatur" of the President of the L.D.S. Washington Stake, says, "We would read it thus: In the beginning was Jesus, and Jesus was with God, and Jesus was [a] God."[49] Jehovah's Witnesses, believing in only one God, print "a god" with a small letter "g"; Mormons believing in many Gods, translate it with a capital "G." But by inserting "a" before "God" both deny the true deity of Jesus Christ who is eternally and essentially one with the Father and the Spirit. John 1:1 still stands! "The Word was God."

Unable to understand and accept the actual deity of Jesus Christ or the doctrine of the Trinity, the Mormons nevertheless believe Jesus was the Messiah.

> We hold that Jesus Christ was the one and only Being fitted to become the Savior and Redeemer of the world, for the following reasons: (1) He is the only sinless Man who has ever walked the earth. (2) He is the Only Begotten of the Eternal Father in the flesh, and therefore the only Being born to earth possessing in their fulness the attributes and power of both Godhood and manhood. (3) He is the One who had been chosen in the primeval council of the Gods and foreordained to this service.[50]

But all such praise of Christ as redeemer falls far short of Christian teaching. If Jesus was not the one true God, He is unable to save. And what is this "council of the Gods"? They are three separately and physically distinct Gods, according to Apostle Talmadge. He explains:

> Three personages composing the great presiding council of the universe have revealed themselves to man: (1) God the eternal Father; (2) His Son, Jesus Christ; and (3) the Holy Ghost. That these three are held to be separate individuals, physically distinct from each other is demonstrated by the accepted records of divine dealings with man.[51]

Then in flatly repudiating the doctrine of the Trinity, Talmadge adds, "This cannot rationally be construed to mean that the Father, the Son, and the Holy Ghost are one in substance."[52]

Why is the unity of the Godhead irrational to Talmadge? Two, let alone three, material things cannot occupy the same space at the same time! And, "Admitting the personality of God, we are compelled to accept the fact of His materiality."[53] Why so? Then it becomes impossible to understand the personality of "intelligences," "spirit-children," "unembodied spirits," and the Holy Spirit! Nevertheless they teach that the Father and Son, if not the Holy Spirit, have literal flesh-and-bones bodies.

We know that both the Father and the Son are in form and stature
perfect men; each of them possesses a tangible body, infinitely pure
and perfect and attended by transcendent glory, nevertheless a body
of flesh and bones.[54]

If, as Talmadge argues, personality requires a flesh-and-bones
body, the Holy Spirit must not be a person. But that contradicts what
Joseph Smith wrote by alleged revelation, when he said, ". . . the
Holy Ghost has not a body of flesh and bones, but is a personage of
spirit" (*Doctrines and Covenants* 130:22). The Christian doctrine
of the Trinity simply says that from all eternity all three members of
the Godhead were personages of the spirit. As such they have no
flesh-and-bones body. They are not therefore bound by the physical
law that two things cannot dwell in the same place at the same time.
As infinite spirits they are unlimited by space and time. In order that
Mormons may see that God is one, and that Jesus Christ is God, they
must be helped to understand that personality does not require a
physical organism.

Christians can help Latter-day Saints by emphasizing that God
is spirit (Jn. 4:24), and that our risen Lord taught, "a spirit hath
not flesh and bones" Lk. 24:39). That is why the Bible says that
God is invisible (I Tim. 1:17; 6:16; Heb. 11:27), and that "No
man hath seen God at any time" (Jn. 1:18; 5:37). And that is why
Joseph Smith is mistaken when He claims to have seen the Father
as well as the incarnate Son. Although there is no literal physical
vision of God, there is another way of "seeing him who is invisible"
(Heb. 11:27). In the faith chapter of the Bible that means not the
sense of sight, but faith. Unfortunately, however, that is not the
kind of vision Joseph Smith claimed. But Mormons today need
not perpetuate his error. On the basis of Scripture they can affirm
their faith that God is invisible spirit.

Knowing that God is spirit, Mormons can then understand that
the Bible employs many figures of speech from the material realm
to designate that which is non-material. God's "eyes," "ears,"
"arms," and "face," are metaphorical terms referring to divine knowledge, strength, and presence. If it is foolish to think that God is a
literal mother hen with wings and feathers (Ps. 91:4), it is equally
foolish to think that God is a big physical man like Brigham Young.
The image of God in man is not physical, but spiritual (Col. 3:10;
Eph. 4:24).

Another Biblical figure of speech for God is "Father." Mormons attempt to take this literally, saying that God literally begets all the spirit-children in the pre-earth stage of existence. Jesus is the first of these literal sons, and hence is called the Son of God. In the Bible the phrase Son of God may be used of Jesus as conceived by the supernatural power of the Spirit (Lk. 1:35), but more frequently is parallel to the figures of "image," and "Word." These terms attempt to express in human language the eternal relationship between the first and second persons of the Trinity. The Second Person is eternally *of* the same divine nature as the Father, not physically, but spiritually. Mormons need help to see that they have become hyperliteralists to the point of contradicting Bible teaching that God is spirit, if not to the point of blasphemy against God Himself.

The doctrine of the Trinity provides an understanding of all the passages that Mormons use in support of a presiding council of separate Gods, and at the same time it incorporates all the passages which assert that God is one. Trinitarians believe, as do Mormons, that Father, Son, and Holy Spirit are three persons. But Trinitarians also believe, as the Bible and the Mormon scriptures teach, that God is one. "The Lord our God is one Lord" (Deut. 6:4). That is not merely a unity of mind or purpose, for as Paul said to the polytheists who called things gods in heaven and earth, ". . . there is none other God but one" (I Cor. 8:4). Only on the basis of Trinitarianism can we integrate Christ's and the Spirit's distinctness from the Father and Their oneness with the Father. Although denying their essential oneness, Lowell L. Bennion admits, "It is not always clear from the context of Scripture which of the three is meant, since their lives and missions are so intimately related."[55] Why not, then, fully affirm with the apostle John, "The Word was God" (Jn. 1:1)? Only those who receive Him have the authority to be called "children of God" (Jn. 1:12).

4. *Redemption*

As a Christian prayerfully attempts to direct a Latter-day Saint's attention to the gospel, he may ask another important question. "Do you believe Christ's shed blood is the only basis for the forgiveness of your sins?"

In answering this query Mormons will extol Christ's atonement. As Talmadge says:

> However incomplete may be our comprehension of the scheme of redemption through Christ's vicarious sacrifice in all its parts, we cannot reject it without becoming infidel; for it stands as the fundamental doctrine of all scripture, the very essence of the spirit of prophecy and revelation, the most prominent of all the declarations of God unto man.[56]

The *Book of Morman* is equally emphatic, "There could be no redemption for mankind save it were through the death and sufferings of Christ, and the atonement of his blood" (Alma 21:9).

Just why do the disciples of Joseph Smith think Christ's death so significant? It has accomplished marvelous things for the entire human race. "All men are thereby exonerated from the direct effects of the Fall (of Adam) in so far as such effects have been the cause of evil in their lives."[57] As a result of Adamic sin all men face physical death. But because of Christ's atonement all men will be raised from the dead. As a result of our first parents' sin all men are born with a natural inclination toward evil with its consequent guilt and condemnation. But because of Christ's death for them, all are "at one(ment)" with God again. Any infant or unaccountable person who dies "will be counted among the redeemed and sanctified."[58]

Wonderful as may be the universal benefits of Christ's atonement, it is of little avail for the normal living Mormon! Christ's death is not the basis of his forgiveness.

> We hold that salvation from sin is obtainable only through obedience, and that while the door to the kingdom has been opened by the sacrificial death and the resurrection of our Lord the Christ, no man may enter there except by his personal and voluntary application expressed in terms of obedience to the prescribed laws and ordinances of the Gospel.[59]

Christ's work only opens the door; man's work must do the rest. Christ makes the down payment; Mormons must make payments all of their lives.

For Mormons, then, the atonement was not completely provided by Christ. Elder Bruce R. McConkie ridicules the Christian belief that salvation is not on the ground of human merit, but of Christ's merit alone.

Christians speak often of the blood of Christ and its cleansing power. Much that is believed and taught on this subject, however, is such utter nonsense and so palpably false that to believe it is to lose ones salvation. Many go so far, for instance, as to pretend, at least, to believe that if we confess Christ with our lips and avow that we accept him as our personal Savior, we are thereby saved. His blood, without other act than mere belief, they say, makes us clean.[60]

Of course the doctrine of justification by faith on the merit of Christ's work alone can be distorted. But the faith that justifies is also the faith that works in love (Gal. 5:6). Whoever holds that the atoning work of Christ provided only an opportunity for people to achieve their own salvation has missed the heart of the Christian message.

Mormons, as desperately as others, need to hear of the good news of the justification by faith. It provides (1) pardon from all sin and (2) the perfect righteousness of Jesus Christ. A Mormon who accepts the teaching of his church fails to realize that keeping laws (even if called the laws of the gospel) never has been the basis of anyone's rightousness in the sight of God. The Scriptures declare, "By the deeds of the law there shall no flesh be justified in his sight: for by the law is the knowledge of sin" (Rom. 3:20). The righteousness the Bible teaches is "without," or apart from the law (Rom. 3:21). Believers are justified "freely by his grace through the redemption that is in Christ Jesus: Whom God hath set forth to be a propitiation through faith in his blood" (Rom. 3:24-25). Not just Christians, but the Scriptures teach that men are pardoned, God's law satisfied, and God's wrath propitiated, by acceptance of the completed atonement of Christ.

Mormon priests, like those of old, perform their works in vain. "And every priest standeth daily ministering and offering oftentimes the same sacrifices, which can never take away sins" (Heb. 10:11). How pitiful that Mormons still think salvation depends upon subservience to such priests, and that there can be no salvation outside their fold! They dare say, "Except men come to these legal administrators and learn of Christ and his laws as newly revealed on earth, they cannot be saved in his everlasting kingdom hereafter."[61] The works of Mormon priests are no more able to save than those of Israel's priests. What a contrast to the full assurance enjoyed by trusting Christ who by one sacrifice for sin "perfected forever them that are sanctified," (Heb. 10:14). Of believers, not law-keepers,

God says, "And their sins and iniquities will I remember no more" (10:17). Let every Mormon who would add his works to Christ's work remember Hebrews 10:18, "Now where remission of these is, there is no more offering for sin."

Tragically, Mormons do not realize that in addition to pardon from all their sin, they may have Christ's perfect righteousness ascribed to them. They have not known the joy David experienced—the blessedness of the man unto whom God imputeth righteousness without works (Rom. 4:6). Your Mormon friends have missed the happiness of Abraham who "believed God and it was counted unto him for righteousness" (Rom. 4:3,5,9,11,13,22). And why was so much written about Abraham's righteousness by faith? "Now it was not written for his sake alone, that it was imputed to him; but for us also, to whom it shall be imputed, if we believe on him that raised up Jesus our Lord from the dead" (Rom. 4:23-24).

Mormons who refuse the free gift of complete pardon and perfect righteousness are much like the Israelites of old. The apostle Paul said of them, ". . . they have a zeal of God, but not according to knowledge. For they, being ignorant of God's righteousness, and going about to establish their own righteousness, have not submitted themselves unto the righteousness of God" (Rom 10:2-3). And with Paul a twentieth century Christian says, "Brethren, my heart's desire and prayer to God for Israel (Latter-day Saints) is that they might be saved" (Rom. 10:1).

5. *The Resurrection of Christ*

A necessary condition of salvation, according to Romans 10:9-10, is belief that Jesus was raised from the dead. Do Mormons confess Christ's resurrection? They do. Talmadge well says:

> The facts of Christ's resurrection from the dead are attested by such an array of scriptural proofs that no doubt of the reality finds place in the mind of any believer in the inspired records.[62]

In support of this statement the usual texts are listed and supplemented with quotations from other Mormon "revelations." The great emphasis in Latter-day Saint writings falls on Christ's resurrection as the firstfruits of the resurrection of all men (Alma 33:22).

Grateful not to find an issue at this point, Christians will proceed more hopefully to the remaining questions.

6. *Personal Trust*

Faith involves intellectual assent to Christ's deity, death, and resurrection. But it involves more than that. The gospel's truths, like a long-awaited registered letter, bring to us something very valuable. By the Spirit of God they bring the living Christ to a sinner. The recipient of the registered letter personally signs that he has received its prized contents. Similarly individuals addressed by the gospel personally "sign" that they have received Christ by complete commitment to Him. Consequently a Christian concerned for a Mormon friend will ask, "Are you personally trusting Jesus Christ Himself as your redeemer and Lord?"

A Mormon who follows the teaching of his religion should have no hesitation in affirming that he has a vital commitment. For Mormonism, as for evangelical Christianity, faith is not mere belief, "merely intellectual assent," or "passive as an agreement or acceptance only." Rather, faith is active, positive, "vivified, vitalized, living belief."[63] It follows that "Faith in a passive sense, that is, as mere belief in the more superficial sense of the term, is inefficient as a means of salvation."[64] The faith that occasions exaltation is

> a principle of power . . . that impels men to resolve and act . . . Faith thus becomes to us the foundation of hope, from which spring our aspirations, ambitions, and confidences for the future. Remove man's faith in the possibility of any desired success, and you rob him of the incentive to strive.[65]

With this active view of faith, Christians heartily agree. But little seems to be written in Mormon literature about fellowship with the living Lord. Individual Mormons seem to be related to God only through the mediation of the institutional church and its sacraments. Since Latter-day Saints may not know the joy of personal communion with God through the one mediator, Jesus Christ (I Tim. 2:5), Christians may help significantly at this point by relating their own experience of fellowship with Christ. Add as well the witness of a mature Mormon who for two years studied the Bible while preparing to teach theology in an L.D.S. Relief Society. Carolyn J. Sexauer, in "My Testimony of the Grace of God," writes:

I came out of Mormonism.

Since that wonderful day when I gave up trying to reconcile the teachings of Mormonism with the Word of God, as found in the Bible, and was "born again" of the Spirit, I have been happier than ever before in my life, and have known in full measure "the peace of God that passeth all understanding."

I live each day rejoicing. Every burden on my heart is gone. Every doubt and fear is gone.

For a long time I have had the desire to bear my testimony to others who are members of the religion into which I was born and in which I have lived most of my life until now.

Space will not permit my going into detail as to my own desperate struggles, my uncertainty and despair before arriving at the truth, but oh I want to make it as clear as these poor words of mine can possibly do, how glorious it is to know the Lord Jesus Christ as my personal Saviour; to be absolutely certain of my salvation apart from anything I have done, or can do; to be a possessor of the indwelling Spirit of Christ — to live under the matchless grace of God.

It is the difference between the darkest night and the brightest day. Having found the Light, no power on earth could cause me to go back into darkness.[66]

In view of testimonies like this, a Mormon who claims to have a vital faith in Christ may not in fact have experienced redemption. He may be trusting not only in Christ, but also in his own works. He may be helped to see this by our last question.

7. *Faith Alone*

"Do you depend upon some achievements of your own for justification or do you rest upon God's grace received through faith alone?" Here a Mormon will take clear exception. He may even call the doctrine of justification by faith a pernicious error.

One wonders if the Mormon attack on the doctrine of justification by faith alone is based on understanding of it. The caricature of the doctrine ridiculed by Talmadge is not taught by the Christian church. As the writer of the standard doctrinal text of Mormonism puts it, "justification by *belief* alone" is "a most pernicious doctrine."[67] Indeed it is. But Christianity has never promulgated a dogma to the effect that "a wordy profession of belief shall open the doors of heaven to the sinner."[68] The atonement of Christ alone opens the doors of heaven. A sinner who by faith identifies himself with Christ is justified, not by what he has done, but by Christ's death. Saved by grace alone, works will follow, as James teaches. But works are not the basis on which God pardons sin and imputes righteousness. This doctrine has yet to be fairly stated and refuted in the Mormon literature.

How then do the Mormons find it possible to say they believe in grace alone? Bruce R. McConkie explains, "All men are *saved by grace alone* without any act on their part, meaning that they are resurrected and become immortal because of the atoning sacrifice of Christ."[69] Although you may be resurrected to judgment, your resurrection is by grace alone! You may be in torment, but your immortality is by grace alone! In addition, "all men by the grace of God have the power to gain eternal life. This is called *salvation by grace coupled with obedience* to the laws and ordinances of the gospel."[70] Then after ridiculing the idea of Christ's shed blood as the sole ground of forgiveness, the same writer adds, "Salvation in the kingdom of God is available because of the atoning blood of Christ. But it is received only on condition of faith, repentance, baptism, and enduring to the end in keeping the commandments of God."[71]

By adding works to faith, Mormons destroy the very essence of grace. According to Romans 11:6 God's election of his people is of grace, "And if by grace, then it is no more of works: otherwise grace is no more grace. But if it be of works, then it is no more grace: otherwise work is no more work." These principles are mutually exclusive because works receive a merited reward but grace is poured out upon those who are undeserving. Grace is unmerited favor, the free gift of God. The Mormon's attempted combination of works and faith reveals a misunderstanding of both. More than that, it destroys the good news. Mormons cannot sing,

> Jesus paid it all,
> All to Him I owe;
> Sin had left a crimson stain,
> *He* washed it white as snow.

Instead, Mormons write, "Does God help those who seek him? Yes,
but all blessings are predicated upon obedience to law."[72] Propitiation
from individual sins comes "through the faith and good works of the
sinner," or "is conditioned on individual effort."[73] The phrase found
so frequently in Mormon works, "the laws of the gospel," is *never*
found in the Bible. As the books of Romans and Galatians state
so emphatically, there can be no mixing of law and gospel or works
and grace as the ground of justification before God.

In spite of Romans and Galatians, Mormon literature abounds
with references to the four basic laws or principles of the gospel.
These are usually listed as: (1) faith, (2) repentance, (3) baptism,
and (4) laying on of hands by the Mormon priesthood for receiving
the Holy Spirit. In view of such Scripture as Ephesians 2:8-10; Rom.
11:6; Gal. 2:16; it seems inconsistent to speak of faith and repentance as works. Together, repentant-faith, is the one act of turning to
God from idols (I Thess. 1:9). As such repentant faith is not an
achievement of man, but a forsaking of every humanly manu-
factured god and a complete casting of oneself upon Christ for
His righteousness. Whoever depends upon his own works for justification has not begun to understand Biblical repentance or faith.
They are the antithesis of human works! How then can they be
classed as the first two works necessary to obey the laws of the
gospel? The sinner who repents and trusts Christ is like the poor
swimmer who finally realizes that left to his own efforts he would
drown, ceases to struggle against the lifeguard, and completely re-
laxes in his care. Whoever claims that faith is just the beginning of
salvation and that you must struggle to keep afloat the rest of your
life has not faith.

The third and fourth principles of the Mormon gospel, baptism
and the laying on of hands, also are believed necessary to justification. "Without these ordinances they could not be saved, says the
scripture."[74] Mormons teach baptismal regeneration. "As a result
of this act of obedience remission of sins is granted."[75] On the
authority of *The Doctrines and Covenants* they hold one who is not
baptized cannot be saved. The passage reads, "And he that believeth
and is baptized shall be saved, and he that believeth not, and *is not
baptized, shall be damned*" (112:29). Mark 16:16 does not add the
last negative which is logically very strong. It is one thing to say,
"He that is of age votes," but quite another to say, "Anyone who does

not vote is not of age." (There could be other reasons for not voting.) It is one thing to say as Mark 16:16 does, "He that believeth and is baptized shall be saved," and quite another to say, as Joseph Smith does, "He that believeth not and *is not baptized* shall be damned." Baptism becomes essential for Mormons because they think it is "the means whereby each sinner may receive a cleansing from his past."[76]

It is not merely baptism that is necessary to pardon from sin, but baptism by the Mormon officials! "Remission of sins comes to the repentant believer through baptism, when it is performed by divine direction and under divine authority."[77] An L.D.S. tract entitled, "Baptism, How and By Whom Administered?" pontificates, "In order for the ordinance to be effectual, it must be performed by one authorized to act in the name of the Lord."[78] That means, called as was Aaron "by the voice of God." Now only Joseph Smith and the Mormon officials meet this test. And the same source insists, Christ "does not acknowledge unauthorized actions." Since baptism by Mormon officials is essential to salvation, it is not difficult to understand why the living are baptized vicariously for the dead Millions died without this ordinance before the time of Joseph Smith, and since his day. People now can be baptized for their relatives. Consequently Mormons pursue "endless genealogies" and think they help many people to salvation by repeated baptisms.

Needless to say, the Bible in its extensive passages on justification (Rom. 3:21 - 5:21; Gal. 2 - 3), does not teach that baptism is a ground of justification. Passages in the Gospels and Acts must be interpreted, then, as intending that repentant-faith is the sole condition of justification, while baptism in water is the immediate outward expression of faith. Normally, every Christian is baptized, but baptism is not that which washes away his sin. A person is justified by faith, not by baptism. Baptism is a work; works are not the basis of imputed righteousness. Baptism is the first act of obedience to the Master whom the believer trusts and loves. And nowhere in the Bible is baptism to be performed by Aaronic priests. The priesthood is done away by the perfect work of Christ (Heb. 5 and 7). Now every believer is a priest of God (I Pet. 2:5,9). Baptism on behalf of the dead is nowhere *taught* in Scripture, although there is an allusion to a practice of baptism for the dead which Mormons often quote (I Cor. 15:29). Whatever its purpose (which may have been very different from that of present-day Mormonism), the practice is not commanded anywhere in Scripture. Surely if souls would be condemned apart from proxy baptism an extensive passage of Scripture would clearly teach this. In fact it should appear in the great commission! Sound Bible interpreters do not base any major doctrine upon one such incidental, ambiguous mention.

There remains the fourth work of laying on hands. Talmadge explains that all the ministries of the Holy Spirit are dependent upon this ceremony.

> The bestowal of the Holy Ghost, which is to be regarded as a conferred right to His ministrations, is effected through the ordinance of the Holy Priesthood, accompanied by the imposition of the hands of him or those officiating.[79]

Scripturally, the Holy Spirit comes upon all who believe (Rom. 8:9, 14; I Cor. 12:13). The apostles in some cases laid hands upon groups previously unassociated with the Jews or unaware of Christ's coming, but these instances in no way prove that after the time of the apostolic eyewitnesses of the risen Christ, this practice should be required of everyone. In all the epistles with their extensive teaching on the work of the Holy Spirit, nothing makes it dependent upon any such human ceremony.

Mormons who think a particular observance of baptism and laying on of hands necessary to salvation, desperately need to be confronted with passages like Galatians 2:16. What did Paul write to these who mixed works and faith in his day?

> Knowing that a man is not justified by the works of the law, but by the faith of Jesus Christ, even we have believed in Jesus Christ, that we might be justified by the faith of Christ, and not by the works of the law: for by the works the law shall no flesh be justified.

As much as any member of legalistic non-Christian religions, Mormons need to learn the truth of Ephesians 2:8-10:

> For by grace are ye saved through faith; and that not of yourselves: it is the gift of God: Not of works, lest any man should boast. For we are his workmanship, created in Christ Jesus unto good works, which God hath before ordained that we should walk in them.

Surely works will follow genuine faith. We are reminded many times by the Mormons that James said, "Faith without works is dead," and Jesus said, "If ye love me, keep my commandments." But what Mormons fail to see is that we are brought into the family of God by acceptance of the Son of God. As regenerated children of God we then behave like sons. That behavior is not the reason we are sons, but the result of sonship (Jn. 1:12-13). Or, as adopted children we behave like sons. But conduct as members of the family does not obtain sonship for us; it demonstrates sonship. If a regenerated and legally adopted son of God should disobey his divine parent — as all do — he does not lose his sonship. He loses fellowship, and the loving Father chastens his sons (Heb. 12:5-11). Christ then becomes the erring child's advocate with the Father (I Jn. 2:1). Parents know that no child can live up to the standards of perfection; they do not disown children for failing to keep every rule. If divine sonship depended on keeping the law there would be no sons! No one ever was saved by keeping the law (Rom. 3:10-23). But children of God by faith lovingly seek to do their divine Father's will. Mormons may say people will then sin that grace may abound (Rom. 6:1). The fact that they raise the same objection to Christian doctrine that was raised against Paul's teaching, is good evidence Christians have the Scriptural view.

Dr. Harry Ironside, once called on by a Mormon missionary, asked, "And now, sir, would you kindly favor us with a short statement of what the gospel really is?"

"Certainly," he replied. "The gospel consists of four first principles. The first is faith; the second, repentance; the third, baptism for the remission of sins by one duly qualified; while the fourth is the laying on of hands of a man having authority, for the reception of the Holy Ghost."

Dr. Ironside then said, "Well, supposing one has gone through all this, is he then saved?"

The Mormon replied, "Oh, of course, no one can know that, in this life. If one goes on to the end, he will be exalted in the kingdom."[80]

That is a clear example of Wesley P. Walter's judgment:

> Mormonism completely misses real salvation *and exaltation* as a free gift of God's grace. The Gospel is reduced to laws and ordinances brought to men by a Christ whose only function as Savior is to guaran-

tee to men a resurrection. To those enmeshed in a religion so materialistic in emphasis and so lacking in reverence, evangelical Christianity must hold out an all-sufficient Savior who saves, sanctifies, *and glorifies* unworthy sinners who place all their confidence in Him alone.[81]

As a result of just such an approach Albert Place, for 29 years a Mormon, found Christ. An earnest Latter-day Saint, he sought to convert others in the army. But Monty Burgeson puzzled him. Monty listened while Albert Place read the *Book of Mormon*, and then quietly said, "But what about Jesus Christ and His salvation?" After attending Monty's church Place gradually began to understand what his friend meant. Let Albert Place give his own witness: "At a Bible conference in the church the speaker taught from the books of Romans and Galatians. For the first time in my life, I realized that salvation comes through faith in Christ's perfect work, not in my own works, regardless of how good. Further Bible study led me personally to make Christ my Savior and Lord."[82] Within a year Place had led his father, mother, brother, and sister to Christ. Now he serves the Lord as a missionary to Mormons in Salt Lake City, Utah. May other missionaries of Joseph Smith become missionaries of Jesus Christ as Christians confront them with the gospel of God's grace!

FOOTNOTES

1. Edwin Scott Gaustad, *Historical Atlas of Religion in America* (New York: Harper & Row, Publishers, 1962), p. 87.
2. *The World Almanac and Book of Facts for 1965*, p. 706.
3. Personal letter of Horace A. Christiansen, President of the Western States Mission, to Gordon Lewis, May 30, 1963.
4. Gordon B. Hinckley, *What of the Mormons?* (Salt Lake City, Utah: The Church of Jesus Christ of Latter-day Saints, 1947), pp. 17-19.
5. *Ibid.,* p. 19.   6. *Ibid.,* p. 30.   7. *Ibid.*
8. "Mormon Dynamo," *Time,* May 20, 1957, p. 48.
9. *The Denver Post,* Dec. 27, 1958, p. 5.
10. Robert W. Fenwick, "Saints on the March," *The Denver Post,* April 7, p. 60.
11. Hartzell Spence, "The Mormons," *Look,* Jan. 21, 1958, p. 57.
12. Horace A. Christiansen, *op. cit.*
13. *A Brief Statement of the Principles of the Gospel* (Salt Lake City: Church of Jesus Christ of Latter-day Saints, 1943), p. 222.
14. James E. Talmadge, *Articles of Faith* (Salt Lake City, Utah: Church of Jesus Christ of Latter-day Saints, 1952), p. 466.
15. *Ibid.,* p. 504.
16. "Statement Regarding the Book of Mormon," Smithsonian Institution, Bureau of American Ethnology, Washington 25, D. C., July 22, 1960.
17. Joseph Smith, *The Pearl of Great Price* (Salt Lake City, Utah: George Q. Cannon and Sons, 1891), pp. 68-69.
18. *Ibid.*
19. Walter R. Martin, *The Maze of Mormonism* (Grand Rapids, Michigan: Zondervan Publishing House, 1962), pp. 42-44 (Reprints the entire letter of Charles Anthon.)
20. Cited by Arthur Budvarson, *The Book of Mormon Examined* (LaMesa, California: The Utah Christian Tract Society, 1959), p. 11.
21. *Ibid.*   22. *Ibid.*
23. John L. Smith, *Has Mormonism Changed?* (Clearfield, Utah: The Utah Evangel Press, 1961), p. 34.
24. Arthur Budvarsson, *op. cit.,* p. 22.
25. Walter R. Martin, *op. cit.,* pp. 51-53.
26. The testimony of the three and eight witnesses is quoted in the introductory pages of the *Book of Mormon.*
27. Cited by G. T. Harrison, *Mormons Are a Peculiar People* (New York: Vantage Press, 1954), p. 91.
28. *Ibid.,* pp. 90-91.
29. James E. Talmadge affirms of only three of the witnesses that they died "in full fellowship" with the church, *op. cit.,* p. 503. All of the three witnesses apostacized, Martin, *op. cit.,* p. 51; and five of the eight witnesses defected from the Church, Budvarson, *op. cit.,* pp. 22, 26.

30. J. H. Beadle, *Life in Utah* (Philadelphia: National Publishing Co., 1870), p. 32.
31. G. T. Harrison, *op. cit.*, pp.12-20; Larry Jonas, *Mormon Claims Examined* (Grand Rapids: Baker Book House, 1961), pp. 30-39, 44.
32. Larry Jonas, *op. cit.*, pp. 21,26.
33. Walter R. Martin, *op. cit.*, pp. 22-25.
34. "Compass," *World Book Encyclopedia*, III, 735.
35. "French Language," *World Book Encyclopedia*, VI, 443.
36. Walter R. Martin, *op. cit.*, p. 53.
37. "Jackson, Andrew," *World Book Encyclopedia*, X, 11.
38. G. T. Harrison, *op. cit.*, p. 167.
39. Cited by Hal Houghey, *Archeology and the Book of Mormon* (Concord, California: Pacific Publishing Co., n.d.), pp. 5-6
40. *Ibid.*   41. *Ibid.*
42. John L. Smith, *op. cit.*, p. 9.
43. Vergilius Ferm, ed., *Religion in the Twentieth Century* (New York: The Philosophical Library, 1948), pp. 289-305.
44. Leo Rosten, ed., *A Guide to the Religions of America* (New York: Simon and Schuster, 1955), pp. 92-93.
45. Rulon S. Howells, *The Mormon Story* (Salt Lake City: Bookcraft, 1963), p. 30.
46. James E. Talmadge, *The Philosophical Basis of Mormonism* (Independence, Missouri: Zion's Printing and Publishing Co., 1915), p. 7.
47. Lowell L. Bennion, *The Religion of the Latter-day Saints* (Salt Lake City: L.D.S. Department of Education, 1940), p. 57.

STAGES AND OPPORTUNITIES IN MAN'S ETERNAL LIFE

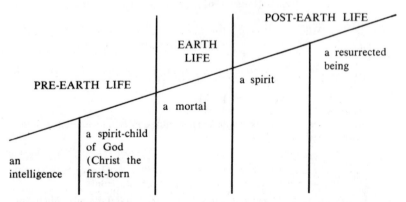

48. Bruce R. McConkie, *What the Mormons Think of Christ* (Salt Lake City: L.D.S. Missionary Committee, n.d.), p. 31.

49. Wallace F. Bennett, *Why I Am a Mormon* (New York: Thomas Nelson and Sons, 1958), p. 216.
50. James E. Talmadge, *op. cit.*, p. 13.
51. James E. Talmadge, *Articles of Faith*, p. 39.
52. *Ibid.*, p. 40.   53. *Ibid.*, p. 43.   54. *Ibid.*, p. 42.
55. Lowell L. Bennion, *op. cit.*, p. 32.
56. James E. Talmadge, *Articles of Faith*, p. 77.
57. James E. Talmadge, *The Philosophical Basis of Mormonism*, p. 15.
58. *Ibid.*, p. 16.   59. *Ibid.*, p. 17.
60. Bruce R. McConkie, *op. cit.*, p. 27.
61. *Ibid.*, p. 7
62. James E. Talmadge, *Articles of Faith*, pp. 385-386.
63. *Ibid.*, pp. 96-97.   64. *Ibid.*, p. 107.   65. *Ibid.*, pp. 102-103.
66. Carolyn J. Sexauer, *My Testimony of the Grace of God* (Helmet, Calif.: Christian Tract Society, n.d.), pp. 3-4.
67. James E. Talmadge, *op. cit.*, p. 107.
68. *Ibid.*, p. 108.
69. Bruce R. McConkie, *op. cit.*, p. 24.
70. *Ibid.*   71. *Ibid.*, p. 28.
72. Gordon B. Hinckley, *op. cit.*, p. 23.
73. James E. Talmadge, *op. cit.*, pp. 87, 89.
74. Samuel O. Bennion, *Fundamental Principles of the Gospel* (Salt Lake City: L.D.S. Missionary Department, n.d.), p. 35.
75. James E. Talmadge, *Articles of Faith*, p. 120.
76. Charles W. Penrose, *Repentance and Baptism* (Salt Lake City: Church of Jesus Christ of Latter-day Saints, n.d.), p. 5.
77. *Ibid.*
78. *Baptism, How, and By Whom Administered?* (Salt Lake City: Deseret News Press, n.d.), p. 2-3.
79. James E. Talmadge, *Articles of Faith*, p. 165.
80. H. A. Ironside, "The Mormon's Mistake," *Religious Research Digest* I (October - December, 1961), pp. 12-13.
81. Wesley P. Walters, "Mormonism," *Christianity Today*, December 19, 1960, p. 10 (230).
82. Albert Place, "I Was a Mormon," *Power*, May 8, 1955, p. 3.

FOR FURTHER STUDY

ARTHUR BUDVARSON, *The Book of Mormon Examined* (La Mesa, Calif.: The Utah Christian Tract Society, 1959). A 47 page booklet with photographic reproductions from the Book of Mormon.

LARRY W. JONAS, *Mormon Claims Examined* (Grand Rapids, Michigan: Baker Book House, 1961). An 85-page booklet with documented evidence answering Mormon claims.

WALTER R. MARTIN, *The Maze of Mormonism* (Grand Rapids, Michigan: Zondervan Publishing House, 1962). A thorough discussion and evangelical appraisal of Mormonism's history and teaching.

JOHN L. SMITH, *Has Mormonism Changed?* (Clearfield, Utah: Utah Evangel Press, 1961). In 62 pages a Southern Baptist preacher who has served many years in Utah shares his experience in witnessing to Mormons. He also publishes: *Hope or Despair?* (35 pp.), *Thirty-five Mormons and One Baptist Preacher* (48 pp.), and *120 Questions to ask Mormon Missionaries.*

SUGGESTIONS FOR TEACHERS

Good Teaching is marked by clarity of purpose. Review the content of this study and attempt to synthesize it in your own mind. This material may best be divided into two sections for two teaching sessions. Put into a few words a statement of objectives for classroom presentation. *Confronting the Cults* differs from some other works on the subject in that its purpose is not primarily negative — refuting false doctrine, but positive — winning cultists to to Christ.

1. Use the lead questions throughout the series to form the major divisions of the teaching sessions. Illustrate the way these questions keep discussion centered on the gospel by moving back to them from irrelevant issues.

2. Anticipate replies Christians may expect to these questions from Latter-day Saints. Evaluate the Mormon position and give specific guidance in answering erroneous beliefs.

3. Build confidence for effective personal witness by helping your group formulate possible approaches and answers. Use simple role playing situations to involve the group in learning the major doctrines of Mormonism. After the material has been studied allow several people to take the position of the cultist in confronting the believer. Let others assume the role of a believer. Simulate a conversation. Try various ways of presenting the truth in the face of error.

4. Secure a copy of the *Book of Mormon* (and possibly also *Doctrines and Covenants* and *Pearl of Great Price*) published by the Church of Jesus Christ of Latter-day Saints, Salt Lake City, Utah. Interested class members also may wish a copy to mark for use in witnessing to members of this cult. Passages revealing contradictions and historical discrepancies could be marked in one way, and verses for leading Mormons to Christ in another way.

5. Ask members of the class to give their personal testimony of salvation by grace apart from works as they would to missionaries of the Mormon church. Especially urge those who depended on a system of works prior to salvation to participate in this.

SAMPLE LESSON PLAN

SESSION 1

Aim

To guide the class to a knowledge of Mormon teaching on divine authority. To help the class develop skills of witnessing to those who accept books other than the Bible as divine revelation.

Approach

Lead a discussion on reasons for the phenomenal growth of Mormonism. What can Christians learn about propagating the faith from Mormons?

Outline

Divine Authority, revelation, inspiration
Question: "Do you base your teachings on revelations other than the Bible?"

A. On a blackboard list inconsistencies in the Mormon revelations.

B. List ways in which these revelations fail to fit facts.

C. List tests of a true prophet and give Joseph Smith a grade of passing or failing.

Conclusion

Sum up answers to Mormon claims of revelation from God in addition to the Bible. Discuss ways of presenting this material to Mormons. Would it be best to start with criticisms of Mormon revelations, or another subject?

SESSION 2

Aim

To guide the class to a knowledge of Mormon teaching about the gospel, Christ, redemption, Christ's resurrection, and personal faith. To help the class members develop skill in handling the Scriptures as they witness to Mormons.

Approach

Review briefly the previous lesson and set an attitude favorable to helping cultists, not embarrassing them.

Outline

   I. The Gospel
      Question: "Is your main business the proclamation of the gospel of Jesus Christ?"

  II. The Doctrine of Christ
      Question: "Do you believe that Jesus is the Christ, the eternal Word of God who has come in the flesh?"

 III. Redemption
      Question: "Do you believe that Jesus died for your sins?"

 IV. The Resurrection of Jesus Christ
      Question: "Do you believe that Jesus Christ arose from the dead bodily?"

  V. Personal Faith
      Question: "Are you personally trusting Jesus Christ as your Redeemer and Lord?"
      Question: "Do you depend upon some achievements of your own to contribute to your justification, or is it only by way of God's grace through faith?"

Conclusion

Sum up the Scriptural teaching on these subjects and challenge the class to be as zealous in witnessing to Mormons as Mormons are in seeking to reach them!

4

The Bible, The Christian, and Christian Science

For all the world's ills Christian Science peddles a panacea. Whoever discovers Mrs. Eddy's secret may triumph over the most grievous sin, the deepest sorrow, the sharpest pain, the most extended sickness and death itself. The optimistic keynote for the religion appears in the "Preface" of the founder's influential work, *Science and Health With Key to the Scriptures,* "To those leaning on the sustaining infinite, today is big with blessing."[1]

How then can a person overcome sorrow, sin, sickness and death? He need only replace the thought of sorrow with the thought of joy, the thought of sin with the thought of righteousness, the thought of sickness with the thought of health, and the thought of death with the thought of life. Mrs. Eddy quotes Shakespeare's famous line, "There is nothing good or bad, but thinking makes it so."[2]

To illustrate the power of mind over sorrow and death, Mrs. Eddy wrote:

> A blundering despatch mistakenly announcing the death of a friend occasions the same grief that the friend's real death would bring. You think that your anguish is occasioned by your loss. Another despatch, correcting the mistake, heals your grief, and you learn that your suffering was merely the result of your belief. Thus it is with all sorrow, sickness and death. You will learn at length that there is no cause for grief, and divine wisdom will then be understood. Error, not Truth, produces all the suffering on earth.[3]

This divine "science" works equally well with the common cold. To the practitioners Mrs. Eddy said, "If your patient believes in taking cold, mentally convince him that matter cannot take cold, and that thought governs this liability."[4] Suppose an objective factor in the environment makes it medically advisable for a person to live in another climate. What then?

> Invalids flee to tropical climates in order to save their lives but they come back no better than when they went away. Then is the time to cure them through Christian Science and prove that they can be healthy in all climates, when their fear of climate is exterminated.[5]

Treat sin in the same manner as sickness. "Expose and denounce the claims of evil and disease in all their forms, but realize no reality in them."[6] Mrs. Eddy explains further:

> A sinner is not reformed merely by assuring him that he cannot be a sinner because there is no sin. To put down the claim of sin, you must detect it, remove the mask, point out the illusion, and thus get the victory over sin and so prove its unreality. The sick are not healed merely by declaring there is no sickness, but by knowing that there is none.[7]

That every difficulty men face can be so neatly disposed of is good news indeed if true. Is it, however, the truth? Is this the gospel of Christ? International lecturer George Channing thinks it is. Mrs. Eddy, he asserts, is "the revelator of truth to this age. She brought the Comforter Jesus foretold. This Comforter is the science of Christianity and is available to all who desire to utilize God's power and God's law as Jesus did."[8] Will this claim stand examination? Is Mrs. Eddy's message the central message of the Scriptures to which the Holy Spirit bears witness? Does her teaching derive its authority from the Bible or from other sources? A clear answer to this vital question may help those who follow Mrs. Eddy.

Authority

Confronting Christian Scientists, then, Christians may ask, "Do you base your teachings on revelations or sacred writings other than the Bible?"

The standard reply is, "As adherents of Truth, we take the inspired Word of the Bible as our sufficient guide to eternal life."[9] Many times Mrs. Eddy reassures her reader (and possibly herself) that the Bible is her only authority.[10] In other passages, however, Mrs. Eddy acknowledges an additional authoritative source of religious truth. She writes, "The testimony of the material senses is neither absolute nor dvine. I therefore plant myself unreservedly on the teachings of Jesus, of his apostles, of the prophets, *and, on the testimony of the Science of Mind.*[11] Alongside Scripture Christian Science places its "scientific demonstrations." As Mrs. Eddy says, "Divine Science derives its sanction from the Bible, and the divine origin of Science is demonstrated through the holy influence of Truth in healing sickness and sin."[12]

When two sources of authority are implied — the Bible and the demonstrations of Divine Science — one must ask which takes precedence over the other. Let Mrs. Eddy reply, "The question, What is Truth, is answered by demonstration — by healing both disease and sin; and this demonstration shows that Christian healing confers the most health and makes the best man."[13]

Even the "truth" of Scripture itself is determined by the demonstrations of "divine science." "The one important interpretation of Scriptures [*not the literal, but*] the spiritual."[14] And Mrs. Eddy goes so far as to say, "Take away the spiritual signification of Scripture, and that compilation can do no more for mortals than can moonbeams melt a river of ice."[15] Where is this indispensable key to the Scriptures? *Science and Health* purports to give the metaphysical, spiritual, and original meanings of Biblical terms. She claims, "In Christian Science we learn that the substitution of the spiritual for the material definition of a Scriptural word often elucidates the meaning of the inspired writer."[16] Note how the exchange of meanings reduces the authority of the Bible to the authority of Mrs. Eddy!

"Adam. Error; a falsity; the belief in 'original sin,' sickness, and death; evil; the opposite of good, . . .

"Angels. God's thoughts passing to man; spiritual intuitions, pure and perfect; the inspiration of goodness, purity, and immortality, counteracting all evil, sensuality, and mortality.

"Baptism. Purification by Spirit; submergence in Spirit.

"Bridegroom. Spiritual understanding . . .

"Children. The spiritual thoughts and representatives of Life, Truth, and Love.

"Children of Israel. The representatives of Soul, not corporeal sense; the offspring of Spirit, who, having wrestled with error, sin, and sense, are governed by divine Science; . . . Christ's offspring.

"Church. The structure of Truth and Love; whatever rests upon and proceeds from Principle.

"Dan (Jacob's son). Animal magnetism; so-called mortal mind; error working out the designs of error; one belief preying upon another.

"Dove. A symbol of divine Science; purity and peace; hope and faith.

"Evening. Mistiness of mortal thought; weariness of mortal mind; obscured views; peace and rest.

"Hell. Mortal belief; error; lust; remorse; hatred; revenge; sin; sickness; death . . .

"Man. The compound idea of infinite Spirit; the spiritual image and likeness of God; the full representation of Mind.

"Mortal Mind. Nothing claiming to be something, for Mind is immortal; mythology; error creating other errors . . .

"River. Channel of thought."[17]

When such meanings are introduced into Scripture from *Science and Health* is it possible to accept a Christian Scientist's assertion that the Bible is the sole sufficient authority? Is there not an additional authority for George Channing who writes, "Christian Scientists feel that Mrs. Eddy's book, *Science and Health with Key to the Scriptures*, offers the *complete* spiritual meaning of the Bible? They believe that this full meaning would not have been available to them without Mrs. Eddy's discovery."[18] Protestants maintain that the Scriptures (without the benefit of an official interpreter) enable a person to be thoroughly furnished for every good work (II Tim. 3:16-17).

Ask Christian Science friends as well, whether *Science and Health* is infallible. Did not Mrs. Eddy, like all others, have a mortal mind? Did her mortal mind (the alleged source of all belief in sin, sickness, and death) in any way affect her writings? To compensate for her limitation Mrs. Eddy claimed to be the recipient of divine revelation. In the *Christian Science Journal*, January, 1901, she said:

I should blush to write of *Science and Health With Key to the Scriptures* as I have, were it of human origin and I apart from God its author, but as I was only a scribe echoing the harmonies of heaven in divine metaphysics, I cannot be super-modest of the Christian Science textbook.[19]

In *Science and Health* she boldly says, "No human pen nor tongue taught me the Science contained in this book."[20] Exploding this claim Walter Martin produces documentary evidence of dependence upon (1) the writings of P. Quimby, (2) *Murray's Reader,* (3) the ideas of Shakerism, and (4) James Henry Wiggin, a retired Unitarian minister who was more a ghost writer than "literary adviser."[21] If the original edition had been given by God, why so many changes since? Current editions of the book contain fourteen chapters; in 1875 it had only eight. The present book has 700 pages; the first only 456. The present is not the one said to be from God. And the original edition was not or it would have been true without corrections. Neither therefore deserves to be placed alongside the Scriptures, much less above them as their complete interpreter!

The Gospel

A second basic question a Christian may put to a Christian Scientist asks whether his main business is preaching the gospel of Jesus Christ. What is the central mission of Christian Science? The movement is best known for healing. Is physical healing the great commission of the Christian Scientists? Not according to Mr. Channing, who writes, "The objective of Christian Science is not *primarily* to heal physical disease but to regenerate human thought through spiritual understanding. Healing has the effect of attaining this regeneration in some degree."[22]

According to Mrs. Eddy, "The central fact of the Bible is the superiority of spiritual over physical power."[23] This spiritual superiority is evident in other ways than healing.

Healing physical sickness is the smallest part of Christian Science. It is only the bugle-call to thought and action, in the higher range of infinite goodness. The emphatic purpose of Christian Science is the healing of sin; and this task, sometimes, may be harder than the cure of disease; because, while mortals love to sin, they do not love to be sick.[24]

How, then, would Christian Science be defined? "As the law of God, the law of good, interpreting and demonstrating the divine principle and rule of universal harmony."[25]

In spite of these protestations to the contrary, healing must be recognized as a major distinctive of Christian Science. Emphasis on healing overshadows the good news of Christ's death, burial and resurrection. As Christian Scientists explain, they have been more successful in demonstrating against sickness than against money, sin, or marriage. And the reason for accepting the whole of Christian Science teaching is its healings. Mrs. Eddy admits:

> I do not maintain that anyone can exist in the flesh without food and raiment; but I do believe that the real man is immortal and that he lives in Spirit, not matter. Christian Science must be accepted at this period by induction. We admit the whole, because a part is proved and that part illustrates and proves the entire principle.[26]

Admittedly, the case for Christian Science rests upon alleged healings. It seems impossible to deny then, that healing rather than the gospel has priority in Christian Science. What has precedence in Scripture? Salvation from sin on the ground of Christ's atonement. Healings were simply signs "that ye may know the Son of man hath power on earth to forgive sins" (Mk. 2:10).

The great need of Christian Scientists, as other cultists, is the gospel of Christ. In confronting them directly with a basic truth of the Gospel Christians may ask, "Do you believe that Jesus is the Christ, the Son of God? Is Jesus the eternal Word who became flesh?" (Jn. 1:1,14).

If the followers of Mary Baker Eddy claim to believe on Jesus Christ their meaning is unbiblical. Consider for example Mrs. Eddy's explanation of Peter's great affirmation, "Thou are the Christ, the Son of the living God." That is:

> The Messiah is what thou has declared - Christ, the spirit of God, of Truth, Life, and Love, which heals mentally . . . It was now evident to Peter that divine Life, Truth, and Love, and not a human personality, was the healer of the sick and a rock, a firm foundation in the realm of harmony.[27]

What lies behind such misinterpretation of Scripture? In *Science and Health* there is a repeated distinction between Jesus and the Christ. "The word *Christ* is not properly a synonym for Jesus."[28] As Mrs. Eddy writes,

> Jesus is the name of the man who, more than all other men, has presented Christ, the true idea of God, healing the sick and the sinning and destroying the power of death. Jesus is the human man, and Christ is the divine idea; hence the duality of Jesus the Christ.[29]

Jesus was born at Bethlehem; Christ was eternal.[30] Jesus suffered; Christ "never suffered."[31] Jesus finally "disappeared"; Christ "continues to exist in the eternal order of divine Science."[32] Jesus was a human being; Christ is Truth,[33] a spiritual or divine idea.[34]

Obviously a Christian Scientist does not assert with Scripture that Jesus is the Christ. The Scientists may say wonderful things about Jesus. "Jesus of Nazareth was the most scientific man that ever trod the globe."[35] "Jesus was 'the best Christian on earth.' "[36] As such Jesus "represented" Christ, "the true idea of God."[37] Jesus "illustrates" the human blending with God that gives dominion over all the earth.[38] "Endowed with the Christ" Jesus became the "wayshower."[39]

Fine as such statements may appear, the Scientists never affirm that Jesus is the Christ. But the Bible declares this affirmation to be the test of genuine Christianity. "Every spirit that confesseth not that Jesus Christ is come in the flesh is not of God: and this is the spirit of antichrist" (I Jn. 4:3). The Gospel of John was written "that ye might believe that Jesus is the Christ" (20:31). To help Christian Science friends, Christians must show that the Bible, the Scientist's alleged authority, declares that Jesus of Nazareth is in fact the eternal son of God become flesh. They say, "Jesus Christ is not God."[40] But John 1 teaches that the Word who became flesh and dwelt among us lived eternally with God and was God (1:14, 1). The same passage says, "As many as received him (who was God), to them gave he power to become the sons of God." (1:12).

How does Mrs. Eddy interpret Jesus' claim, "I and the Father are one" (Jn. 10:30)? She explains, "that is, one in quality, not in quantity."[41] Of course it was not a "quantitative" oneness since

God is spirit and occupies no space. Nevertheless Jesus is one with the Father in His eternal Being as John 1:1 teaches. Mrs. Eddy's interpretation contradicts not only John 1 but also the context in John 10. The context records Jesus' power to keep His own as identical with that power on the part of the Father. Because Jesus claimed more than oneness of quality He was stoned.

Since Jesus is not the Christ for Christian Scientists He is not the second Person of the eternal Trinity. "The true Logos (Word, Jn. 1:1) is demonstrably Christian Science, the natural law of harmony which overcomes discord."[42] This law is eternal for "The Christ dwelt forever an ideal in the bosom of God."[13] Plainly then, the Christ is impersonal idea, truth or law. Jesus is a person; the Christ is impersonal. Neither are the Spirit and the Father persons. Christian Science is avowedly anti-trinitarian. Mrs. Eddy says, "The theory of three persons in one God suggests polytheism rather than the one, ever-present I am."[44] She does teach, however, that

> Life, Truth, and Love constitute the triune Persons called God, - that is, the triply divine Principle, Love. They represent a trinity in unity, three in one, - the same in essence though multiform in office; God the Father-Mother; Christ the spiritual idea of sonship; divine Science or the Holy Comforter. These three express in divine Science the three-fold essential nature of the infinite. They also indicate the divine Principle of scientific being, the intelligent relation of God to man and the universe.[45]

The relation of Jesus to the eternal Christ Principle is but one example of the relation of every human being to God. "As a drop of water is one with the ocean, a ray of light with the sun, even so God and man, Father and Son, are one in being."[46] Men may not always appear to be divine, but we cannot trust appearances. "Man's real existence" is "as a child of God."[47] Explicitly contradicting Scripture (Gen. 2:7; I Cor. 15:47-79, etc.) Mrs. Eddy adds, man is "not of the earth, earthy, but coexistent with God."[48] Discounting the evidence of the physical senses she also writes, "Man is not the offspring of flesh, but of Spirit, of Life, not matter. Because Life is God, Life must be eternal, self-existent."[49] Thus "Science reveals Soul as God, untouched by sin and death."[50] So the real man, in contrast to the visible man, is but one part God. God is "all-inclusive."[51] "All reality is in God and His creation, harmonious and eternal."[52] All appearances to the contrary, and the Bible notwithstanding, "All is divine Mind, or God and His idea."[53]

Two inferences follow from the pantheistic belief that all reality is divine. First, since God is all and God is spirit, all is spirit in reality. There is no matter. Mrs. Eddy explains, "God is all, therefore matter is nothing beyond an image in mortal mind."[54] What then of the Biblical evidence that Jesus had a body? And what about the physical sciences? On the authority of Mrs. Eddy, Christian Scientists insist, "Natural science as it is commonly called, is not really natural nor scientific, because it is deduced from evidence of the material senses."[55] Any reference to matter is therefore simply "error of statement."[56] There are not two bases of being, matter and mind, but one alone, — Mind.[57] So the "visible" Jesus was not the real Jesus. The real Jesus was invisible divine principle. His divinity is in principle no different than that of any other man's. He was not different from other men, except in degree. He was not the unique, only begotten Son of God (John 3:16; Col. 1:15; Heb. 1:3-13).

A second inference from the pantheism of Mary Baker Eddy relates, not to matter, but to evil. Since all that is real is divine and God is good, all is good. There is no evil, sin, sickness or death. The Christian Science textbook explains the common acceptance of evil as real.

> The only reality of sin, sickness, or death is the awful fact that unrealities seem real to human, erring belief, until God strips off their disguise. They are not true, because they are not of God. We learn in Christian Science that all inharmony of mortal mind or body is illusion, possessing neither reality nor identity though seeming to be real and identical.[58]

From the perspective of Mrs. Eddy, "Nothing is real and eternal, — nothing is spirit, — but God and His idea. Evil has no reality. It is neither person, place, nor thing, but is simply a belief, an illusion of material sense."[59] Since sin is unreal there need be no atonement for it. Mrs. Eddy's pantheism makes Christ's atonement a needless mirage. But in the gospel atonement for sin receives indispensable priority.

Redemption

So real is sin from the Biblical perspective that no man can be right before God "without the shedding of blood." Propitiation is possible according to Romans 3:25 only by faith in Christ's blood. Therefore we ask Christian Scientists, "Do you believe that Christ's shed blood is the only basis for the forgiveness of your sins?"

For followers of Mrs. Eddy the eternal Christ did not suffer in the flesh, but Jesus of Nazareth did, or appeared to. However, his suffering and death did not propitiate the Father.[60] "Jesus aided in reconciling man to God by giving man a truer sense of Love."[61] His atonement is "the exemplification of man's unity with God."[62] "The efficacy of the crucifixion lay in the practical affection and goodness it demonstrated for mankind," and "Every pang of repentance and suffering, every effort for reform, every good thought and deed, will help us to understand Jesus' atonement for sin and aid its efficacy."[63] As men practice divine Truth and Love sin (illusion) is destroyed. "Being destroyed, sin needs no other form of forgiveness."[64] Overcoming error in the daily walk, men achieve their own "at-one-ment" with Truth and Love. "Christians do not continue to labor and pray, expecting because of another's goodness, suffering, and triumph, that they shall reach his harmony and reward."[65]

Apparently thinking that her doctrines were destined to prevail, Mrs. Eddy predicted, "The time is not distant when the ordinary theological views of atonement will undergo a great change."[66] But people who accept no other authority than Scripture never will agree that "The material blood of Jesus was no more efficacious to cleanse from sin when it was shed upon 'the accursed tree' than when it was flowing in his veins."[67] Should we abandon grace for works? She says, "One sacrifice, however great, is insufficient to pay the debt of sin. The atonement requires constant self-immolation on the sinner's part."[68] Salvation by grace through faith without works, is according to Mrs. Eddy "the safety valve for wrong-doing."[69] Not so according to Ephesians 2:8-10:

> For by grace are ye saved through faith; and that not of yourselves: it is the gift of God: Not of works, lest any man should boast. For we are his workmanship, created in Christ Jesus unto good works, which God hath before ordained that we should walk in them.

So, for Christian Science sin is not real enough to require atonement. God is not propitiated by the sacrifice of Christ, nor are sins forgiven through His precious blood. Jesus simply provided an example of love in which His followers are always to walk.

But the Bible plainly teaches that Jesus the Christ suffered (I Pet. 3:18) and died (I Cor. 15:3). The Bible teaches furthermore that by another's act believers are declared righteous (II Cor. 5:21; II Pet. 2:21-24; I Jn. 2:2). That redeeming act was the death of Jesus Christ or the shedding of His blood (Lev. 17:11; Mt. 26:28; Rom. 5:9; Eph. 1:7; 2:13; Col. 1:20; Heb. 9:22; 10:19; 13:12; I Pet. 1:18; Rev. 1:5). On the cross Jesus cried, "It is finished," for His death once and for all completed all that could be done for man's salvation (Jn. 19:13; Heb. 9:26; 10:10,12,14).

The Resurrection of Christ

Another essential in the gospel message concerns Christ's resurrection. We ask Christian Scientists, then, "Do you believe that Jesus Christ died, was buried and rose again from the dead?"

According to Christian Scientists there is in reality no physical body and no death. However they admit the presence of very strong illusions based upon deceptive sensory evidence to the reality of bodily death. From that illusion men must be saved. "As soldiers of the cross we must be brave," Mrs. Eddy writes, "and let Science declare the immortal status of man, and deny the evidence of the material senses, which testify that man dies."[70] Resurrection from the dead amounts to deliverance "from the belief in death."[71] In an Easter morning message, Mrs. Eddy asked, "What is it that seems a stone between us and the resurrection this morning? It is the belief of mind in matter. We can only come into the spiritual resurrection by quitting the consciousness of Soul in sense . . . We must lay aside material consciousness, and then we can perceive Truth, and say with Mary, 'Rabboni!' - Master!"[72]

Jesus did not really die, but went through "what seemed to be death."[73] Apparently also he seemed to rise from the dead. "Resurrection from the grave awaits Mind or Life, for the grave has no power over either."[74]

Why then did Jesus give these appearances of death, burial and resurrection to material sense? To prove the truth of Christian Science! The resurrection, according to Mrs. Eddy, "was the great proof of Truth and Love,"[75] "it glorified the supremacy of Mind over matter"[76] and "served to uplift faith to understand eternal Life, even the Allness of Soul, Spirit, and the nothingness of matter."[77]

Here is a prime example of wresting the Scriptures to one's own destruction. So real was the body of the risen Christ that Jesus said, "A spirit hath not flesh and bones as ye see me have" (Lk. 24: 39). Christ's physical body could be seen, heard and touched. The fact of the bodily resurrection is plainly taught in Scripture as read by any sound principles of interpretation (Mt. 28; Mk. 16; Lk. 24; Jn. 20-21; I Cor. 15). Christian Scientists must be willing to deny Scripture in order to follow Mrs. Eddy when she says, "To accommodate himself to immature ideas of spiritual power, — for spirituality was possessed only in a limited degree even by his disciples, — Jesus called the body, which by spiritual power he raised from the grave, 'flesh and bones.' "[78] Far from an accommodation for purposes of communication, the resurrection of Christ from the grave is indispensable to Christianity. Paul writes "If Christ be not risen then is our preaching vain, and your faith is also vain . . . ye are yet in your sins" (I Cor. 15:14,17).

Christians are concerned for the salvation of Christian Scientists, for belief in the resurrection of Christ from the dead is one condition of salvation. Romans 10:9 declares, "If thou shalt confess with thy mouth the Lord Jesus, and shalt believe in thine heart that God hath raised him from the dead, thou shalt be saved." The resurrection of Christ, far from a mere appearance to the immature, is one of the central realities of Christianity. However good the motivation it cannot be dismissed as a farce or a stage managed trick.

Personal Trust

A Christian's love for his neighbor requires that he introduce him to his living Lord. Lovingly, then, ask Christian Scientists, "Are you personally trusting Jesus Christ as your Savior and Lord?"

Christian Scientists put their faith, not in a person, but in Principle. They have faith in "the truth of being" or "the divine

Principle of health."[79] They disavow the faith that trusts one's welfare to another in favor of a faith which understands divine Love and how to work out one's 'own salvation with fear and trembling' . . . [It] "demands self-reliant trustworthiness which includes spiritual understanding and confides all to God."[80] Mrs. Eddy also says, "The prayer that reforms the sinner and heals the sick is an absolute faith that all things are possible to God - a spiritual understanding of Him, an unselfed Love."[81] And if the object of faith is medicine or drugs rather than Deity men commit idolatry.[82] Worshiping an impersonal God Christian Scientists do not enjoy personal communion or fellowship with the Father or with his Son Jesus Christ (I Jn. 1:3).

Although claiming to repudiate the blind faith, Christian Scientists close their eyes to sensory evidence for faith.[83] In her glossary of terms Mrs. Eddy defines believing as "firmness and constancy; not a faltering nor a blind faith, but the perception of spiritual truth." This faith is inspired by "spiritual perception of Scripture."[84] On Mrs. Eddy's authority, then, Christians can direct Christian Scientists to study the written word and trust the Holy Spirit through it to evoke personal faith in Jesus Christ Himself.

Grace Alone

One additional basic question may help Christian Scientists see their need for God's gospel of grace. A chain with one link of human works is too weak to hoist men to heaven. For the sake of the eternal well-being of Christian Science friends, urge them to consider this destiny-determining question. "Do you depend upon some acts of your own for your salvation, or is your trust in the grace of God alone?"

How is a Christian Scientist likely to answer? Although claiming to be in the line of Christian tradition, indeed of Protestant tradition,[85] the Scientists repudiate justification by faith and forge every link in the chain of redemption out of human rather than divine activity. An impersonal principle cannot act in behalf of unworthy sinners. No hope of pardon can bring peace to a guilty heart. Mrs. Eddy lays down the unqualified pronouncement, Salvation cannot be received through pardon, but through reform.[86] "We must prove our faith by demonstration."⁸⁷ Those who depend upon belief instead of demonstration commit an error fatal to a knowledge of Science.⁸⁸

The fatal spurning of God's great grace occurs all too frequently in the writing of Christian Science. Propagating the official views, the *Christian Science Sentinel* of September 26, 1925, reported,

> A four year old Christian Scientist was once asked, "How do we get to God?" and he answered, "By being good." Surely there is no other way . . . the little child was right. If we are expressing Humanity, honesty, affection, compassion, hope, faith, meekness, temperance, those beautiful transitional qualities we need never fear; for each day we are drawing nearer to our Father-mother God.

Unfortunately for those whose trust is in being good, no one but Christ in all Biblical history was ever good enough. The best of men fall far short of God's glory. Abraham's righteousness was not earned, but imputed to him. David, chosen of the Lord to lead His people, illustrated the murderous and adulterous potential of the human heart. Paul, dismissing his outstanding background and religious devotion, considered himself the chief of sinners. Try as one may, no human being of himself can continuously be all that he ought. If from the moment of this reading he could henceforth be perfect, that would not atone for his past sin. Biblical history gives us no reason to hope for perfection from the flesh.

And according to all Biblical teaching no fallen man can rise above his own sinful nature. The human heart is not good or morally neutral, it is desperately wicked (Jer. 17:9; Jn. 3:6; Rom. 7:18; Eph. 2:4; 4:18). No aspect of man's being escapes the debilitation of his sin. Not even his best efforts at reasoning about God are unaffected by "mortal mind" (Rom. 8:7-8; I Cor. 2:14; II Cor. 4:4; Eph. 4:18; I Tim. 6:5; Tit. 1:15). Even if one could always think correctly his conduct would be tainted by his sin-twisted will (Prov. 1:25,30; Isa. 30:9; Ez. 3:7; Rom. 6:16, 20; 7:14-25). If a person is ever to live in a way pleasing to God he must be born again. He must receive from God's Holy Spirit a new heart, a new spiritual life (Jn. 3:1-8). Apart from this divine renewal no man — sincere though he may be — will see the kingdom of God.

Unquestionably the greatest need of Christian Scientists is the gospel of God's grace. On the authority of Mrs. Eddy the Bible's central message is flatly denied. Jesus is not the Christ, He did not die for the sins of the world, nor did He rise from the dead. No personal relation with the living God is admitted and salvation is not by divine grace but human effort.

Christian Science teachings are the antithesis of Christianity. No Bible believer can consistently accept the teaching of *Science and Health With Key to the Scriptures.* But every Bible believer must feel his Lord's compassion upon those who, seeking to establish their own righteousness, have failed to submit themselves to the righteousness that comes from God (Rom. 10:1-3).

FOOTNOTES

1. Mary Baker Eddy, *Science and Health With Key to the Scriptures* (Boston: First Church of Christ Scientist, 1932), p. vi.
2. *Ibid.*, p. iii.　　　3. *Ibid.*, p. 386.　　　4. *Ibid.*, p. 377.
5. *Ibid.*　　6. *Ibid.*, p. 447.　　　7. *Ibid.*
8. George Channing, "What Is a Christian Scientist?" Leo G. Rosten, ed. *A Guide to the Religions of America* (New York: Simon & Schuster, 1955), p. 22.
9. *Science and Health*, p. 497.
10. *Ibid.*, viii, 110, 126.　　　11. *Ibid.*, p. 269.　　　12. *Ibid.*, p. 146.
13. *Ibid.*, p. viii.　　　14. *Ibid.*, p. 320.　　　15. *Ibid.*, p. 241.
16. *Ibid.*　　　17. *Ibid.*
18. George Channing, *op. cit.*, p. 22.
19. Cited by Walter R. Martin, *The Christian Science Myth* (Grand Rapids: Zondervan Publishing House, 1955), p. 55.
20. *Ibid.*
21. Walter R. Martin, *op. cit.*, chapters 3 and 4.
22. George Channing, *op. cit.*, p. 25.
23. *Science and Health*, p. 131.
24. Mary Baker Eddy, "Rudimental Divine Science," *The Unity of Good and Other Writings* (Boston: First Church of Christ Scientist, 1936), p. 2.
25. *Ibid.*, p. 1.
26. *Science and Health*, p. 461.
27. *Ibid.*, pp. 137-138.　　　28. *Ibid.*, p. 333.　　　29. *Ibid.*, p. 473.
30. *Ibid.*, p. 29.　　　31. *Ibid.*, p. 38.　　　32. *Ibid.*, p. 334.
33. *Ibid.*, p. 18.　　　34. *Ibid.*, p. 334.　　　35. *Ibid.*, p. 313.
36. *Ibid.*, p. 360.　　　37. *Ibid.*, p. 316.　　　38. *Ibid.*
40. *Ibid.*, 361.　　　41. *Ibid.*　　　42. *Ibid.*, p. 134.
43. *Ibid.*, p. 29.　　　44. *Ibid.*, p. 256.　　　45. *Ibid.*, pp. 331-332.
46. *Ibid.*, p. 361.　　　47. *Ibid.*, pp. 288-289.　　　48. *Ibid.*, pp. 68-69.
49. *Ibid.*, pp. 289-290.　　　50. *Ibid.*, p. 310.　　　51. *Ibid.*, p. 310.
52. *Ibid.*, p. 472.
53. *Ibid.*, p. 372. To trace different interpretations of the material realm by Christian Scientists see Charles S. Braden, *Christian Science Today* (Dallas: Southern Methodist University Press, 1958), pp. 297-335.
54. *Ibid.*, p. 116.　　　55. *Ibid.*, p. 274.　　　56. *Ibid.*, p. 277.
57. *Ibid.*, p. 279.　　　58. *Ibid.*, pp. 472-473.　　　59. *Ibid.*, p. 71.
60. *Ibid.*, p. 18.　　　61. *Ibid.*, p. 19.　　　62. *Ibid.*, p. 18.
63. *Ibid.*, pp. 24, 29.　　　64. *Ibid.*, p. 339.　　　65. *Ibid.*, p. 21.
66. *Ibid.*, p. 24.　　　67. *Ibid.*, p. 25.　　　68. *Ibid.*, p. 23.
69. *Ibid.*, p. 6.
70. Mary Baker Eddy, "Is There No Death?" *Unity of the Good & Other Writings* (Boston: First Church of Christ Scientist, 1887), p. 39.
71. *Ibid.*, p. 41.

72. Mary Baker Eddy, *Miscellaneous Writings 1883-1896* (Boston: First Church of Christ Scientist, 1896), p. 179.
73. *Science and Health*, p. 46.   74. *Ibid.*, p. 291.
75. *Ibid.*, p. 25; ff. p. 44.   76. *Ibid.*, p. 45.   77. *Ibid.*, p. 497.
78. *Ibid.*, p. 313   79 *Ibid.*, pp. 146, 401, 319.   80. *Ibid.*, p. 23.
81. *Ibid.*, p. 1.   82. *Ibid.*, p. 146.   83. *Ibid.*, pp. 12, 23, 297, 398.
84. *Ibid.*, p. 547.
85. Arthur J. Todd, "Christian Science," *Twentieth Century Religion*, Vergilius Ferm, ed. (New York: The Philosophical Library, 1948), p. 360.
86. *Ibid.*, p. 285.   87. *Ibid.*, 329.   88. *Ibid.*, 286.

FOR FURTHER STUDY

ANTHONY A. HOEKEMA, *The Four Major Cults* (Grand Rapids: Eerdmans Publishing Company, 1963), pp. 171-221. A competent doctrinal study.
WALTER R. MARTIN and NORMAN H. KLANN, *The Christian Science Myth* (Grand Rapids: Zondervan Publishing House, 1955). A critical examination of the movement's founder, Mrs. Eddy, the history, beliefs and healings of the movement.
CHARLES S. BRADEN, *Christian Science Today: Power, Policy, Practice* (Dallas: Southern Methodist University Press, 1958). A perceptive description of the contemporary movement.

SUGGESTIONS FOR TEACHERS

Good teaching is marked by clarity of purpose. Review the content of this study and attempt to synthesize it in your own mind. This material may best be divided into two sections for two teaching sessions. Put into a few words a statement of objectives for classroom presentation. *Confronting the Cults* differs from some other works on the subject in that its purpose is not primarily negative — refuting false doctrine, but positive — winning cultists to Christ.

1. Use the lead questions throughout the series to form the major divisions of the teaching sessions. Illustrate the way these questions keep discussion centered on the gospel by moving quickly back to them from irrelevant issues.

2. Anticipate replies Christians may expect to these questions from Christian Scientists. Evaluate the Christian Science position and give specific guidance in answering erroneous beliefs.

3. Build confidence for effective personal witness by helping your group formulate possible approaches and answers. Use simple role playing

situations to involve the group in learning the major doctrines of Christian Science. After the material has been studied allow several people to take the position of a believer. Simulate a conversation. Try various ways of presenting the truth in the face of error.

4. Secure a copy of Mary Baker Eddy's *Science and Health With Key to the Scriptures* (in a second-hand book store). Interested class members may also wish a copy to mark for use in witnessing to members of this cult. Passages contradicting Bible teaching could be marked in one way, and verses for leading Christian Scientists to Christ in another way,

5. Ask members of the class to give their personal testimony of salvation by grace from the reality of sin as they would to representatives of the Christian Science church.

SAMPLE LESSON PLAN

SESSION 1

Aim

To guide the class to a knowledge of Christian Science teaching on divine authority, the priority of the gospel, and the Person of Jesus Christ. To help the class develop skills of witnessing to those who accept books other than the Bible as divine revelation.

Approach

Lead a discussion on reasons for the appeal of Christian Science. What can Christians learn from the Christian Science movement?

Outline

Divine authority, priority of the gospel and Christ.

A. Authority
Question: Do Christian Scientists base their teachings on revelations other than the Bible?

B. The Gospel's Priority
Question: Is the main business of Christian Science the proclamation of the gospel of Jesus Christ?

C. The Doctrine of Christ
Question: Do Christian Scientists believe that Jesus is the Christ, the eternal Word who became flesh?

Conclusion

Sum up the Christian Science position and the best ways to help Christian Scientists see the truth about Scripture, the gospel, and Christ.

SESSION 2

Aim

To guide the class to a knowledge of Christian Science teaching about redemption, Christ's resurrection, and personal faith in God's grace.
To help class members develop skill in handling the Scriptures as they witness to Christian Scientists.

Approach

Review briefly the previous lesson and set an attitude favorable to helping cultists, not embarrassing them.

A. Redemption
   Question: Do Christian Scientists believe that Jesus died for their sins?

B. The Resurrection of Jesus Christ
   Question: Do Christian Scientists believe Jesus Christ arose from the dead bodily?

C. Personal Faith
   Question: Do Christiant Scientists personally trust Jesus Christ as redeemer and Lord?
   Question: Do Christian Scientists depend on some achievements of their own to provide justification or is it only by God's grace through faith?

Conclusion

Sum up the Scriptural teaching on these subjects and challenge the class to confront their Christian Science friends with the gospel.

5

The Bible, The Christian, and
Seventh-day Adventists

or

Is Seventh-day Adventism Evangelical?

In a sound Baptist church just prior to the Sunday morning service a mature deacon loudly acclaimed the message he had just heard on a radio broadcast called "The Voice of Prophecy." Upon learning that it was Seventh-day Adventist he was chagrined. Unsuspecting evangelicals may be equally impressed with the Adventists' television program, "Faith for Today," or personal copies of the Review and Herald Publishing Association's *Bible Readings for the Home Circle*.

Evangelicals also may be counted among the avid readers of some of the Adventists' strikingly beautiful magazines: *Life and Health*, a national journal, *Signs of the Times*, a prophetic monthly, *These Times*, dedicated to strengthening the moral, physical and spiritual life of the individual reader, and *Liberty*, a magazine of religious freedom.

All these sources have much truth in them. They have far more truth than the propaganda of other cults. As a matter of fact, they have so much truth that Christian laymen may be excused for asking if Adventists are not, after all, evangelical. And laymen have the company of some ministerial leaders in challenging the customary designation of Seventh-day Adventism as a cult.

In order to determine the facts of the matter Rev. Walter R. Martin and the late Donald Grey Barnhouse for two years probed Adventism's leading spokesmen. In September, 1956, an editorial in *Eternity* magazine stated Dr. Barnhouse's tradition-breaking conclusion. No longer can Seventh-day Adventists be classed as a cult

and its adherents non-Christian, he declared. Adventists are "redeemed brethren and members of the body of Christ."[1] And
Walter Martin, who had roundly denounced Christian Science and
Jehovah's Witnesses as cults, now argued as vehemently that
Seventh-day Adventism is evangelical. In spite of some secondary
deviations from orthodox Christian teaching, Martin said, the Adventists "have always as a majority, held to the cardinal, fundamental doctrines of the Christian faith which are necessary to
salvation, and to growth in grace that characterizes all true
Christian believers."[2]

The Adventists' response to Martin appeared in a 700-page
volume called *Questions on Doctrine*. "Prepared by a Representative Group of Seventh-day Adventist Leaders, Bible Teachers and
Editors," the book came out in 1957 from the Washington, D. C.,
Review and Herald Publishing Association. Although not an official
statement adopted by the General Conference in quadrennial
session, "this volume can be viewed as truly representative of the
faith and beliefs of the Seventh-day Adventist Church."[3]

Three years and much controversy later, Zondervan Publishing
House printed Martin's complete analysis, *The Truth About
Seventh-day Adventism*. The "Foreword" by Dr. Barnhouse nar-
rowed the previous thesis that the majority of Adventists had
always held an evangelical position. He wrote, "Let it be understood that we made only one claim; i.e., that those Seventh-day
Adventists who follow the Lord in the same way as their leaders
who have interpreted for us the doctrinal position of their church,
are to be considered true members of the body of Christ."[4] In
supporting this thesis Martin explicitly assumes: (1) that the Adventist leaders contacted were honest and (2) that *Questions on
Doctrine* is "*the* primary source upon which to ground an evaluation of Adventist theology."[5] On this basis Martin concluded
the leadership is evangelical, and as we shall see, evangelical with
an Arminian system of theology which denies eternal security.

But not all evangelicals were willing to grant these assumptions
or, if they did, not all concurred in Martin's conclusion. That conclusion was challenged by Professor Harold Lindsell, then Dean of
Fuller Theological Seminary, in *Christianity Today*, March 31,
1958. Dr. Lindsell concurred that Seventh-day Adventism is not
a cult like Christian Science or Jehovah's Witnesses, since it does

not deny the absolute deity of Christ nor reject His atoning sacrifice on Calvary. But, Lindsell suggested, Seventh-day Adventism is not therefore evangelical. Like Romanism, it denies the sufficiency of Christ's death for man's salvation. Mixing works with grace Adventism errs with the legalism Paul disputed in Galatians. Grace simply supports man's will so that through his good works he may obtain eternal life. Works remain the basis of man's hope.[6] This differs from Arminianism, which makes faith as distinct from works the single condition of salvation.

Herbert S. Bird, home from a decade of missionary service, acknowledged that evangelicals have much to learn from Seventh-day Adventism, but concluded, an approach "which views it as just another evangelical denomination cannot help but bring about greater confusion in the Christian world than exists already."[7] The reasons for this judgment are given more fully in Bird's book entitled, *Theology of Seventh-day Adventism*, published by Eerdmans in 1961. The strongest of these is Adventism's legalism,

> Here not even ninety-nine percent is necessarily a passing grade. In all probability the Galatian Judaizers, whose message the apostle Paul anathematized, agreed with him on almost everything but the one issue of the necessity of circumcision and the observance of sundry ceremonial practices for salvation. Wherefore, then, Paul's refusal to admit their teaching is essentially Christian and to move themselves into the group of those who are brethren in Christ? . . . The reason is that for Paul the problem was not that of the number of doctrines on which the people agreed with Biblical Christianity, but that of whether the details on which they disagreed, whether these details were few or many, were in areas of truth so vital that their denial subverted the gospel of the grace of God.[8]

In reviewing Martin's book, *The Truth About Seventh-day Adventism*, Dr. Merrill Tenney, Professor of New Testament at Wheaton College, raised a question about Martin's second assumption. "Is the doctrinal platform of Seventh-day Adventism determined by what a few of its scholars defined, or by what the majority of its followers believe and practice?" Tenney apparently feels that though Martin did not compromise on the level of the leaders' teaching, he failed to give sufficient consideration to the movement's policies and practices and to the bulk of its teachings.[9]

Norman F. Douty, in a book entitled *Another Look at Seventh-day Adventism* (Baker Book House, 1962), not limiting himself to *Questions on Doctrine*, found that the movement denied doctrines the church has always declared, and taught doctrines the church as a whole has always denied. In spite of the differences he said, "It is our duty to manifest love and kindness toward those who are in Adventism."[10] But Douty concluded, "They who would be loyal to God rather than be swayed by sentiment must avoid any alliance with the Adventist system. No other course is open to them."[11]

And in 1963 Anthony A. Hoekema, Associate Professor of Systematic Theology at Calvin Theological Seminary, published a book categorizing Seventh-day Adventism as one of *The Four Major Cults*. Any group in which five specified criteria play a leading role he classifies as a cult. On each count Hoekema finds Seventh-day Adventism guilty, although with inconsistency and ambivalence. The five tests: An extra-biblical source of authority, denial of justification by grace alone, devaluation of Christ, the group as the exclusive community of the saved, and the group's central role in eschatology.[12] Because Hoekema's conclusions are carefully stated and reveal some of the specific problems to look for in studying Adventism, they deserve our careful attention.

> Seventh-day Adventists do have an extra-Scriptural source of authority in the writings of Ellen G. White, which are accepted by them as inspired counsels from the Lord.[13]

> Though Seventh-day Adventists claim to teach justification by grace alone their doctrine of the investigative judgment and their views of the sabbath command are inconsistent with that claim.[14]

> While appreciating the Adventist's recognition of Christ as fully divine, however, we must reluctantly observe that there are aspects of Seventh-day Adventist teaching which detract from the splendor of Christ's deity and do in fact constitute a devaluation of Him.[15]

> Though theoretically granting that people outside their community can be saved Seventh-day Adventists actually undermine that concession by their teaching on the remnant church. Since they claim to be *the* remnant church in distinction from all other Christian bodies, they do manifest the cultist trait under discussion, though in a somewhat ambivalent manner.[16]

For Seventh-day Adventists . . . eschatology is the arena in which the glorification of their own movement completes itself and in which they shall be completely vindicated over against their enemies. Since the Sabbath will be the great test of loyalty in the last days, we see that the antithesis between God and Satan becomes in the end the antithesis between Seventh-day Adventism and those who refuse to follow its special teaching. We conclude that since Seventh-day Adventists do picture themselves as playing a central role in eschatology this distinctive trait of the cult is also clearly applicable to their movement.[17]

This brief sketch of the revolutionary attempt to regard Seventh-day Adventism evangelical and of its disclaimers reveals some of the issues which must now be faced in any study of that movement. Our answer to these issues will determine our approach to Adventist friends. If they are still considered non-Christian cultists we shall endeavor to win them to the Lord. If they are classed with Romanists in their legalism we must approach them as Paul did the people at Galatia. If they are evangelical we may fellowship and work together in the evangelistic cause while engaging in intramural debates on issues not affecting salvation. Or it may be that no generalization can be made about the movement as a whole, and we must deal with each individual upon the basis of his own stated beliefs.

The approach of *Confronting the Cults* suggests seven questions to use in discussion with people to help distinguish cultic from Christian organizations and lead people to Christ. Evangelicals may use these questions to guide discussions they may have with Adventists.

Authority

What must a man do to be saved? Our answer to that question is determined by its source and basis. To help Adventists see where their controversial beliefs may have arisen we must ask, "Do you base your teachings on revelations or sacred writings other than the Bible?"

In answer, Adventists usually present one of their "Fundamental Beliefs." The group's official denominational teaching states "that the Holy Scriptures of the Old and New Testaments were given of God, contain an all-sufficient revelation of His will to men, and are the only unerring rule of faith and practice (II Tim. 3: 15-16)."[18] Among the doctrines shared with conservative Christians, the writer of *Questions on Doctrine* included this, "That the Scriptures are the inspired revelation of God to men; and that the Bible is the sole rule of faith and practice."[19] To be even more explicit they add, "We belive that all theological beliefs must be measured by the living Word, judged by its truth, and whatsoever is unable to pass this test, or is found to be out of harmony with its message is to be rejected."[20]

Despite these strong affirmations of the supremacy and sufficiency of Scripture, ambiguity persists concerning the status of Ellen G. White's writings. Because Adventists believe Mrs. White had the gift of prophecy (Eph. 4:11), she is called a prophetess. She gave "testimonies" as did the prophets throughout the Old Testament (Rev. 10:10),[21] and entitled one of her works, *Testimonies*. In a popular booklet, *Your Friends the Adventists*, Arthur S. Maxwell remarks about the "authority" of Mrs. White's works and adds, "Many believe that Mrs. White spoke with more than human wisdom. Read one of her books yourself and see what you think."[22] The writers of *Questions on Doctrine* hold her writings in "highest esteem" because "the Holy Spirit opened to her mind important events and called her to give certain instructions for these last days." Consequently, "we as a denomination accept them as inspired counsels from the Lord. But we have never equated them with Scripture."[23]

If Mrs. White's writings are not equivalent to Scripture why are both said to be "inspired"? Walter R. Martin sympathetically reasons that "inspiration" in connection with Mrs. White's works "has a rather different meaning from the inspiration of the Bible." Nevertheless, even Martin concludes that "the Adventists are defending a situation which is at best paradoxical and at times contradictory."[24] Until this confusion is cleared up in their statements about inspiration it is difficult to understand without qualification the Adventist's claim "that we do not regard the writings of Ellen G. White as an addition to the sacred canon of Scripture . . . in the same sense as the Holy Scriptures."[25]

In order to help Seventh-day Adventists more clearly to distinguish Mrs. White from the Biblical prophets and thus avoid cultism we may ask a question suggested by Dr. Harold Lindsell. "Did Mrs. White err at any point theologically or in ethical and personal life, or was she inerrant in all her teachings, pronouncements and ethics?"[26] If Adventists continue to defend her every word and action they put her on a pedestal even higher than the Christian Scientists put Mary Baker Eddy or the Latter-day Saints put Joseph Smith. To regard Mrs. White, or any such person, as God's single spokesman for the end times is to supplant the ultimate authority of Scripture. If one differs with Mrs. White does he necessarily differ with God?

The evidence does not support Mrs. White's infallibility. Adventists cannot simply assume "that Mrs. White's writings are free from theological and exegetical errors," Walter Martin points out, "*for they are not.*"[27] This charge is documented, for one thing, by indications of plagiarism. In parallel columns Martin lists passages from Mrs. White and from Conybeare and Howson's *The Life and Epistles of the Apostle Paul*, J. A. Wylie's *History of the Waldenses*, and D'Aubigne's *History of the Reformation*.[28] Then, on Mrs. White's own authority it may be shown that she erred, even in her "inspired" *Testimonies*. She admitted, "Under these circumstances I yielded my judgment to that of others and wrote what appeared in Number Eleven in regard to the Health Institute, being unable to give all that I had seen. *In this I did wrong.*"[29] Who can say that Mrs. White did not yield upon other occasions to the pressure of circumstances or opinions in exercising her "gift of prophecy"?

May God help any Adventists who have not already done so to admit as plainly as did Mrs. White her fallibility. Then they cannot establish doctrine on her authority, but must always discover doctrine in Scripture and test her works by Scripture. Any Adventist who confesses this and dispenses with the proof texts from Mrs. White shows that he holds the Bible alone infallible and sufficient to all matters of faith and practice. As far as this point is concerned, such Adventists are welcome to the camp of evangelicals. But any Adventist who continues to equivocate on the inerrancy of Mrs. White thereby excludes himself from unqualified acceptance among evangelicals. Our prayer is that every Adventist would in fact hold that there is but *one* infallible rule of faith and practice, the Bible, and so on this issue be evangelical.

The Gospel's Priority

Another question must be asked Adventists, "Is your primary business preaching the gospel?"

Many evangelicals would expect a sincere Adventist answer to say their main business was preaching the law. Some have wondered whether the Adventists' radio and television ministry was truly representative of their beliefs. The Adventist leaders faced this forthright question:

> Are not the spiritual content and evangelical emphasis of your "Voice of Prophecy" radio program and "Faith for Today" telecast a rather far cry from the doctrinal and legal core of Adventism? Are they not rather a bid for good will, and subtle attempt to draw those who enroll in your proffered Bible courses to gradually accept the doctrinal and legal heart of Adventism?

To this frank question, the Adventists replied:

> There is no attempt at subtlety or effort to deceive. The heart of the Advent message is Christ and Him crucified . . . We believe that Christianity is a real experience with Christ. Christianity is a relationship to a Person — our blessed Lord and Saviour Jesus Christ . . . We also believe that a specific message is due the world today, and that we were called into being to have a part in proclaiming it. But again, that message is simply the everlasting gospel in the setting of God's great judgment hour, the imminent second coming of our Lord, and the preparation of men to meet God . . . We repeat, this emphasis is not something subtle, as suggested in the question. It is not a lure, or trick, or bait. It is, instead, a serious endeavor to put first things definitely first in our public presentations, and to let the world see and know that the heart burden of Adventism is Christ and His salvation.[30]

Plainly, the writers of *Questions on Doctrine* intend that the primary business of the Adventists is preaching not law, but gospel.

The same conclusion is required by Arthur S. Maxwell's essay entitled, "What is a Seventh-day Adventist?" In a series on different religions in a popular magazine, Maxwell wrote:

> A Seventh-day Adventist is one who, having accepted Christ as his personal Savior, walks in humble obedience to the will of God as revealed in the Holy Scriptures. A Bible-loving Christian, he seeks to pattern his life according to the teachings of this book, while looking

for the imminent return of his Lord. He lives under a sense of destiny, believing it is his duty to warn mankind that the end of the world is at hand.[31]

Unless one presumes adversely to judge the motivation of these leaders, he can conclude that as they see it, their primary business is preaching the gospel. If keeping the seventh day or an Old Testament diet appears to be the prominent feature, we may have misjudged. Or there may be differences in the movement itself. On the leaders' own affirmation of the priority of the gospel, we must conclude that those they represent do take an evangelical stance. It may be wise to reserve final judgment, however, until we have analyzed more fully their position on the elements of the gospel message.

Christ

One basic element of the gospel which in the New Testament distinguished true Christianity from counterfeits concerned the nature of Jesus Christ. Let us ask Adventists, then, this leading question: "Do you believe that Jesus is the Messiah, the Christ, the eternal Word who has come in the flesh?" What answer may be anticipated?

Among the Adventist's "Fundamental Beliefs" is this fine summary of Biblical teaching:

> Jesus Christ is very God, being of the same nature and essence as the Eternal Father. While retaining His divine nature He took upon Himself the nature of the human family, lived on the earth as a man, exemplified in His life as our example the principles of righteousness, attested His relationship to God by many mighty miracles, died for our sins on the cross, was raised from the dead, and ascended to the Father, where He ever lives to make intercession for us.[32]

On the deity of Christ and the fact of His incarnation Seventh-day Adventists stand squarely with evangelical Christians. The Biblical doctrines are made explicit objects of faith for salvation in Scripture, the Adventists assert. By the Scriptural test adopted in this study, then, Adventists in their view of Christ's Person are evangelical.

Some critics of Adventism, however, in evaluating the movement employ the more detailed and full doctrinal statements. By these standards the Adventists' understanding of Christ's human nature is challenged. The Adventists differ from the historic Christian church in their notion of human nature, and consequently in their doctrine of Christ's human nature. Man is not an entity with two parts, a body and a soul. They teach that "the soul of man represents the whole man, and not a particular part independent of the other component parts of man's nature; and further that the soul cannot exist apart from the body, for man is a unity."[33] When Christ became man, He took upon Him human flesh and human nature, but no human soul as a distinct immaterial substance. In the final judgment of Norman F. Douty, then, the Adventist's doctrine is like that of Apollinaris, whose view was pronounced heretical by the church.[34] To the early Christians this teaching detracted from Christ's full humanity. The orthodox doctrine maintains that Christ took upon Himself not only a human body, but also a human soul or spirit.

A second aspect of Adventist teaching about Christ has been criticized. While orthodox Christians have held that His human nature was like that of Adam before the fall, Adventists have held it was like that of Adam and the race after the fall. It was necessary for Christ to share fallen human nature, Adventists insist, in order to be tempted in all points as we are. Numerous quotations in standard Adventists' writings are cited by Bird and Douty to the effect that Christ had a sinful nature.[35]

Of course the Bible teaches Christ had no sin. The child born of Mary was not sinful but holy (Lk. 1:35). Jesus said Satan had nothing in Him (Jn. 14:30). Peter called Him a lamb "without blemish and without spot" (I Pet. 1:19) and declared He did no sin, "neither was guile found in his mouth" (I Pet 2:22). And John who knew him so well could write, "In him is no sin" (I Jn. 3:5).

Seventh-day Adventist writers unite in affirming that Christ never sinned, but they may contradict each other on the issue of the sinfulness of his human nature. The writers of *Questions on Doctrine*, however, adopt the orthodox position and insist that Christ took sinless human nature.[36] In alluding to Christ's sinful human nature other Adventists denied the least participation in sin, but assumed Christ suffered the liabilities inherent in human nature. Christ was genuinely tempted in all points as men are tempted, and identified Himself with the sinners He came to save.[37]

In their views of Christ, then, are Adventists evangelical? If to be evangelical one must affirm the full details of orthodox doctrine, then on one point they fall short. They do not assert that Christ took a human spirit or soul as an immaterial substance distinct from the human body in His incarnation. The leaders who wrote *Questions on Doctrine* emphatically deny that His nature was sinful. For those they represent, the one issue that remains can hardly of itself exclude from evangelicalism people who affirm the absolute deity of Christ, the doctrine of the Trinity and the literal incarnation.

Historically, there have been sound men who have held a similar view of the soul, and some hold it today. Biblically, Adventists receive the Word who was God and became flesh (Jn. 1:1, 12,14). Who then, when thinking of their view of Christ, can say that they have not the authority to be called sons of God? They affirm that Jesus has come in the flesh (I Jn. 4:1-3). Who then will say that they are antichrist? They believe that Jesus is the Christ (Jn. 20:31). Who then will dare to question whether they have life through His name? On this issue it appears that Bird and Douty either raise too detailed a standard for evangelicalism, or have abandoned the issue concerning the Adventist's evangelicalism. If the Adventists represented by *Questions on Doctrine* are not part of the body of Christ, it is not because of their view of Christ's Person. Christians will not initially help Adventists by debating these detailed issues about Christ's human nature. Rather, Christians should rejoice in the testimony of an Adventist's belief in Christ's deity and incarnation, and move on to other issues.

Redemption

The gospel includes an affirmation not only concerning Christ's person, but also concerning His work. Christians interested in helping Adventists will ask: Do you believe Christ's shed blood is the only basis for the forgiveness of your sins?

A similar question came to the leaders: "Seventh-day Adventists have frequently been charged with teaching that the atonement was not completed on the cross. Is this charge true?"[37] The answer was as blunt. "May we state most earnestly and explicitly that Seventh-day Adventists do *not* believe that Christ made but a partial or incomplete sacrificial atonement on the cross."[38] What they do stress, is the difference between Christ's completed work and its application to individuals.

> Most decidedly the all-sufficient atoning sacrifice of Jesus our Lord was *offered and completed* on the cross of Calvary. This was done for all mankind. (Jn. 2:2). But this sacrificial work will actually benefit human hearts *only* as we surrender our lives to God and experience the miracle of the new birth. In this experience Jesus our High Priest *applies to us the benefits* of His atoning sacrifice. Our sins are forgiven, we become children of God by faith in Christ Jesus, and the peace of God dwells in our hearts.[39]

Clearly this is an evangelical position as stated. If, however, the application of the atonement's saving benefits depends upon some additional work of Christ, such as the alleged cleansing of the heavenly sanctuary in 1844, it raises the issue of the completeness of the work at Calvary. Furthermore, if eventually all sin must be put upon Satan as a scapegoat, the atonement at the cross seems incomplete.

How did the ideas of the investigative judgment in the heavenly sanctuary and the scapegoat originate? Adventists interpreted the Old Testament day of atonement typologically. On that day participants were judged (Lev. 23:29-30) and the goat was sent off into the wilderness (Lev. 16:20-28). Typological interpretations of these events (rather than explicit Scriptural teaching) became the basis of doctrine.[40] How this developed is a story in itself.

In 1844, because of William Miller's prediction of the end of the world, a flurry of excitement ended in a great disappointment. Miller had found a basis for predicting Christ's return in Daniel 8:14. The 2300 days until the cleansing of the sanctuary were taken to be 2300 years. Starting at 457 B.C., when Artaxerxes decreed the Israelites could rebuild their ruined capital city, the period ended in 1844. But Jesus did not return to Jerusalem.

On October 23, 1844, the day following the scheduled return of Christ, a Millerite named Hiram Edson walked alone through a cornfield, when, suddenly there burst upon his mind the thought that there were *two* phases to Christ's ministry in the heaven of heavens, just as in the earthly sanctuary of old . . . He (Christ) for the first time *entered* on that day the second apartment of that (heavenly) sanctuary to perform in the Most Holy before coming to this earth.[41]

But what in the heavenly sanctuary needed to be cleansed? Explaining this, Mrs. White wrote, "Sin was not canceled by the blood of the victim. A means was thus provided by which *it was transferred to the sanctuary*. By the offering of blood, the sinner was not yet entirely released from the condemnation of the law."[42] Since the record of good and evil deeds still stands in heaven, the authors of *Questions on Doctrine* admit, "Acceptance of Christ at conversion does not seal a person's destiny."[43]

Pardon from all sin as a benefit of Christ's atonement, according to Adventists, is not received upon believing. Justification before God Himself in the holy of holies awaits another work of Christ, His investigative judgment. There even the believer may lose his salvation. "When any have sins remaining upon the books of record, unrepented of and unforgiven, their names will be blotted out of the book of life, and the record of their good deeds will be erased from the book of God's remembrance."[44]

On what basis do men stand or fall in the investigative judgment? Not their union with Christ by faith, not their new birth by the Holy Spirit, not their propitiation by the blood of Christ, say Seventh-day Adventists. "The law of God is the standard by which the characters and the lives of men will be tested in the judgment."[45] Ameliorating this, Adventists emphasize that Christ the great high priest becomes the believer's advocate, and in the heavenly court He never lost a case. But this comfort is snatched away when they add, "To us, it seems clear that we must continue our allegiance throughout life if we expect Christ to represent us in the judgment."[46] Quite the contrary, the Bible explains that it is precisely because no sinner could keep the law that we need an advocate in case he sins. "My little children, these things I write unto you that ye sin not, And if any man sin, we have an advocate with the Father, Jesus Christ the righteous" (I Jn. 2:1).

So long as the outcome of the investigative judgment is determined not by faith, but by law-keeping, it is difficult to conclude that Adventists consistently regard the blood of Christ the sole ground for salvation. Evangelicals must confront Adventists, not so much with their error in timing divine judgment or their literalistic concept of the heavenly sanctuary or the unwise practice of basing a major doctrine on an Old Testament type alone, but with their consequent contradiction of Scriptural teaching on justification by faith. That involves complete pardon from all sin and the imputation of Christ's perfect righteousness. So a believer in Christ, crucified and risen, need never fear judgment or condemnation (Rom. 8:1; Jn. 3:18). "Be it known unto you therefore, men and brethren, that through this man is preached unto you the forgiveness of sins: and by him all that believe are justified from all things from which ye could not be justified by the law of Moses." In the context of Acts 13:38-39 "law of Moses" is not distinct from, but includes the Ten Commandments. Let Adventists hear again Romans 3:38, "Therefore we conclude that a man is justified by faith without the deeds of the law." (Cf. Rom. 4:6; 11:6; Eph. 2:2-9; Gal. 2:16; Tit. 3:5.) Whatever Daniel 8:14 may mean, it cannot overthrow the foundational teaching throughout Scripture that the just shall live by faith in Christ's complete atoning work, not in their ability to keep the law. Believers have redemption "through his blood, the forgiveness of sins, according to the riches of his grace" (Eph. 1:7).

Where then does the scapegoat come in? The name of the goat the high priest sent out into the wilderness on the day of atonement was Azazel. Adventists, as well as many orthodox interpreters, think Azazel designates Satan.[47] The meaning of the name is not the crucial issue. Do Adventists hold that Satan in some way provides atonement for sin not completed by Christ?

Contemporary Adventists as represented by the authors of *Questions on Doctrine* flatly deny that Satan in any way completes the atonement. But, they say, Satan is not unrelated to our sin. In all sin, they teach, there is a twofold responsibility: "first my responsibility as the *perpetrator*, agent, or medium; and second, Satan's responsibility as the instigator, or temptor, in whose heart sin was first conceived."[48] So when Satan is said to carry away our sins, they mean he is paying for instigating them, not that he is providing an atonement for them. "Satan makes no atonement for our sins. But Satan will ultimately have to bear the retributive punishment for his responsibility in the sins of all men, both righteous and wicked."[49]

For two reasons, Adventists argue, Satan could not be a vicarious sin-bearer: (1) the transaction with the scapegoat took place *after* the atonement had been accomplished, and (2) it was not slain—and without the shedding of blood there is no remission (Heb. 9:22). Seventh-day Adventists therefore repudiate *in toto* any idea, suggestion, or implication that Satan is in any sense or degree our sin-bearer. The thought is abhorrent to us, and appallingly sacrilegious."[50] On this basis then, evangelical Christians may choose not to follow the Adventist's interpretation of the scapegoat, but they cannot justifiably charge those who accept it with heresy affecting salvation. One could only wish their position on the investigative judgment was as emphatically aligned with Biblical teaching on Christ's atonement. On that point the denomination has yet consistently to state the evangelical position. Its legalism is further considered in question seven.

The Resurrection of Christ

Faith in another aspect of the gospel, Christ's triumph over the grave, is an explicit condition of salvation (Rom. 10:9). Out of concern for an Adventist, then, ask, "Do you believe that Jesus Christ rose from the dead?"

In agreement with orthodox Christians, Adventists hold "that Jesus Christ arose literally and bodily from the grave."[51] To avoid possible misunderstanding they further explain, "The resurrection of Christ is not to be understood in a spiritual sense. He actually rose from the dead. He who came from the tomb was the *same* Jesus who lived here in the flesh."[52] In support of the resurrection Adventists amass the same evidences as evangelicals, and they take a similar position on its doctrinal significance. The strongest opponents of Adventism do not question the Adventist's belief in Christ's resurrection. So evangelicals will rejoice that their faith in Christ's victory over death is shared by Seventh-day Adventists.

Personal Trust

Christians concerned to win not mere arguments, but persons, may also ask Adventists, "Are you personally trusting Jesus Christ as your redeemer and Lord?"

Much like evangelicals, Adventists repeatedly stress the indispensability of faith.[53] In those discussions Hebrews 11:3 frequently occurs, "Without faith it is impossible to please God." Furthermore they distinguish between a mere intellectual belief and total commitment. Mrs. White explained that there is

> a kind of belief that is wholly distinct from faith. The existence and power of God, the truth of His Word, are facts that even Satan and his hosts cannot at heart deny. The Bible says that "the devils also believe and tremble"; but this is not faith. Where there is not only a belief in God's Word, but a submission of will to Him; where the heart is yielded to Him, the affections fixed upon Him, there is faith, — faith that works by love, and purifies the soul.[54]

A similar emphasis upon both belief and faith appears in Mrs. White's famous *Steps to Christ*.[55]

And in *Questions on Doctrine* justification is said to be by a faith that lays hold upon the power of God.

> Even in the days of old, men were not justified by works; they were justified by faith" (Heb. 2:4; compare Rom. 1:17; Gal. 3:8, 11; Phil. 3:9; Heb. 10:38). God calls upon man to be righteous; but man is naturally unrighteous. If he is to be prepared for the kingdom of God, he must be made righteous. This is something man cannot do in and of himself. He is unclean and unrighteous. The more he works, and the greater his effort, the more he reveals the unrighteousness of his own heart. Therefore, if man is ever to become righteous, it must be by a power entirely outside himself — it must be by the power of God.[56]

With the Seventh-day Adventist view of faith as such, evangelicals do not take issue. But evangelicals know that it is one thing to preach the need for personal faith and another to exercise that faith personally. In conversations with Adventists as with others we may help by testifying of our own unconditional trust in our living Lord.

Faith Alone

For Adventists the final question becomes crucial. "Do you depend upon some achievements of your own to contribute to salvation or is it only by God's grace through faith?"

Many Adventist statements related works to faith in an orthodox manner. In *Steps to Christ* Mrs. White wrote:

> There are two errors against which the children of God — particularly those who have just come to trust His grace —especially need to guard. The first, . . . is that of looking to their own works, trusting to anything they can do, to bring themselves into harmony with God. He who is trying to become holy by his own works in keeping the law, is attempting an impossibility. All that man can do without Christ is polluted by selfishness and sin. It is the grace of Christ alone, through faith, that can make us holy.
>
> The opposite and no less dangerous error is, that belief in Christ releases men from keeping the law of God; that since by faith alone we become partakers of the grace of Christ, our works have nothing to do with our redemption.
>
> But notice here that obedience is not a mere outward compliance, but the service of love. The law of God is an expression of His very nature . . . If our hearts are renewed in the likeness of God, . . . will not the law of God be carried out in life? . . . Obedience - the service and allegiance of love - is the true sign of discipleship . . . Instead of releasing man from obedience, it is faith, and faith only, that makes us partakers of the grace of Christ which enables us to render obedience.[57]

"The faith which justifies," comments *Bible Readings for the Home Circle* on Galatians 5:6, "is the faith which works."[58] Arthur S. Maxwell explains, "Acceptance of divine grace brings a man under a thousandfold greater compulsion to obey God — the compulsion not of force but of love . . . Being under grace is not an excuse for sin, but an added reason for righteous living."[59] Asked point-blank if Adventists teach that people must obey the Ten Commandments in order to be saved, Maxwell answered,

> No. Salvation is by grace alone. There is only one way of salvation. That is faith in the atoning death of Jesus Christ. No one can "work his way" into the kingdom of God. No degree of obedience, no works of penance, no amount of money entitles anyone to any divine favor. Nevertheless, "faith without works is dead." Keeping the commandments is the result, the evidence, of salvation. It is a matter of love, not legal duty. "If ye love me," said Jesus, "keep my commandments" (Jn. 14:15).[60]

And the contributors to *Questions on Doctrine* concur:

> Salvation is not now, and has never been, by law or works; salvation is only by the grace of Christ . . . Nothing men can do, or have done, can in any way *merit* salvation. While works are not a *means* of salvation, good works are the inevitable *result* of salvation. However, these good works are possible only for the child of God whose life is inwrought by the Spirit of God . . . This relationship and sequence is imperative, but is often misunderstood or reversed.[61]

Even as the fruit of faith, however, Adventists do not expect believers to keep all the varied commands of the Old Testament. The ceremonial law of Moses as distinct from the moral law of God in the Ten Commandments, was but a shadow of Christ's work to come. Since His crucifixion the ceremonial law has been done away. It is carnal and enslaves anyone who attempts to keep it. But the Ten Commandments are not abolished. They are spiritual and bless with liberty the one who keeps them."[62] With a different interpretation of the fourth commandment many orthodox Christians would agree with this distinction. Others would insist that even the Old Testament moral law as stated in the Ten Commandments inscribed in stone is done away (II Cor. 3), but nine of the Ten Commandments are then maintained as stated in the New Testament.

But one wonders how the Adventists, consistent with their own view, advocate Old Testament dietary requirements. Some Adventists may declare their freedom from them as legal taboos, but find the distinction between clean and unclean animals prior to Moses and keep them as a health program.[63] But a popular booklet sent by the Adventists to a letter of inquiry teaches something quite different. In *Just What Do You Believe About Your Church?* Fordyce W. Detamore writes:

> As long as Isaiah 66:15-17 is in this Book, how dare I tell you it doesn't make any difference whether or not you eat swine's flesh and other unclean foods? . . . It would be much easier for me to say, "Go ahead and eat as you please; you needn't worry about those things any more." But God says those who are eating unclean things when He comes will be destroyed. Wouldn't you rather I put it plainly so that you'll not be deceived and be destroyed at our Lord's coming?[64]

Threats like this are difficult to harmonize with the assurances that salvation is by grace through faith and not of works.

The same confusion seems to exist with respect to the Ten Commandments. On one page Detamore says, "We keep the law of God because we are saved, not because we can save ourselves by lawkeeping." But on another page he asserts, "Everywhere the Bible stresses the imperativeness of obedience if one would be saved." He concludes a section captioned "Standard of Judgment":

> The best summary of the requirements for salvation is found in the counsel Jesus gave the rich young nobleman (Matthew 19:15-21), "If thou wilt enter into life, (1) keep the commandments, . . . and (2) follow me." There is no other hope of salvation. By the standard of God's holy law we shall be judged in the day of reckoning.[65]

In order to help, observe that no human has ever kept the law. No one was ever saved by keeping its requirements. It actually serves not to save but to show men how desperately they need to be saved. The law speaks "that all the world may become guilty before God. Therefore by the deeds of the law shall no flesh be justified in his sight: for by the law is the knowledge of sin" (Rom. 3:19-20). By quoting the commandments Christ sought to show the rich young ruler his need of "righteousness without the law . . . even the righteousness of God which is by faith of Jesus Christ unto all and upon all them that believe" (Rom. 3:20-21). The young man's claim to have kept all the law from his youth revealed his failure to perceive its fundamental import. This Jesus brought out by asking him to sell all that he possessed, and give it to the poor. Sorrowfully he did not love God with his whole heart or his neighbor as himself. But upon these two commandments rests the whole law (Mt. 22:37-40).

The acid test of Adventist views on the law is the doctrine of the Sabbath. From the creation to the end times the fourth commandment is held to be part of God's unchanging moral law. Roman Catholic papal authority changed the day of worship from Saturday to Sunday, Adventists teach. And Protestantism has not completed the reformation by continuing seventh-day worship. In the end times, now upon us, the truth is being restored. Those who receive this light and conviction are responsible for obedience to this command. As the final great religious crisis breaks upon mankind papal power will head up forces in opposition to God, requiring first-day worship (Dan. 7:25; Rev. 13:16,17) as the mark of the beast. At this future time the day of worship will be a worldwide test of loyalty to Christ or antichrist.[66]

Those who do not now see the obligation of the fourth commandment are not punished, but in the future crisis Sunday worship will be sufficient grounds for condemnation. Then all who keep the commandments of God (Rev. 12:17) will join the remnant church in worshiping on Saturday. Unquestionably salvation in the future is by faith and Saturday worship, by grace and law keeping. While at present God overlooks Sunday worshipers' ignorance, and does not execute the deserved penalty for flouting His commandment, the Sunday worshipers have in fact committed gross sin. All evangelicals are still daughters of Babylon; they bear the mark of the beast. This, Herbert S. Bird predicts, "will not appeal to many as being a solid basis for Christian fellowship."[67] And it is not more solid for asserting without qualification that salvation is by grace through faith.

The Adventist's case for seventh-day worship does not hold up. If the fourth commandment is a moral principle it may be kept by worship on one day of the seven, Sunday. Nowhere does the New Testament reaffirm the fourth commandment, although it repeats the other nine. As a matter of fact whoever makes sabbath days a test of fellowship disobeys the New Testament. And in the Biblical context weekly sabbaths are not excluded (Col. 2:13-17; Gal. 4:9-11; Rom. 13:8-10; 14:4-6,10,12,13).

Considering the centuries of tradition in which the Jewish writers of the New Testament were saturated, it is remarkable that they so emphasized the first day of the week. On the first day Jesus rose from the dead (Jn. 20:1). He appeared to the ten disciples on that same day (Jn. 20:19). One week later he appeared to the eleven disciples (Jn. 20:26). The promised Pentecostal coming of the Holy Spirit occurred on Sunday (Lev. 23:16). That significant Sunday after the first message proclaiming Christ's death and resurrection, 3000 received the Word, were baptized and added to the church (Acts 2). At Troas the Christians assembled for worship the first day of the week (Acts 20:6-7). And on the first day of the week the Corinthians made their contributions. As the Sabbath commemorated not only creation but also divine deliverance from Egypt (Deut. 5:15) it is fitting that the first day commemorate the Creator's mighty deliverance of Christ from the grave.

The change in the day of worship was not made, as Adventists claim, centuries after New Testament times by the Pope. It was already in the New Testament and it was recognized by writers shortly thereafter. References to first-day worship may be found in the writings of Ignatius, Bishop of Antioch A.D. 110; Justin Martyr, A.D. 100-165; Barnabas, A.D. 120-150; Irenaeus, A.D. 178; Bardaisan, A.D. 154; Tertullian, A.D. 200; Origen, A.D. 225; Cyprian, A.D. 200-258; Peter of Alexandria, A.D. 300; and Eusebius, A.D. 315.[68]

These historical facts undermine the whole Adventist interpretation of first-day worship as the mark of the Beast. If the Roman Pope is the Beast, no particular significance can be attributed to his alleged change of the day of worship. And first-day worship cannot be any particular "mark" of the Beast. It follows that no special place can be given to the keeping of the fourth commandment in interpreting the reference to those who keep the commandments of God (Rev. 14:12). Neither is it necessary to apply the power designated in Daniel 7:25 to Rome.

The great test of allegiance to God distinctively proclaimed by Adventists is not an explicit, unmistakable Scriptural test. It is a theory of well-meaning, but mistaken men and women. No such human fabrication should be made a fundamental of faith, rending the body of Christ. And surely no such theory should be added to the simple gospel invitation. Salvation never has been or will be conditioned upon the seventh-day worship. Nowhere do we read, "Believe on the Lord Jesus Christ and keep the seventh day and thou shalt never come into condemnation." But repeatedly we read, "If there had been a law given which could have given life, verily righteousness should have been by the law. But the scripture hath concluded all under sin, that the promise by faith of Jesus might be given to them that believe (Gal. 3:21-22). However commendable a law may be, added to faith it destroy's God's way of salvation. The Bible teaches, "If by grace, then it is no more of works: otherwise grace is no more grace. But if it be of works, then is it no more grace: otherwise work is no more work" (Rom. 11:6). Much as we should like to say Adventists base their hope on grace alone, some of their positions on Old Testament dietary requirements and seventh-day worship seem to contradict it. Would to God that every Adventist could give the testimony of Rev. Don Phillips, who came to realize the full meaning of grace. In a *Power* account of his conversion from Seventh-day Adventism he testified, "It is wonderful to be free from legalism, and to *know* that I can serve and glorify Him (the Lord)."[69]

In view of apparent Adventist inconsistency on keeping the law for salvation, how can Walter R. Martin pronounce Adventism evangelical? Martin's judgment follows from his interpretation of the position in terms of Arminianism. Among evangelicals is a school of thought named after James Arminius (1560-1609) which opposes Calvinism's stress on divine election and eternal security. Arminians often deny eternal security, teaching that a person may believe, enjoy the saved life for a time, and then forfeit salvation by unbelief. Seventh-day Adventists classify themselves as Arminians. In *Questions on Doctrine* they teach,

> that God, by an eternal and unchangeable decree in Christ before the world was, determined to elect from the fallen and sinning human race to everlasting life those who through his grace believe in Jesus Christ and *persevere* in faith and obedience; and, on the contrary, had resolved to reject the unconverted and unbelievers.[70]

This seems to make divine election conditional not only upon faith, but continued works. In the judgment of Walter Martin, the Adventist position,

> though tinged with legalism has its roots in the basic Arminian position that one receives salvation as a free gift of God, but once he has received this gift, the believer is responsible for its maintenance and duration, and the chief means of accomplishing this is "commandment-keeping" or "obedience to all the laws of God."[71]

From this interpretation Martin's conclusion follows.

> Since Adventists are basically Arminian, we may logically deduce that, in a sense, their salvation rests upon legal grounds. But the saving factor in the dilemma is that by life and by world-wide witness, Adventists, like other so-called Arminians, give true evidence that they have experienced the "new birth" which is by grace alone, through faith in our Lord and His sacrifice upon the cross. One would be callous and uncharitable indeed not to accept their profession of dependence upon Christ alone for redemption, even though there *is inconsistency in their theological system*.[72]

While declaring Adventists evangelical, as sympathetic an interpreter as Martin admits their system is tinged with legalism and is contradictory. But over against this deficiency he sets their life and service. Others like Bird, Douty and Hoekema respect the life and service but feel the doctrinal divergence is far more serious than that between Calvinism and Arminianism. In pointing out Adventist errors, however, these writers do not regard *Questions on Doctrine* representative of Adventism or fail to limit marks of evangelism to Scripturally explicit conditions of eternal life.

In contrast, this study has evaluated the Seventh-day Adventism that is represented by *Questions on Doctrine* and has employed Scripturally explicit tests related to salvation for determining whether the movement is evangelical. What, then, are the results by these standards?

The Seventh-day Adventist position is evangelical in respect to statements about the priority of the gospel, the deity of the incarnate Christ, His substitutionary atonement, His resurrection from the dead and the necessity of personal faith in Christ.

One can hardly acknowledge the many agreements with evangelical and orthodox theology and at the same time class the Adventists with cults which deny the priority of the gospel, the deity of Jesus Christ, the need for substitutionary atonement, the bodily resurrection or the necessity of personal faith. In all fairness it seems overly harsh to class Seventh-day Adventism with Jehovah's Witnesses, Mormonism, and Christian Science.

There remains reason to question, however, whether Seventh-day Adventism is evangelical in respect to an infallible source of truth in addition to Scripture (Mrs. White's writings), the doctrine of investigative judgment detracting from the completeness of Christ's atonement, and the necessity of law-keeping as a condition of justification.

Are these differences typical of those between Calvinists and Arminians within evangelicalism? If one denies that Adventism is evangelical, does he exclude all who deny eternal security from evangelicalism? These differences, in all three cases, are not characteristic of Arminianism. Arminians do not claim an authoritative body of writings like Mrs. White's. Arminians have not constructed a doctrine like that of the heavenly sanctuary or the investigative judgment compromising the completeness of Christ's work at Calvary. And Arminians do not make any such legalistic use of the commandments as a whole or of the fourth comamndment in particular. The interpretation that takes Adventist doctrine to be Arminian — even in *Questions on Doctrine* — seems too generous.

If Adventism is not ardent evangelicalism or typical cultism then how shall it be classified? The evidence supports Dr. Lindsell's judgment that it is similar to Romanism. Like Romanism Adventism has added to the Scripture a body of tradition it seems reluctant to break. Like Romanism Adventism depreciates the completeness of Christ's work of atonement, and like Romanism Adventism adds to grace the necessity of human works as a condition of salvation. Needless to say, both Adventism and Romanism assert the deity of Christ, His atonement for sinners, and His resurrection from the dead. In other respects their systems may not be analogous except in asserting that the Pope changed the day of worship, but these are highly significant.

The error of Romanism and Adventism resembles that of the Galatians. Adding to the apostolic authority, the Galatians who started with grace were told not to continue in the flesh (Gal. 3:3). They gave ground to those who would pervert the gospel (1:7). But there are not two gospels. Only one message can be identified with the gospel of Christ which Paul had delivered to them. It was not a man's gospel — Paul received it not from man but God (1:11-12). When that gospel was jeopardized by others who believed it but added the Old Testament requirement of circumcision, Paul asked, How can you compel the Gentiles to live like Jews (1:14)?

The Adventists under an influence beyond Scripture (Mrs. White) seem similarly to pervert the gospel by asking Gentiles to live on the sabbath like Jews. Paul underlined the fact that a person is not made righteous due to works of the law, but through faith in Christ. By the works of the law, Paul insisted, no flesh shall be justified (2:16). He then argued if righteousness were through law, Christ died to no purpose (2:21), and that anyone who thought he could be saved by the law, if he did not obey all the laws, was under a curse (3:10). What a tragedy if Adventists today find themselves under that curse when long ago Christ liberated us from it by being made a curse in our place (3:13)! We are not children of the slave woman who represents Mount Sinai (4:24) and the earthly Jerusalem, but we are the children of the free woman and her children.

Although there may be agreement otherwise, Christ's death does not benefit those who depend on circumcision or Sabbath-keeping (5:2). Whoever aims at justification by law-keeping has been dissevered from Christ and has fallen from grace (5:3-4). A bit of yeast raises the whole lump of dough. Believers conduct their lives not according to fleshly cravings, but by the Spirit. But those guided by the Spirit are not under law (5:18). For even the keeping of God's law may be motivated by fleshly desires (6:12-13). With Paul our boast should be in the cross of Christ. What counts is not Saturday-keeping or Sunday-keeping, but a new creation (6:15).

The evangelical's great concern, then, is for individuals in Adventism to be new creatures. Whatever the evaluation of Adventism in general, evangelicals must confront individual Adventists with the one true gospel. If an Adventist will admit that Mrs. White was fallible, that no record in heaven could possibly bring a believer into condemnation, and that works of the law such as Sabbath-keeping are not necessary conditions of salvation, then, other things being equal, he should be acknowledged an evangelical. On the other hand, if the Adventist persists in defending Mrs. White's infallibility, the investigative judgment and the necessity of Old Testament diet and Sabbath-keeping, he chooses for himself the Galatian heresy and places himself under the curse of the law (Gal. 3:10) and of preaching another gospel (Gal. 1:8-9).

FOOTNOTES

1. Donald Grey Barnhouse, "Are Seventh-day Adventists Christians?" *Eternity*, VII (September, 1956), p. 45.
2. Walter R. Martin, "What Seventh-day Adventists Really Believe," *Eternity*, VII (November, 1956), p. 43.
3. *Questions on Doctrine* (Washington, D. C.: Review and Herald Publishing Association, 1957), p. 9.
4. Walter R. Martin, *The Truth About Seventh-day Adventism* (Grand Rapids: The Zondervan Publishing House, 1960), p. 7.
5. *Ibid.*, p. 10.
6. Harold Lindsell, "What of Seventh-day Adventism?" *Christianity Today*, April 14, 1958, pp. 13, 15.
7. Herbert S. Bird, "Another Look at Adventism," *Christianity Today*, April 28, 1958, p. 16.
8. Bird, *Theology of Seventh-day Adventism*, (Grand Rapids: Wm. B. Eerdmans Publishing Company, 1961), p. 129.
9. Merrill C. Tenney, "Review of the Truth About Seventh-day Adventism," *Eternity*, May, 1960, p. 40.
10. Norman F. Douty, *Another Look at Seventh-day Adventism* (Grand Rapids: Baker Book House, 1962), p. 189.
11. *Ibid.*, p. 188.
12. Anthony A. Hoekema, *The Four Major Cults* (Grand Rapids: Wm. B. Eerdmans Publishing Company, 1963), pp. 377-388.
13. *Ibid.*, p. 389.   14. *Ibid.*, p. 394.   15. *Ibid.*
16. *Ibid.*, p. 400.   17. *Ibid.*, p. 403.
18. *Questions on Doctrine*, p. 11.
19. *Ibid.*, p. 22.   20. *Ibid.*, p. 28.
21. *Bible Reading for the Home Circle* (Washington, D. C.: Review and Herald Publishing Association, 1931), pp. 189-194.
22. Arthur S. Maxwell, *Your Friends the Adventists* (Mountain View, California: Pacific Press Publishing Association, 1960), p. 87.
23. *Questions on Doctrine*, p. 93.
24. Walter R. Martin, *The Truth About Seventh-day Adventism*, pp. 96-97.
25. *Questions on Doctrine*, p. 93.
26. Harold Lindsell, "What of Seventh-day Adventism?" *Christianity Today*, March 31, 1958, p. 7.
27. Walter R. Martin, *The Truth About Seventh-day Adventism*, p. 113.
28. *Ibid.*, pp. 100-104.
29. Ellen G. White, *Testimonies* I, 563, cited by Martin, p. 107. Italics his.
30. *Questions on Doctrine*, pp. 101-102.
31. Arthur S. Maxwell, "What Is a Seventh-day Adventist?" *A Guide to the Religions of America*, ed. Leo Rosten (New York: Simon and Schuster, 1955), p. 133.
32. *Questions on Doctrine*, pp. 11-12.
33. *Ibid.*, p. 515.

34. Norman C. Douty, *op. cit.*, pp. 48-50.

35. *Ibid.*, pp. 52-64; Herbert S. Bird, *Theology of Seventh-day Adventism*, pp. 64-71.

36. *Questions on Doctrine*, pp. 650-652.

37. *Ibid.*, pp. 653-658.   38. *Ibid.*, p. 349.   39. *Ibid.*, p. 350.

40. *Ibid.*, pp. 362-364.

41. Leroy E. Froom, *The Prophetic Faith of Our Fathers* (Washington, D. C.: Review and Herald Publishing Association, 1954), IV, 661.

42. Ellen G. White, *The Great Controversy* (Washington, D. C.: Review and Herald Publishing Association, 1911), p. 420.

43. *Questions on Doctrine*, p. 420.

44. Ellen G. White, *op. cit.*, p. 483.

45. *Ibid.*, p. 482.

46. *Questions on Doctrine*, p. 442.

47. Samuel Zwemer, E. W. Hengstenberg, J. V. Rotherham, and J. Russell Howden in the *Sunday School Times* (Jan. 15, 1927), cited in Walter Martin, *The Truth About Seventh-day Adventism*, pp. 184-188.

48. *Questions on Doctrine*, pp. 397-398.   49. *Ibid.*, p. 400.

50. *Ibid.*, pp. 399-400.   51. *Ibid.*, p. 22.   52. *Ibid.*, p. 66.

53. *Bible Readings for the Home Circle*, 551; 83.

54. Ellen G. White, *Steps to Christ* (Mountain View, California: Pacific Press, 1908), p. 68.

55. *Ibid.*, p. 55.

56. *Questions on Doctrine*, pp. 141-142.   57. *Ibid.*, pp. 65-66.

58. *Bible Readings for the Home Circle*, p. 137.

59. Arthur S. Maxwell, *Your Friends the Adventists*, p. 38.

60. Maxwell, "What Is a Seventh-day Adventist?" p. 136.

61. *Questions on Doctrine*, p. 141.

62. *Ibid.*, pp. 121-134.   63. *Ibid.*, pp. 622-624.

64. Fordyce W. Detamore, *Just What Do You Believe About Your Church?* (Nashville, Tennessee: Southern Publishing Association, n.d.), p. 22-23.

65. *Ibid.*, pp. 32-34.

66. *Questions on Doctrine*, pp. 149-185 (emphasis mine).

67. Herbert S. Bird, *Theology of Seventh-day Adventism*, p. 117.

68. Walter R. Martin, *The Truth About Seventh-day Adventism*, pp. 152-153.

69. Don Phillips, "Taboo: I Was a Seventh-day Adventist," *Power*, Vol. 22, No. 3 (August 16, 1964), p. 6.

70. *Questions on Doctrine*, p. 404 (emphasis mine).

71. Walter R. Martin, *op. cit.*, p. 205.

72. *Ibid.* (emphasis mine).

FOR FURTHER STUDY

ANTHONY A. HOEKEMA, *The Four Major Cults.* (Grand Rapids, Michigan: Wm. B. Eerdmans Publishing Company, 1963). A forceful argument attempting to show that Seventh-day Adventism must be classified as a cult.

HAROLD LINDSELL, "What of Seventh-day Adventism?" *Christianity Today*, Part I (March 31, 1958), p. 6-8; Part II (April 14, 1958), p. 13-15. Presents the view that Seventh-day Adventism is neither cultic nor evangelical, but closest to the legalism of Roman Catholicism.

WALTER R. MARTIN, *The Truth About Seventh-day Adventism.* (Grand Rapids, Michigan: Zondervan Publishing House, 1960). Martin's three years of personal contact and research resulted in this case for accepting Seventh-day Adventism as evangelical.

WALTER R. MARTIN, *The Kingdom of the Cults* (Grand Rapids, Michigan: Zondervan Publishing House, 1965). Against Hoekema and others, Martin writes an appendix replying to those who continue to call Seventh-day Adventism cultic.

Seventh-day Adventists Answer Questions on Doctrine. (Washington, D. C.: Review and Herald Publishing Association, 1957). In response to extensive questioning, this book of more than 700 pages was prepared by a representative group of Seventh-day Adventist leaders, Bible teachers, and editors.

SUGGESTIONS FOR TEACHERS

Good teaching is marked by clarity of purpose. Review the content of this study and attempt to synthesize it in your own mind. This material may best be divided into two sections for two teaching sessions. Put into a few words a statement of objectives for classroom presentation. *Confronting the Cults* differs from some other works on the subject in that its purpose is not primarily negative — refuting false doctrine, but positive — winning cultists to to Christ.

1. Use the lead questions throughout the series to form the major divisions of the teaching sessions. Illustrate the value of these questions in keeping discussion centered on the gospel by moving quickly back to them from irrelevant issues.

2. Anticipate replies Christians may expect to these questions from Seventh-day Adventists. Evaluate the Adventist's position and give specific guidance in answering erroneous beliefs.

3. Build confidence for effective personal witness by helping your group formulate possible approaches and answers. Use simple role playing

situations to involve the group in learning the major doctrines of Seventh-day Adventists. After the material has been studied allow several people to take the position of the Adventist in confronting the evangelical believer. Let others assume the role of evangelicals. Simulate a conversation.

SAMPLE LESSON PLAN

SESSION 1

Aim

To guide the class to a knowledge of Seventh-day Adventist teaching on divine authority, the priority of the gospel and Christ.

To help the class develop skills of witnessing through the use of questions and proper handling of Scripture.

Approach

Lead a discussion on the attempt to consider Seventh-day Adventism evangelical.

Outline

I. Divine Authority — Revelation
   Question: "Do you base your teachings on revelations other than the Bible?"

II. The Gospel's Priority
   Question: "Is your main business the proclamation of the gospel of Jesus Christ?"

III. The Doctrine of Christ
   Question: "Do you believe that Jesus is the Christ, the eternal Word of God who has come in the flesh?"

Conclusion and Summation

SESSION 2

Aim

To guide the class to a knowledge of what Seventh-day Adventists believe about redemption, Christ's resurrection, faith and grace.

To help the class members develop skill in handling the Scriptures as they contact Seventh-day Adventists.

Approach

Review briefly the three key questions of the previous session.

Outline

   I. Redemption
      Question: "Do you believe that Jesus died for your sins?"

  II. The Resurrection of Christ
      Question: "Do you believe that Jesus Christ arose from the dead bodily?"

 III. Personal Faith
      Question: "Are you personally trusting Jesus Christ as your redeemer and Lord?"

 IV. Grace and Law Keeping
      Question: "Do you depend upon some achievements of your own to contribute to justification, or is it only by God's grace through faith?"

Conclusion and Summation

6

The Bible, The Christian, and
Students of Unity

"Are you dissatisfied with your life and the way in which things are turning out for you? Have you felt, deep inside, that there should be something better for you but that you have not yet been able to find the way to attain it?" Questions like these introduce some 50 million pieces of literature published annually by The Unity School of Christianity, Lee's Summit, Missouri.

In place of personal discontent Unity promises all-around satisfaction. "Do you truly desire sufficiency in all things, freedom from fear, health and harmony, wisdom and fulfillment? If you sincerely want a change in your pattern of life, if you want to be happy and free and whole, there is a way you can have all these things — and much more besides!"[1] A school rather than a church, Unity seeks to help anyone, regardless of church affiliation, "to find health, peace, joy and plenty through his day-by-day practice of Christian principles."[2]

"What have you found in Unity?" Professor Marcus Bach asked people in many Unity centers. They said: an honesty about religion, a teaching that makes sense, physical healing, the inspiration of *Daily Word* (a devotional booklet), a challenge, a religion that can be lived, practical teachings, a wonderful Sunday School for my children, a new approach to religion, no talk about sin or punishment, a happy religion, a God of love, the creative power of thoughts and words, prosperity, the meaning of prayer, not to be afraid of God, and the real meaning of Jesus Christ.[3]

Unity reveals its secret of abundance most popularly in *Daily Word* and *Weekly Unity*. Adapting the program to varied needs, Unity publishes several monthlies: for working people *Good Business*, for youth *Progress*, for boys and girls *Wee Wisdom*, and for the sick *Unity*. Annually some fifty books and numerous pamphlets flow from Unity presses.

Furthermore, spiritual counseling and prayer are always available at Lee's Summit or Unity churches in many large cities. Twenty-four hours a day you may pick up the phone and "Dial-a-Prayer." Or you may submit your request to the local center and know that others will pray with you. If you wish, a duplicate of your petition will be sent to Lee's Summit. An average of 7,000 letters a day require the prayer of 150 Silent Unity workers in relays of 6 to 8 continuously. Symbolizing the unbroken stream of silent prayers for over 70 years a light at headquarters is always burning.

> Go to a telephone wherever you may be, at any part of the earth, at any moment of the day or night, and call LAclede 4-3550, Lee's Summit, Missouri. From a room where the light shines a voice will ring out for your heart to hear, "Silent Unity!" and the light that shines in this window will begin to shine for you.[4]

The story of Unity begins in 1886 when Myrtle Fillmore, who had suffered for years from tuberculosis and malaria, heard Dr. E. B. Weeks, a mental healer. One of his statements transformed her life: "I am a child of God and therefore I do not inherit sickness." Since life is intelligent, she began to reason, it can be directed by thinking and talking. "Then it flashed upon me," Mrs. Fillmore wrote, "that I might talk to the life in every part of my body and have it do just what I wanted. I began to teach my body and got marvelous results." Mrs. Fillmore spoke words of truth to each life center silently and aloud until the organs responded. After asking divine forgiveness for misusing her body she determined to entertain no anxious or negative thoughts. In two years Myrtle Fillmore was no longer an invalid.[5]

A cripple from infancy, her husband several months later finally applied the healing principle. Gratified with the results Charles Fillmore wrote, "My chronic pains ceased. My hip healed and grew stronger, and my leg lengthened until in a few years I dispensed with the steel extension that I had worn since I was a child."[6]

Through the Fillmores' counsel and prayer others found healing. In order to share more widely the principles of health Charles Fillmore left the real estate business and published his first paper in 1889. Long before more recent emphases on the power of positive thinking, his journals featured abundance, health, self-confidence and courage. Today thousands follow the Fillmores' affirmation of life. "Live!" they proclaim, "Live free! Live whole! Live eternally!"[7] One rainy morning Unity workers were heard to exclaim,

> Our happy hearts just sing and sing!
> We thank Thee, God, for everything![8]

And one of the Unity favorites is Hannah More Kohaus' "The Prayer of Faith":

> God is my help in every need;
> God does my every hunger feed;
> God walks beside me, guides my way
> Through every moment of the day.
>
> I now am wise, I now am true,
> Patient, kind, and loving, too.
> All things I am, can do, and be,
> Through Christ, the Truth that is in me.
>
> God is my health, I can't be sick;
> God is my strength, unfailing, quick;
> God is my all, I know no fear,
> Since God and love and Truth are here.[9]

Because Unity is much more interested in meeting human needs than in formulating doctrines,[10] Christians may anticipate difficulty in obtaining specific answers to questions. In an early issue of *Modern Thought* editor Fillmore said,

> He who writes a creed or puts a limit to revelation, is the enemy of humanity. . . . Creeds have ever been the vampires that sucked the blood of spiritual progress in the past, and life can only be kept in the present movement by latitude of thought tempered always by the power that moves the world, love.[11]

It was 30 years before Fillmore's students induced him to write a statement of faith. Even then he added, "We are hereby giving warning that we shall not be bound by this tentative statement of what Unity believes. We may change our mind tomorrow on some of the points, and if we do, we shall feel free to make a new statement."[12]

Nevertheless Unity writings often allude to Truth with a capital "T." Admittedly, no lasting fulfillment in life is possible through self-delusion. Temporary success apart from truth would lead only to greater despair. For their own well being, then, students of Unity should be willing to consider the basis on which to know whether our religious beliefs are true or false.

Authority

Christians may introduce the discussion by asking, "Do you base your teachings on revelations or sacred writings other than the Bible?" Students of Unity will reply, indeed, we do! Each individual frequently receives disclosures of God's life-changing reality for himself.

> Divine revelation is much more common than is understood. The Spirit of truth is revealing the hidden wisdom to thousands on every hand. Poets and writers of Truth are being inspired of the Most High. Quiet citizens in every walk of life are the recipients of the divine word. Every man who has earnestly asked for divine guidance, or who has earnestly desired to do right in the sight of God and man, is being taught by the Holy Spirit.[13]

Revelation, Unity teaches, conveys more than information; it engenders a personal experience of divine life and love. Mrs. Cady, author of the Unity textbook, *Lessons in Truth*, explains,

> We want a revelation of God in us as life, to be made our own personal consciousness as health. We no longer care to have somebody just tell us words from the outside. We want a revelation of God as love within us so that our whole being will be filled with love.[14]

How does an individual recognize a very personal revelation from God? According to H. Emilie Cady, "while you are using the words of Truth, they will suddenly be illumined and become to you the living word within you — the true light which lights every man who comes into the world."[15] Students of Unity identify divine revelation with a sudden intuition which needs no further corroboration to produce a conviction of its truth. Such a self-authenticating insight is considered to be "a flash of the Most High within your consciousness."[16] A silent prayer proposed in *Unity* magazine for repetition on December 3, 1961, read, "I listen to the voice of God and hear it in my convictions."[17] The human mind, then, "is the connecting link between man and God."[18] God's Word is indistinguishable from flashes of insight bringing strong conviction.

The Bible may stimulate revelatory insights, but it is not God's Word. God's Word is "the agency by which God reveals Himself in some measure to all men, but to greater degree to highly developed souls; the thought of God or the sum total of God's creative power."[19] The Bible only "bears 'witness unto the Word' of God" (Acts 14:3).[20] The sacred writings of other religions, although in lesser degrees, also witness to God's creative Word.[21]

> The Scriptures alone are not sufficient to impart spiritual understanding. The Pharisees were inveterate students of the Hebrew Scriptures, but Jesus accused them repeatedly of lack of understanding. The Bible is a sealed book to one whose own spiritual understanding has not been quickened by the living word.[22]

Identification of the Bible with the living Word of God, Unity students insist, has diverted Christians' attention from the one creative Word. Of all the world's sacred writings, however, the Bible receives most frequent mention. When asked why she employed so much Scriptural terminology, Mrs. Cady replies, "I use Scriptural terms simply because I prefer them."[23]

Unity students select the Bible's statements, however, only when they displace its normal meaning with a spiritualized meaning. Charles Fillmore maintained, "It is the spirit rather than the letter of the text, that those worship who have within them the true Christ principle."[24] So every Biblical name is given a "metaphysical" significance — the inner, esoteric meaning as it applies to every unfolding individual.[25] "Our interpretation of the problems, our own ideals, interests and needs."[26] Admittedly, the Unity interpretation of Scripture is made to the measure of the Fillmores' preconceived ideals and interests. After claiming a Biblical basis for all the teachings of Unity, Elizabeth Sand Turner concedes, "It presents the interpretation that came to Charles and Myrtle Fillmore, the co-founders of the Unity School of Christianity, as the result of years of study and prayer."[27]

Examples of the Fillmores' "metaphysical" meanings show how Unity perverts the Bible's message.

> Bread, in the language of mysticism, is substance; that invisible energy of Divine Mind which is the essence of all form. When we say, "Give us this day our daily bread," we are asking of our heavenly Father, "Give us all that we need of Thy spiritual substance in whatever form we need it this day."[28]

In the *Mysteries of John* Charles Fillmore interprets the eleventh chapter concerning Lazarus' resurrection esoterically. "Out of a torpid condition of soul like that of Lazarus the I AM (Jesus) calls forth the living Spirit of the Spirit of the Christ, and reawakens by one word the consciousness of true understanding in man and the quickened perception of his faculties." Every detail conceals a "deep" meaning. "Jesus was at Bethany near Jerusalem. Metaphysically Jerusalem represents a point in consciousness where the spiritual energy of life is strong enough to vitalize adjacent body substance (Bethany, 'home of bread')."[29]

The Bible's last book, Revelation, does not tell about future events when Christ returns. "The Revelation, when interpreted metaphysically tells the story of the unfoldment of the individual soul, and it is filled with lessons that will help us to make our own spiritual overcoming as we meet the dragons and earthquakes of our own experiences in the world."[30]

And what does this practical mysticism find in Jesus' miracle of changing the water to wine? It "represents the change that goes on in the waters of life, or the nerve fluids, as they are brought into vibration by a spiritually quickened man or woman." And, we are told, there is a still more interior meaning. "The six waterpots indicate that, when the six great nerve centers in the body are purified . . . the vibratory power of the voice will become so great that by the spoken word a vessel filled with water may be changed into wine."[31]

Unity's *Metaphysical Bible Dictionary* reveals the hidden meanings of hundreds of Biblical proper names. The "Preface" says that they are "suggestions by no means final," and that no one can "truthfully say that a certain text means such or such a thing and nothing else. A dozen persons may get inspiration in a dozen different ways from one Scripture text."

To help people influenced by Unity teaching, the Christian may first establish that a given sentence, although it may have many applications, has but one meaning. No appeal to Scripture can be decisive until it is admitted that an author intends by a sentence to assert one thing in his context of thought. For example, quotations from Unity publications cannot ethically be used to support views contrary to the author's intention. No amount of "inspiration" could justify that unwarranted procedure. Of course an author's devotional thought may be differently applied by a mother, a teen-ager, a rancher and an astronaut. But the devotional thought must remain unchanged if it be ascribed to the author. Similarly applications of Scripture may vary. But when we claim Biblical authority for an idea, we must be prepared to show from the grammar, the history, the culture and the context that the writer in fact taught that idea. Otherwise the Bible is not used but abused.

The attempt to discover hidden levels of meaning in the Bible is not new. The long history of the Christian church has produced numbers of allegorizers, mystics, pietists, and spiritualizers. Serious students of Unity owe to themselves a survey of interpretations which their forerunners invented in order to get an esoteric blessing. (For this purpose a useful book is Bernard Ramm's *Protestant Biblical Interpretation*, Boston: W. A. Wilde Co.). Contradictory approaches to the Bible have led to the establishment of carefully formulated principles of Biblical interpretation. The sooner Unity students adopt sound ways of getting the Bible's meaning the more they stand to gain. The genuine blessings come from Scripture, not wishful thinking.

Christians may also point out to students of Unity that the Bible is an objective source and norm of truth whether a person subjectively accepts it or not. Surely a person must "see" or intuitively grasp the Bible's meaning before it actually governs his life. But Unity stresses this half of the truth to the exclusion of the objective. Whoever claims to follow the example of Jesus Christ should regard the Scriptures as He did. In the life and faith of the "Way Shower" the Bible was God's Word written. Its teaching did more than witness to the divine Word, it was God's Word written. The human words did more than point to the divine Word. By the inspiration of the Holy Spirit what the Bible writer said, God said (Jn. 5:46-47; 10:35).

That is why Jesus exclaimed, "O foolish men and slow of heart to believe all that the prophets have spoken!" (Lk. 24:25).

Unity students rightly endeavor to apply truth to their practical lives. But to do this they need not destroy the Bible's objective validity. The Lord met life's most severe temptations by applying relevant Scripture literally understood (Mt. 4:1-11). He who perfectly lived "came not to abolish the law and the prophets, but to fulfill (Mt. 5:17). In emphasizing the spirit He did not negate the letter. As a matter of fact He could not have said more emphatically, "For truly I say to you, until heaven and earth pass away, not the smallest letter or stroke shall pass away from the Law until all is accomplished" (Mt. 5:18). The Bible's contrast between letter and spirit (II Cor. 3) is directed not against the sacred writings, but against their hyperliteral misuse. Pharisaic legalism had missed the weightier matters in its magnification of incidentals. Some of Unity's interpretations from geographical associations and other incidentals deserve the same denunciation. Furthermore Judaizers thought they could deliver themselves from the guilt and power of sin by keeping the Ten Commandments. In no way does Paul's accentuation of the Spirit's regeneration challenge the written law's validity for revealing sin's sinfulness. The Pharisees' mistake came in thinking the law could do what God's Spirit alone can do — create spiritual life. So as the Spirit illumines Scripture, He does not destroy the intent of the wording He originally inspired!

By reason of the Holy Spirit's inspiration of Biblical writers, Christians believe the Bible has a unique place in God's redemptive plan. Apart from Scripture men may see God's wisdom and power in His handiwork (Ps. 19:1-6; Rom. 1:18-20). They may also be aware of certain divinely given moral standards (Rom. 2:14-15). But apart from God's prophets and apostles men do not perceive God's gracious plan of redemption. The sacred writings "are able to give you the wisdom that leads to salvation through faith which is in Christ Jesus" (II Tim. 3:15). Furthermore the Bible is a sufficient revelation of truth. Continued redemptive revelation is unnecessary. It is precisely the Bible that God inspired "for teaching, for reproof, for correction, for training in righteousness; that the man of God may be adequate, equipped for every good work" (II Tim. 3:16-17). However noble the intentions, no one enriches his life by reducing the Scriptural message of redemptive grace to natural insights of theistic moralism. Unity's reinterpretations may be just such a reduction.

The Priority of the Gospel

In order to focus attention on the Bible's central message a Christian may ask people in the Unity School of Christianity, "Is your main business the preaching of the gospel of Jesus Christ?" The Biblical gospel offers hope for men who have defied God and championed sin. In order that the guilty may be acquitted and God remain just, Christ endured their deserved penalty. Is this truth at the heart of Unity's teaching? By no means.

Man has committed no sins deserving punishment, according to Unity. And for this notion H. Emilie Cady claims New Testament authority. "Sins in the original text," she says, "does not mean crime deserving punishment. It means any mistake or failure which brings suffering."[32] Furthermore, "Nowhere in the New Testament is the idea conveyed that Jesus Christ came that there might be, after death, a remission of the *penalty* for sin." Why then did Christ come? Christ came that there might be "salvation from mistakes and failures here and now."[33] No one need pray for divine forgiveness from guilt, and "there is no such thing as spiritual death."[34] A short definition of sin is "ignorance."[35]

In our ignorance and lovelessness we may mistakenly criticize and condemn others. "So it is a wholesome thing once in a while to go to God and say, 'I realize that humanly I haven't been perfect; therefore, forgive my sins, forgive my trespasses, and let's start all over again.' "[36] How this plea to an impersonal God can without any just basis change inexorable moral laws remains unexplained. What a man sows, Unity writers often say, he will reap.

Although men make mistakes they find in themselves the power to correct them. As children of God they can release the power to change their thought and consciousness. "Man's sins are forgiven when he ceases to sin and opens his mind to the fact that he is heir only to the good."[37] Sin is first in the mind and is redeemed by a mental process. Wrong thinking is erased from consciousness when we cast all error out of our minds.[38] The power to do this comes from "the Christ." "Turn to His Spirit within you; He will lift you

up, renew and revive you, make you strong, and keep you steady."
The explanation follows. "How will God do it? He works through
His powerful spiritual ideas. The power is in the idea. When you
think the idea, the spiritual power becomes active in you."[39]

This then is Unity's major message: creative ideas cause every
human condition. "The spoken word is the first projection of the
creative power of mind into the realm of form, and further manifestation always follows."[40] Potentially our false ideas create a world
of limitation, evil and misery; our true ideas create a world of unlimited goodness and joy. The power to create a perfect world is
called: the Spirit, the divine spark, the Christ, or the kingdom of
God within you. "The Christ is the invisible activity, substance and
law of all that appears as effect."[41] That is why Emmet Fox can say
in *Life Is Consciousness* that "Before you change your state of
consciousness nothing else can change."[42] By changing your conscious thought, however, all things are possible.

Every problem can be solved by this very simple method:
"*Stop thinking about the difficulty, whatever it is, and think about
God instead.* This is the complete rule, and if only you will do this,
the trouble, whatever it is, will presently disappear. It makes no
difference what kind of trouble it is."[43] We are only admonished to
leave the question of ways and means strictly to God. The possibilities are seriously meant to be absolutely unlimited. When men
fully grasp this power of Divine Mind they "will bring forth offspring
without physical birth; that is, restore life to an organism, or even
form a new organism out of the universal Substance, and breathe
into it the breath of life."[44]

Unity's main business is not to report what Jesus Christ has
done for sinful men, but what sinful men must do to save themselves.
What is the gospel according to the Unity School of Christianity?
"If you want to get nearer to God . . . you must change your
thought and keep it changed."[45] Man's only hope lies in thought control. "Thought control is established by aligning the thoughts with the
mind of Christ, bringing every thought into a harmonious relation
to eternal, unchangeable principles."[46] Nothing Jesus did can control
your thought for you. This you must do for yourself. No one else can
think for you.

The means by which to control your thought are Unity's famous denials and affirmations. For example, when confronted with an appearance of poverty you should "deny that it has any place in God's will for you." One of Georgiana West's ten commandments for prosperity: "Thou shalt not speak the word of lack or limitation." Rather, affirm constantly: "I have faith in the power of my word. I speak only that which I desire to see made manifest." Then decree stedfastly: "I am a living expression of God's abundant good. I receive and distribute His never-failing bounty."[47]

When students of Unity claim to believe the gospel of Christ, Christians must understand that they believe in the unlimited power of their own affirmations. Charles Fillmore explains,

> The gospel of Jesus is that every man can become God incarnate. It is not alone a gospel of right living, but also shows the way into dominion and power equal to and surpassing that of Jesus of Nazareth. "He that believeth on me, the works that I do shall he do also; and greater works than these shall he do; because I go to my Father (Jn. 14:12).[48]

The Unity "gospel" allegedly comes directly from the "Holy Spirit" (an intuitive flash) its only authorized interpreter.

Christians must remind adherents of Unity that the Holy Spirit first gave the one and only gospel of Jesus Christ. Whoever — a devoted apostle like Paul or a holy angel from heaven — teaches any other gospel comes under the Bible's severest condemnation (Gal. 1:8-9). The Holy Spirit does not contradict Himself. The question is not how good and sincere Unity leaders may have been; the question is whether their main business is Christianity's main business. Plainly, the suggestion that men by creative thought can achieve perfection for themselves and their world is not the gospel of God's grace. Unity's fundamental thesis contradicts the faith once for all given to the saints.

What the Christian gospel denies Unity affirms. Biblically, fallen men are incapable of liberating themselves from the slave market of sin. Their moral and spiritual likeness to God was lost in revolt. Blinded to spiritual truth (II Cor. 4:4), they find it impossible to see things as God sees them. Try as they may, they cannot continuously think God's thoughts after Him. The mind by nature set on the flesh is hostile to God; it does not subject itself to the Law of

God, for it is not even able to do so" (Rom. 8:7). So the gospel
seems to be foolishness (I Cor. 2:14). No amount of denial will
change man's spiritual plight. Endless affirmations at best produce
but a temporary, counterfeit comfort. The Biblical gospel denies that
man can save himself; Unity affirms that man is his own savior.

And what the gospel affirms Unity denies. What men could
not do for themselves Jesus Christ alone has done. He came to seek
and save the lost (Lk. 19:10). The good shepherd will recover
them at immeasurable cost. He must give his life a ransom (Mk.
10:45) and a propitiation (Rom. 3:24-25) as a ground for their
redemption (I Pet. 1:18-19) and reconciliation (II Cor. 5:18-21).
These concepts so crucial to Christianity are not even mentioned in
Unity's massive *Metaphysical Bible Dictionary*. The narrow way to
eternal life is emphatically denied. Jesus said, "No man comes to the
Father but by me" (Jn. 14:6). But Unity denies that Jesus' is the
only name under heaven given among men, by which we must be
saved (Acts 4:12).

Christians of course admit a measure of truth in Unity's emphasis on the power of mind to influence the body. Research shows
that functional diseases are often related to mental conditions. These
psychosomatic illnesses require treatment of the mind as well as the
body. But medical science does not attribute all illness to undesirable
thought patterns. There are structural problems which remain unaffected by anxiety or peace of mind. Within limits the Bible itself
recognizes a power of mind over body (Prov. 15:13; 17:22; 23:7).

Christians also recognize, however, the reality of demonic forces.
God is not the one and only reality. Divine power is not the only
causal agency at work in the world. Satan and his hosts have rebelled
against the Creator. And God has not purposed to remove all the
effects of sin at present. For reasons both wise and holy, God
permits men to face real difficulty, testing, illness and death. Like
Christian Science, Unity defines all evil as "unreality; error thought;
a product of the fallen human consciousness; negation." And like
Christian Science, Unity assumes that "Apparent evil is the result
of ignorance, and when Truth is presented the error disappears."[50]
Evil involves far more than the mind. The whole person, like Satan
himself, rises up against his Creator. From the inside out he must be
regenerated, not by any act of human flesh but by a direct act of

God (Jn. 1:13; 3:3-8). Until students of Unity realistically recognize the radical nature of evil they will not see the need for Christ's objective atonement or for the Holy Spirit's subjective regeneration. What the Christ of Calvary and the Spirit of Pentecost can do, can never be done by any mere thought control. Unity will never meet sinful man's deepest need so long as its main business is "a spiritualized course in how to win friends and influence people!"[51] A Christian's major task is proclaiming the gospel of Jesus Christ (I Cor. 15:1-4).

Christ

Distinctively Christian faith is directed by the Biblical gospel to truth concerning Jesus Christ Himself. Christians believe something very significant about Him. Therefore they ask friends in Unity: "Do you believe that Jesus is the Christ, the eternal Word who was God and became flesh?"

Typical statements in reply will convey "metaphysical" meanings. According to Unity the Father, the Son, and the Holy Spirit are not three Persons. So Christ cannot be the second Person of the Trinity. Unity teaches that the Father is Principle, the Son the Ideal, and the Holy Spirit the formative Word.[52] For the religious terms, Father, Son, and Spirit, Mr. Fillmore substituted the "metaphysical" terms mind, idea, and expression, or thinker, thought, and action.[53] Rejecting the orthodox doctrine of three persons in one essence, Unity maintains that the all-encompassing Mind, the all-loving Mind, and the all-active manifestation are "one fundamental Mind in its three creative aspects."[54]

When students of Unity speak of the Christ, they do not refer to the second person of the Trinity, but to divine ideas, and particularly the ideal of a perfect man. Before God created man the Christ-ideal was envisioned. In so far as that perfect pattern has been achieved in a person he is in Christ. Just as the eternal Word or idea was God, so the higher spiritual self is divine. "The Christ is the higher self of man."[55]

Each of us has within him the Christ, just as Jesus had, as we must look within to recognize and realize our sonship, our divine origin and birth, even as He did. By continually unifying ourselves with the Highest by our thoughts and words, we too shall become sons of God, manifest.[56]

Jesus of Nazareth was not the Christ but a man who perfectly expressed the eternal Christ principle. Since all men may realize the Christ ideal in them as Jesus did, He is not uniquely divine. Jesus, Unity maintains, is not God's only begotten Son. Like Christian Scientists, students of Unity fail to affirm that Jesus of Nazareth is the eternal Christ. "Jesus represents God's idea of man in expression; Christ is the idea in the absolute."[57]

Every event in the life of Jesus is interpreted as an expression of God's ideal for man. Jesus' first coming portrays "The dawning in mind that spiritual man is the real Son of God."[58] Jesus' birth at Bethlehem of Judea teaches that, "the principles of Truth have laid hold of the intelligent substance of Spirit (Bethlehem), and through praise (Judea) have brought the Christ into manifestation."[59] Herod, the personal ego, tries to destroy the Christ in us. Christ is taken down into the subconscious (Egypt) for protection. In the temple at the age of twelve Jesus represents man's growing consciousness of sonship with God. As healer Jesus pictures the I AM harmonizing all mental and bodily conditions. The "twelve" disciples typify the twelve faculties of the human mind functioning under the direction of I AM. Ella Pomeroy's *Powers of the Soul* devotes a chapter to each of the twelve: faith, strength, wisdom, love, power, imagination, will, understanding, order, zeal, elimination, and life.[60]

Jesus' temptation shows that the place of overcoming is within man's consciousness. The devil is the adverse consciousness built up in ignorance and disregard of divine law. What did Jesus demonstrate when He went up into the mountain to pray and was transfigured?

> Prayer always brings an exalted or rapid radiation of mental energy, and when it is accompanied by faith (Peter), love (John), and judgment (James) there is a lifting up of the soul that electrifies the body; the raiment (the aura surrounding the body) shines with glistening whiteness.[61]

Riding into Jerusalem on an ass Jesus represented the Christ taking charge of animal nature and inaugurating a new order. Judas illustrated "the personal self of the body whose center of consciousness is in the sex function." At the crucifiixion of Jesus the human consciousness of a perishable body died. Jesus resurrected the body by putting into it the true state of consciousness. We can resurrect our body just as Jesus resurrected His. In sum, "If the mind has grasped the capacity and power of spiritual ideas then the appearance of Jesus will be understood."[62]

Because Jesus so perfectly demonstrated the power of positive thoughts, students of Unity call Him the "Way-Shower." He came, they say, "to awaken man to the possibilities of his own nature."[63] All may demonstrate thought control as He did. This should be kept in mind when evaluating the fact that each class session begins, "Jesus Christ is the head of Unity School. We are now open, receptive, and obedient to His instruction and guidance."[64]

Counting on an openness to the Lord's directives, Christians may present to students of Unity Jesus' view of Himself. Did the Master declare Himself a human being who more perfectly than any other demonstrated the creative power of thought? Or did Jesus Christ claim that before the foundation of the world He was with the Father? Jesus told about His glory with the Father before the world was (Jn. 17:5). Neither Jesus nor the Jews to whom he spoke had a merely representative sense in mind when He said, "Truly, truly, I say to you, before Abraham was born, I AM" (Jn. 8:58). Contrasting Himself with God's prophets, Jesus related the parable of the vineyard (Mk. 12:1-6). The vine-growers, having killed the owner's hired servants, also killed the owner's beloved son who was sent into the vineyard (Mk. 12:7-8). Jesus clearly looked upon his relationship with the Father as different in kind, not merely degree, from that of created representatives. Having already existed, the Father sanctified Him and sent Him into the world (Jn. 3:17; 10:36).

Furthermore Jesus claimed prerogatives that no merely human representative of God has. He could forgive sins (Lk. 7:48; Mk. 2:10-11). He deserved the same honor as the Father because he has the power to raise and judge the dead (Jn. 5:21-22). Charles Fillmore made some stupendous affirmations, but never went so far as to say, "He who does not honor the Son does not honor the Father who sent Him" (Jn. 5:23). When Jesus said "I and the Father are one" (Jn. 10:30), He meant far more than a oneness of mind and purpose such as believers may have with God. In the context He claimed the power for sustaining eternal life equal with that of the

Father. He said, "I give eternal life to them; and they shall never perish, and no one shall snatch them out of my hand." After asserting the same thing of the Father He concluded, I and the Father are one (i.e., in eternal and irresistible power) (Jn. 10: 27-30). No great man in Unity or any other religion could say, "I am the way, and the truth, and the life; no one comes to the Father but through me" (Jn. 14:6). At His trial Jesus declared, "But from now on the Son of Man will be seated at the right hand of the power of God." They asked, "Are you the Son of God, then?" and He said to them, "Yes, I am" (Jn. 22:70). And following His resurrection our Lord left His disciples with these words, "All authority has been given to me in heaven and on earth" (Mt. 28:18).

Whoever desires to follow the teaching of Jesus must confess Him to be the Son of God in a sense far more profound than other men are. While men are created in the likeness of God, Jesus alone was eternally begotten of God (Jn. 1:1). There is a vast difference between making and begetting. A carpenter makes a house, something very different from himself. But a carpenter begets a son, a being of the same nature as himself. Men bear some traces of their creator's skill, but are very different from God. Jesus, on the other hand, as the only begotten Son is of the same nature as God the Father.

From all eternity Jesus was not mere idea in the Father's mind, but a divine Person in fellowship with the Father. He was the object of the Father's love (Jn. 17:24) and glorification (Jn. 17:5). Now in heaven He actively intercedes for believers as their great High Priest (Heb. 4:14-16). No mere idea does that. It was the eternal, personal Christ who became flesh and dwelt among us (Jn. 1:14,18). Therefore Christians believe not that Jesus merely represented the Christ, but that Jesus of Nazareth was the Christ! And that is what men believe in order to receive eternal life. The gospel of John was written, not that interpreters might make mysteries out of each word, but "that you may believe that Jesus is the Christ, the Son of God; and that believing you may have life in His name" (Jn. 20:31). Because standard Unity doctrine does not assert that Jesus of Nazareth was the eternal Christ, Christians lovingly ask whether students of Unity have the life which is in His name alone.

In coming to earth in human form the eternal Christ chose to live as a servant and subject Himself even to the cross. During His life, therefore, Jesus did not at all times exercise His divine powers. Intentionally He put Himself in the position of those who are mere creatures. That is why He could say, "The Father is greater than I" (Jn. 14:28). He was no less God's eternal Son; He was God's unique Son procuring redemption in human flesh.

It was as difficult for some in New Testament days as it is for students of Unity today to believe that the babe of Bethlehem was God. The problem in earlier days was that human flesh was thought to be the source of evil and would contaminate a holy God. So some thought the Christ could not actually inhabit human flesh. Unity faces a similar problem because it denies the reality of all matter. According to Fillmore's *Revealing Word* matter is

> man's limited concept of divine substance that he has "formed" in consciousness; a thought of substance as dense, solid, weighty, and separate from the spiritual life that underlies it. When man is quickened by the Spirit he knows the Spirit to be all in all, and he gives all thought to this reality.[65]

Matter, however, as part of God's creation is not inherently evil, and not to be ignored. The eternal Word who was in the beginning with God and who was God (Jn. 1:1) became flesh (Jn. 1:14). This very point became the test of genuine Christian faith before the New Testament was completed. That test of true teaching from God's Spirit is highly relevant to people in Unity today. "By this we recognize the Spirit of God: Every spirit that acknowledges Jesus Christ as having come incarnate is from God: while every spirit that does not acknowledge Jesus is not from God; it is the spirit of Antichrist" (I Jn. 4:1-3). May students of Unity yield to God's Spirit and confess that the eternal Christ Himself "became flesh" and lived among us (Jn. 1:1,14,18).

Redemption

According to the gospel, Jesus Christ died for our sins (I Cor. 15:3). In all the affirmations of Unity is this one found? To help focus on the exact point ask students of Unity, "Do you believe that Jesus Christ's shed blood is the one ground on which God forgives your sin?"

At first Unity replies may sound Biblical. "The blood of this Christ man is the very essence of His life. It will cleanse our life if we accept it, and we shall become new creatures." Christians must ask what Unity's references to Christ's blood mean. "The crucifixion of Jesus illustrates the crossing out of the son of man, which is followed by the resurrection of the Son of God. The blood thus shed on the cross represents the denial or erasing of the natural life from consciousness and the Resurrection, the substitution in its place of the life of the spiritual man."[66] At the cross Jesus exemplified the divine ideal for man. Just as the Father gave up Jesus we must give up false ideas our minds have begotten. We must replace the illusion that man inevitably sins with the "truth" that men are really perfect sons of God. In that way Jesus' blood cleanses our lives and we become new creatures.[67]

The tract, *Jesus Christ's Atonement*, by Charles Fillmore, correctly says, "Unless you perceive that there is something more in the doctrine of Jesus than keeping up a worldly moral standard as preparation for salvation after death, you will fall far short of being a real Christian." A negative "Thou shalt not" moralism must be replaced, Fillmore then proposes, by the dynamic power of ideas. Mental discipline day after day and night after night overcomes the mind's inertia and produces a consciousness of ourselves as sons of God right here and now, regardless of appearances to the contrary.[68] In this entire work nothing is said about Jesus' objective atonement for our sins. According to Unity the spiritually dead must raise themselves. Jesus did nothing more than set an example of creative thought.

Christians fully appreciate the hollowness of a merely objective atonement which does not produce new creatures. And Christians devoutly try to follow the great example set forth by Jesus Christ. His death is an example of love (Eph. 5:1-2), humility (Phil. 2:3-8), endurance under hostility (Heb. 12:1-3), and suffering for the sake of others (I Pet. 2:21-25).

But the atonement of Jesus Christ is far more than an example. By giving His life Jesus Christ provided a ransom to liberate men from the slave market of sin (Mt. 20:28; Jn. 8:36; Rom. 8:2; Eph. 1:7; Tit. 2:14; I Pet. 1:18; Rev. 5:9). Jesus also propitiated (appeased) God's righteous wrath by offering Himself a sacrifice in place of sinners who deserved death (Isa. 53:5-6; Rom. 3:25; II

Cor. 5:21; Gal. 1:4; Eph. 5:2; Heb. 9:28; I Pet. 3:18; I Jn. 2:2; 4:10; Rev. 1:5). Furthermore Christ's death provided the basis for the sinner's reconciliation to God (Rom. 5:10; II Cor. 5:19-20; Eph. 2:12-16; Col. 1:20-22).

Christ's objective sacrifice is the *sine qua non* of pardon for sin against God. "Without shedding of blood there is no forgiveness" (Heb. 9:22). No endless affirmations to the contrary will change that divine law. The power of Fillmore's words cannot nullify the power of God's Words! Unity's efforts to produce new life are doomed so long as God's basis for granting eternal life is rejected. Only on that basis can God remain just and justify believers (Rom. 3:26). Repeated subjective affirmations do not reconcile sinners to God. That is done only by the once-for-all objective atonement of Jesus Christ.

Renewal of the mind (Rom. 12:1) is the fruit of reconciliation with God. Having received Christ's free gift of righteousness (Rom. 5:12-21), the believing sinner is transformed from the inside out. He is created by God anew (II Cor. 5:17), raised from a spiritual grave (Eph. 2:1-6), and born a second time (Jn. 3:1-7). So by God's grace the good tree will bring forth good fruit. As the Christian grows in grace he will also grow in knowledge. He is progressively renewed in knowledge according to the image of the One who created him (Col. 3:10). Those disappointed in their efforts to change their own hearts by thought control may freely cast themselves upon the mercy of God. The noble goals they had hoped to accomplish by their own decrees will become a genuine possibility through Jesus Christ who died that all who believe may have life.

The Resurrection of Christ

The good news does not end with Jesus Christ's death for sinners. It reports His triumphant resurrection from the grave. The Bible conditions salvation upon belief that God raised Him from the dead (Rom. 10:9-10). Christians wonder whether students of Unity have met that condition. Therefore they ask, "Do you believe that Jesus Christ, having died and been buried, actually rose from the tomb?"

The *Metaphysical Bible Dictionary* plainly says, "Jesus was raised from the dead." What do adherents of Unity mean by affirmations of Jesus' resurrection? Keeping in mind Unity's distinction between the temporal Jesus and the eternal Christ, we may begin to glimpse Charles Fillmore's meaning when he writes, "We know that Christ, the spiritual man, could not have experienced death, burial, and resurrection. The experiences were possible only to the mortal man, who was passing from the natural to the spiritual plane of consciousness."[69]

No miracle occurred the first Easter. An electrical engineer knows how to generate energy through conforming to the laws governing electricity. This energy can be converted into innumerable forms, such as light, heat, and power. Similarly, Georgianna West explains, "The metaphysician knows that Divine Mind, which is living intelligence, has already created the energy that man converts into the forms he desires."[70] Jesus, then, simply chose to withdraw the idea of death with its physical expression and to affirm the idea of life converting it into physical form.

Resurrection, according to Unity teaching, is "The raising of man's mind and body from sense to spiritual consciousness . . . . the lifting up of the whole man into the Christ consciousness."[71] To some degree, we are told, there are resurrections taking place each day in the lives of us all. In the pamphlet *Daily Resurrections* Cleda Reyner declares, "Each moment someone is experiencing resurrection: restoration, revival, a rising again. Every time we doubt, every time we fumble or stumble or fall but gather our forces together and proceed again, we are, I think, experiencing resurrection."[72]

Unsatisfied with "little daily resurrections," the Fiilmores actually taught that they could overcome the processes of old age and death itself. People grow old because they let the youth idea fall asleep. This idea is not dead but is sleeping, and the understanding I AM (Jesus) goes to awaken it."[73] All evidences of old age can be put away by renewing every organ and every part within and without the body. By the principles of Unity Fillmore hoped furthermore, to construct houses in the air and to levitate his body.[74] Fillmore apparently predicted his own resurrection, "I shall with Jesus attain eternal life in the body." At the age of 92 he wrote,

Subscribers are now asking if I mean that I shall live forever in the
flesh body. . . . I expect to associate with those in the flesh and be
known as the same person that I have been for ninety-two years, but my
body will be changed in appearance from that of an old man to a
young man with a perfectly healthy body. . . . Some of my friends
think it is unwise for me to make this public statement that I shall
overcome death, that if I fail it will be detrimental to the Unity cause.
I am not going to admit any such possibility; I am like Napoleon's
drummer boy. I do not know how to beat a retreat and am not going
to learn.[75]

Like the illusion of Napoleon's drummer boy the illusion of
Charles Fillmore met more than its match in actual facts. On July 5,
1948, Fillmore died. His whole approach would seem to be discredited. But a neat rationalization had been provided: reincarnation.
The souls of the departed by sheer desire create other bodies until
they do demonstrate the power of their affirmations over the grave!
The doctrine of reincarnation is admittedly "not a part of the divine
plan and does not lift a man out of moral limitations. It is not an aid
to spiritual growth, but merely a makeshift until full Truth is discerned."[76] The great aim of Unity is resurrection; the idea of the
soul's reincarnation is but a temporary expedient.[77]

To help a student of Unity see the implications of his belief,
a Christian might ask how a soul whose ideas and affirmations are
too weak to sustain bodily life can possibly hope by sheer desire
and affirmation to create another living body. Nowhere does the
Bible teach the possibility of reincarnation. Rather, it everywhere
assumes the urgency and eternal finality of the destiny sealed in the
present life. Already under condemnation men must hear God's
urgent summons commanding all men everywhere to repent (Acts
17:30). "It is appointed unto man once to die and after that the
judgment" (Heb. 9:27). Christ's account of the rich man and
Lazarus provides no ground for hope of deliverance from torment
by some future bodily existence (Lk. 16:19-31).

In the context of New Testament thought, furthermore, to believe that Jesus was raised from the dead (Rom. 10:9-10) was to
believe a miracle. No mere exercise of "right thinking," it demonstrated the power of God freely to act apart from the natural laws of
a fallen world. No man can change the facts of sin and death. The
soul that sins, it shall die. Death passes upon all men because all
sinned (Rom. 5:12). Under divine judgment for all men's sins, the

spotless lamb of God gave up His life. Only the Lord of all could raise Him from the dead. So it served as a "sign" of divine power when the ruined "temple" of His body lived again (Jn. 2:19-22). Jesus' resurrection assures all men that He is no mere man practicing principles of mental healing, but the divinely appointed judge of all men (Acts 17:31).

Believers in the risen Christ receive God's graciously given power for new life. The Christian has genuine basis in God's almighty power for "little daily resurrections." Baptism portrays the Christian's death to the old life and resurrection to the new (Col. 2:12-13). Setting his affections on things above he puts off the unworthy characteristics of his former life and puts on the characteristics of Christ (Col. 3:1-17). All that students of Unity hope to find in their spiritualizing of the resurrection story may be had by accepting its literal truth and applying it daily. Here is a realistic basis for demonstrating the powers of divine life here and now. Beyond that, it provides a solid ground for trusting that because He rose we too shall rise (I Cor. 15). The Christian need not despair at the grave of his loved one. Neither need he resort to a notion of reincarnation. One day the powers of the grave will be turned back by the power of the risen Christ!

Personal Trust

Christianity is no mere philosophy, it is a life of personal fellowship with the Person of Christ. Christians who enjoy this communion with their Creator and Redeemer hope to share it with others. It is only natural then that they should ask people in Unity, "Are you personally trusting Jesus Christ Himself as your redeemer and Lord?"

Unity has much to say about faith. It must not be a blind "hope-so," but confidence based on principle. No mere belief, genuine faith must produce results. It is not mere faith in faith, but as Marcus Bach found, faith in an operative reality.[78] The eternal impersonal principles may be counted on. "Faith is built up through denial of all doubt and fear and continuous affirmations of loyalty to the divine idea, the higher self."[79]

Unfortunately Unity confuses faith with magic. Faith becomes a means for compelling God to do what men wish. In Lowel Fillmore's

New Ways to Solve Old Problems a chapter is actually devoted to "Faith the Magic Wand." He says, "Faith becomes the manifestation in tangible substance of the things we behold in our visions (imaginations)."[80] The danger is that faith may become a means to get what we want, not what God wants. "Faith," says Charles Fillmore, "is a deep inner knowing that that which is sought is already ours for the taking."[81]   H. Emilie Cady explains, "Desire in the heart for anything is God's sure promise sent beforehand to indicate it is yours already in the limitless realm of supply, and whatever you want you can have for the taking."[82]

The prayer of faith is not a request dependent upon God's will. God always wills that his people have perfect health and abundant wealth. "God's will for us is not sorrow, loneliness, death, and all other forms of suffering that we usually associate with the expression 'Thy will be done.' "[83] The prayer of faith, then, is more than a request, it is a command. "Listen! 'If Thou wilt' brings no visible answer to prayer. But a definite, positive will-not-be-put-off attitude, a determined 'I will have Thy will done in this matter' is a force that always brings results into manifestation."[84]

The Bible teaches that prayer is no magical compulsion of God's power to suit our purposes. Rather prayer is a means by which to align our purposes with God's. Faith trusts God's wisdom and will more than man's. "And this is the confidence which we have before Him, that, if we ask *anything according to His will*, He hears us" (I Jn. 5:14). Jesus Himself prayed, "My Father, if it is possible, let this cup pass from me; yet not as I will, but as thou wilt" (Mt. 26:39). And the Father's will permitted Him to die for the sins of the world. Three times the apostle Paul asked God to remove his thorn in the flesh. God did not choose to give Paul perfect health, but the grace and strength to triumph over bodily ills (II Cor. 12:8). If any ever had the faith to compel God to grant their desires Jesus and Paul did. Students of Unity would do well to join them in the faith that trusts the Father even through pain and death. In the wilderness Israel demanded some material provisions of the Lord, "So He let them have what they wanted but sent leanness within their soul" (Ps. 106:5).

Before sin entered the world God's purposes excluded sickness and death. Now God allows sin to produce death, but He takes no pleasure in it. For man's ultimate good God may punish (Gen.

3:16-19), chastise (Heb. 12:5-11), discipline (Jn. 15-2), and prove (Job 1:8-12; 2:3-6) fallen men. He is far less interested in our luxuries than in our learning. Persecutions caused Christians to go everywhere preaching the gospel (Acts 8:1-4). Bodily afflictions cause some to trust Christ (Mt. 8:23-27; Jn. 9:3; 11:6,11,15). Nowhere does the Bible minimize or deny the reality of sin or suffering. Rather, it realistically faces sin and all its effects and proclaims God's just and loving plan of salvation. The God-given hope for students of Unity as all others is not Pharisaic pride, but the publican's prayer, God be merciful to me a sinner.

Christians trust Christ, not the creative power of their own thoughts. Jesus Christ is a person, not a principle. And He forgives the sins of all who confess to Him (I Jn. 1:9). If we say we have no sin we deceive ourselves, make Him a liar, and show that His truth is not in us (I Jn. 1:8, 10). But cleansed by faith in the blood of Christ we have fellowship with God and one another (I Jn. 1:3,7). The Christian's prayer is that students of Unity might repent and believe. They may more fully understand genuine communion with Jesus Christ as Christians testify of their own personal fellowship with the living Lord.

Faith Alone

A final question may clarify the Christian gospel for people in Unity. Ask, "Do you depend upon some achievements of your own to contribute to salvation or is it by God's grace through faith alone?"

Little is said in Unity about grace. H. Emilie Cady's *Lessons in Truth* does not teach the fact that sinners who deserve God's wrath may receive His undeserved favor. The *Metaphysical Bible Dictionary* does not define "grace." Apart from one reference in *The Revealing Word* Unity has overlooked one of the most precious aspects of Christianity.

The one mention of divine grace is misconstrued. Although said to be "aid from God in the process of regeneration" (Eph. 2:5), grace is provided not by Christ's cross but His exemplary life "in establishing for the race a new and higher consciousness in the earth."[85] But the Biblical view of Christ's grace is no mere pattern or example that men must try to follow as best they can. Acquittal before God comes "as a gift by His grace through the redemption which is in Christ Jesus whom God displayed publicly as a propitiation in His blood through faith" (Rom. 3:24-25). Not one reason remains for humans to boast (Eph. 2:8,9).

> He saved us, not on the basis of deeds which we have done in righteousness, but according to His mercy, by the washing of regeneration and renewing by the Holy Spirit, whom He poured out upon us richly through Jesus Christ our Savior, that being justified by His grace we might be made heirs according to the hope of eternal life (Tit. 3:5-7).

Unity ignores this perfect relationship to God, including complete pardon before divine justice, imputation of Christ's righteousness, and personal fellowship with God Himself. Unity's concern is so earthly, that it may be of little heavenly good. Human striving is Unity's central emphasis. Cady writes, "Our ways of thinking make our happiness or unhappiness, our success or nonsuccess. We can by effort, change our ways of thinking."[86] It is true that Unity emphasizes this as the outworking of the Christ in you. It is true that Charles Fillmore proclaimed as the greatest words ever spoken: "Christ in you, the hope of glory" (Col. 1:27).[87] But by "Christ" he meant an impersonal, eternal principle. The Christ of Unity turns out not to be the loving Lord who became flesh, lived, died, and rose to renewed joy with the Father, but a person's higher self! Where there is no belief in a personal God there can be no belief in free grace. Students of Unity must come to see that they are not trusting another (Jesus Christ) to release them from divine condemnation, but they are depending upon their own inadequate efforts. Because no man, even in his "better self" could keep God's perfect standards, every student of Unity is doomed to disappointment. All have sinned and come short of the glory of God — Abraham, David, Matthew, John, Paul, Augustine, Luther, and Billy Graham. All deserved God's wrath. But by simple faith in Christ's sacrifice all were reconciled to God. The Fillmores and all their followers also have come short of their own standards, not to mention God's. Christians therefore plead with them to trust the One who died for their sins and rose from the dead. Our only hope of glory is not in our higher self, but in union by faith with the Lord of life, sin, and death.

Summing up we must observe that while claiming to be a school of Christianity, Unity differs from the Christian faith in seven essential respects. (1) The Bible is not divine revelation, but merely fallible human witness to revelation. It may be reinterpreted at will in accord with Fillmore's flashes of insight. (2) Man's primary problem is not sin before a holy God, but mistakes in thinking. So man's primary need is not for the gospel of redemption but examples of denials and affirmations. (3) Jesus is not God incarnate but a man who effectively demonstrated the Christ ideal. (4) At Calvary Jesus made no real atonement for man's sin but exemplified the power of mind over matter. (5) Christ's resurrection was no miracle but another demonstration of thought control. (6) Faith is a magic wand which uses divine principle to satisfy personal desires. (7) In place of divine grace through faith alone Unity stresses human striving to overcome the lower by the higher self.

Zealously seeking to establish their own righteousness, students of Unity have failed like the Israelites of old to submit to the righteousness which comes from God. Our heart's desire and prayer to God is that they might be saved (Rom. 10:1-3).

FOOTNOTES

1. Fannie Sue Grasso, "You Name It," *Weekly Unity*, November 12, 1961, p. 1.
2. *Unity School of Christianity* (Lee's Summit, Missouri: Unity School of Christianity, n.d.), p. 1.
3. Marcus Bach, *The Unity Way of Life* (Englewood Cliffs, N. J.: Prentice-Hall, 1962), pp. 150-51.
4. *The Light That Shines for You* (Lee's Summit, Missouri: Unity School of Christianity, n.d.), p. 7.
5. James Dillet Freeman, *The Story of Unity* (Lee's Summit, Missouri: Unity School of Christianity, 1954), pp. 44-49.
6. *Ibid.*, p. 55.   7. *Ibid.*, p. 195.
8. Marcus Bach, *op. cit.*, p. 94.
9. J. D. Freeman, *op. cit.*, p. 75.
10. J. D. Freeman, *What Is Unity?* (Lee's Summit, Missouri: Unity School of Christianity, n.d.), p. 4.
11. Cited by Marcus Bach, *They Have Found a Faith* (New York: The Bobbs-Merrill Company, 1946), p. 227.
12. J. D. Freeman, *What Is Unity?* p. 5.
13. Charles Fillmore, *The Revealing Word* (Lee's Summit, Missouri: Unity School of Christianity, 1963), p. 170.
14. H. Emilie Cady, *Lessons in Truth* (Kansas City, Missouri: Unity School of Christianity, 1940), pp. 88-89.
15. *Ibid.*, pp. 78-79.   16. *Ibid.*, pp. 18, 79.
17. George E. Carpenter, ed. *Unity*, December, 1961, p. 54.
18. Freeman, *op. cit.*, p. 10.
19. C. Fillmore, *The Revealing Word*, p. 212.
20. *Ibid.*, p. 23.
21. Elizabeth Sand Turner, *What Unity Teaches* (Lee's Summit, Missouri: Unity School of Christianity, n.d.), p. 4.
22. Charles Fillmore, *Mysteries of John* (Kansas City, Missouri: Unity School of Christianity, 1946), p. 65.
23. H. Emilie Cady, *op. cit.*, p. 83.
24. Cited by Freeman, *The Story of Unity*, p. 56.
25. *Metaphysical Bible Dictionary* (Lee's Summit, Missouri: Unity School of Christianity, 1962), p. 6.
26. *Unity School of Christianity*, p. 14.
27. E. S. Turner, *op. cit.*, p. 5. Cf. *Metaphysical Bible Dictionary*, p. 5.
28. Georgiana Tree West, *Prosperity's Ten Commandments* (Lee's Summit, Missouri: Unity School of Christianity, 1963), p. 15.
29. C. Fillmore, *Mysteries of John*, pp. 107, 109.
30. Winifred Wilkinson, *Your Personal Revelation* (Lee's Summit, Missouri: Unity School of Christianity, n.d.), p. 7.
31 *Metaphysical Bible Dictionary*, p. 8.

32. H. Emilie Cady, *How I Used Truth* (Kansas City, Missouri: Unity School of Christianity, 1941), p. 27.
33. *Ibid.*
34. *Attaining Immortality* (Lee's Summit, Missouri: n.d.), p. 3.
35. C. Fillmore, *Mysteries of John*, p. 90.
36. Joel S. Goldsmith, *A Lesson to Sam* (Honolulu, Hawaii: Joel S. Goldsmith, 1959), p. 12.
37. "Sin," *Metaphysical Bible Dictionary*, p. 620.
38. C. Fillmore, *The Revealing Word*, pp. 179-80.
39. *Unity Prayer Guide: Rise Up* (Lee's Summit, Missouri: Unity School of Christianity, n.d.), p. 2.
40. G. West, *op. cit.*, pp. 42-43.
41. Joel S. Goldsmith, *The Fourth Dimension of Life* (Honolulu, Hawaii: Joel S. Goldsmith, 1953), p. 9.
42. Emmet Fox, *Life Is Consciousness* (Lee's Summit, Missouri: Unity School of Christianty, 1962), p. 8.
43. Emmet Fox, *The Golden Key* (Lee's Summit, Missouri: Unity School of Christianity, 1936), p. 5.
44. *Attaining Immortality*, p. 17.
45. Emmet Fox, *The Mental Equivalent* (Lee's Summit, Missouri: Unity School of Christianity, 1962), p. 23.
46. "Thought," *Metaphysical Bible Dictionary*, p. 654.
47. G. West, *op. cit.*, pp. 45-47.
48. C. Fillmore, *The Revealing Word*, p. 88.
49. *Ibid.*, p. 64.   50. *Ibid.*
51. M. Bach, *They Have Found a Faith*, p. 248.
52. C. Fillmore, *Mysteries of John*, pp. 93, 136.
53. "Trinity," *Metaphysical Bible Dictionary*, p. 664.
54. C. Fillmore, *The Revealing Word*, p. 199.
55. "Christ," *Metaphysical Bible Dictionary*, p. 150.
56. *Ibid.*
57. "Jesus," *Metaphysical Bible Dictionary*, p. 345.
58. C. Fillmore, *The Revealing Word*, p. 35.
59. "Jesus," *Metaphysical Bible Dictionary*, p. 346.
60. Ella Pomeroy, *Powers of the Soul* (New York: Island Press, 1948), pp. 1-152.
61. "Jesus," *Metaphysical Bible Dictionary*, p. 347.
62. *Ibid.*, p. 350.
63. C. Fillmore, *The Revealing Word*, p. 111.
64. M. Bach, *The Unity Way of Life*, p. 85.
65. C. Fillmore, *The Revealing Word*, p. 130.
66. L. Fillmore, *New Ways to Solve Old Problems* (Kansas City, Missouri: Unity School of Christianity, 1939), p. 151.
67. *Ibid.*
68. Charles Fillmore, *Jesus Christ's Atonement* (Lee's Summit, Missouri: Unity School of Christianity, 1960), pp. 13, 21.

69. C. Fillmore, *Mysteries of John*, p. 92.
70. G. West, *Prosperity's Ten Commandments*, pp. 123-24.
71. "Resurrection," *Metaphysical Bible Dictionary*, p. 554.
72. Cleda Reyner, *Daily Resurrections* (Lee's Summit, Missouri: Unity School of Christianity, n.d.), pp. 6-7.
73. C. Fillmore, Mysteries of John, p. 110.
74. *Ibid.*, pp. 174-75.
75. Freeman, *The Story of Unity*, pp. 198, 219-11.
76. C. Fillmore, *The Revealing Word*, p. 166.
77. *Ibid.*
78. M. Bach, *The Unity of Life*, p. 148.
79. C. Fillmore, *The Revealing Word*, p. 69.
80. L. Fillmore, *op. cit.*, p. 25.
81. C. Fillmore, *op. cit.*, p. 67.
82. H. E. Cady, *Lessons in Truth*, p. 57.
83. Cady, *God a Present Help* (Kansas City, Missouri: Unity School of Christianity, 1942), p. 25.
84. *Ibid.*, p. 36.
85. C. Fillmore, *op. cit.*, pp. 88-89.
86. H. E. Cady, *Lessons in Truth*, p. 25.
87. Elizabeth Sand Turner, *Your Hope of Glory* (Lee's Summit, Missouri: Unity School of Christianity, 1959), p. 8.

FOR FURTHER STUDY

MARCUS BACH, *The Unity Way of Life* (Englewood Cliffs, New Jersey: Prentice-Hall, 1962). An interesting and sympathetic account of life and thought in Unity.

H. EMILIE CADY, *Lessons in Truth* (Kansas City, Missouri: Unity School of Christianity, 1940). The leading textbook in the movement.

WALTER R. MARTIN, *The Kingdom of the Cults* (Grand Rapids, Michigan: Zondervan Publishing House, 1965), Chapter 14. An evangelical's critique.

JAN KAREL VAN BAALEN, *The Chaos of Cults*, 3rd revision (Grand Rapids, Michigan: Wm. B. Eerdmans Publishing Company, 1960). Chapter 7. A brief evangelical assessment.

SUGGESTIONS FOR TEACHERS

Good teaching is marked by clarity of purpose. Review the content of this study and attempt to synthesize it in your own mind. This material may best be divided into two sections for two teaching sessions. Put into a few words a statement of objectives for classroom presentation. *Confronting the*

Cults differs from some other works on the subject in that its purpose is not primarily negative — refuting false doctrine, but positive — winning cultists to Christ.

1. Use the lead questions throughout the series to form the major divisions of the teaching sessions. Illustrate the way these questions keep discussion centered on the gospel by moving quickly back to them from irrelevant issues.

2. Anticipate replies Christians may expect to these questions from students of Unity. Evaluate the Unity position and give specific guidance in answering erroneous beliefs.

3. Build confidence for effective personal witness by helping your group formulate possible approaches and answers. Use simple role playing situations to involve the group in learning the major doctrines of Unity. After the material has been studied allow several people to take the position of the cultist in confronting the believer. Let others assume the role of a believer. Simulate a conversation. Try various ways of presenting truth in the face of error.

4. Ask members of the class to give their personal testimony of salvation by grace as they would to students of Unity.

SAMPLE LESSON PLAN

SESSION 1

Aim

To guide the class to a knowledge of Unity's teaching on religious authority and the gospel's importance.

To help the class develop skills of witnessing to those who accept the Fillmores' insights as a major source of religious truth.

Approach

Trace the origin of Unity. List factors in its present appeal.

Outline

A. Authority
   Question: "Do students of Unity base their teachings on revelations other than the Bible?"

B. The Gospel's Priority
   Question: "Is the main business of Unity the proclamation of the gospel? What is Unity's major emphasis? Is that the Biblical gospel?"

Conclusion

Sum up the Unity position and the best ways to help people in Unity see the unique importance of the Bible and the gospel.

SESSION 2

Aim

To guide the class to a knowledge of Unity teaching on the person of Christ, His death and resurrection and the need for personal trust in Christ and His grace alone.

Approach

Review briefly the previous lesson and set an attitude favorable to helping students of Unity, not embarrassing them.

Outline

A. The Person of Christ
    Question: "Does the Unity School believe that Jesus is the Christ, the eternal Word who became flesh?"

B. Redemption
    Question: "Do students of Unity believe that Jesus died for their sins?"

C. The Resurrection of Jesus Christ
    Question: "Do people in Unity believe that Jesus Christ arose from the dead?"

D. Personal Faith
    Question: "Do people in Unity personally trust Jesus Christ as redeemer and Lord?"
    Question: "Do students of Unity depend on some achievements of their own to provide justification or is it only by God's grace?"

Conclusion

Sum up the Scriptural teaching on these subjects and challenge the class to confront people in Unity with the gospel.

7

The Bible, The Christian, and Spiritualists

Tearfully we finally leave behind a loved one's fresh grave. In this life we shall not again hear his familiar voice; we shall not again see his familiar form. Not, that is, unless we become Spiritualists!

According to Spiritualism we may see our departed loved one again. His familiar form may materialize before our eyes. Or we may become clairvoyant and see him in the spirit-world. He may communicate with us through coded rappings, or we may hear him speak by clairaudience. At first we may lack sufficient sensitivity to vibrations from the spirits and require the help of a psychically perceptive medium. But the bereaved need not remain in uncertainty or sorrow concerning the departed's continued existence and happiness. Through many different means, Spiritualists insist, the possibility of communication with the dead is very much alive.

Capitalizing upon people's deepest emotions, some swindlers deliberately deceive the sorrowing with stage-managed tricks. Or they use bona fide spiritistic phenomena for unethical purposes. Frauds like these, Palmer Emerson explains, might be called spiritists, but not spiritualists.[1] Their interest is limited to the strange phenomena and "the loaves and fishes" of material profit. Spiritualists, on the other hand, not only know Spiritualism as a science, but accept it as a philosophy and practice it as a religion. Recognizing the reality of the spirit world, the Spiritualist endeavors to mold his or her character and conduct in accordance with its highest teachings. Emphasizing the golden rule, spiritualists may be fine relatives, good neighbors and dependable employees.

Not all interest in Spiritualism is profiteering or religious. While both the insincere and sincere forms probably go back to Old Testament history, recently an attempt has been made to examine spirit-communication from a strictly scientific perspective. Such psychical research includes as well, other forms of extrasensory perception. Parapsychology studies "psychological events which seem to go beyond the normal, recognized, everyday activities of the psyche, providing evidence which seems inexplicable except in terms either of the intervention of some entity other than ourselves or the play of some function other than our known faculties and the senses recognized by contemporary physiology."[2] Although this field is still relatively young, its existence and findings ought not be ignored in religious discussions of Spiritualism.

In one form or another Christians are likely to confront Spiritualism's claims with increasing frequency. Since 1848, when "Old Splitfoot's" raps told the Fox sisters of Hydesville, New York, that his body was buried beneath their house and named his murderer, modern Spiritualism has surged forward. The house rebuilt in Lily Dale, New York, is now a Mecca for thousands of Spiritualists every summer.[3] The *Centennial Book of Modern Spiritualism in America*, issued by The National Spiritualist Association in 1948, described one hundred years of growth in United States Spiritualist Churches.

In 74 years the Brazilian Spiritual Federation claims 3,600 centers and 10 million of Brazil's 61 million population, rating *Time* Magazine's designation as the nation's "fastest growing cult."[4] Normandy may be the beachhead for Spiritualism in France, with hundreds of sorcerers practicing in 300 Spiritualist temples.[5] In all of France, it is estimated, some 75,000 diviners and clairvoyants of all kinds receive annually about 750,000,000 francs (roughly $2,000,000).[6] The English healing medium, Harry Edwards, who frequently receives 2,000 letters a day, compiled statistics showing improvement in 80% of his patients and cures with 30%.[7] Every Sunday night a quarter of a million people in Britain attend meetings to receive messages from the spirits.[6] Attunement with spirit power is becoming big business.

What shall evangelical Christians think of Spiritualism as a religion? Is it a form of Christianity? Are Spiritualist acquaintances forgiven their sins and in fellowship with God? How may a believer in Christ help a Spiritualist? Seven questions may guide discussions to the central message of Christianity and the basis on which it rests.

Authority

In order to help Spiritualists consider the unique importance of Scripture inspired by the Holy Spirit, Christians may ask them, "Do you base your religious teachings on revelations or sacred writings other than the Bible?"

In reply Spiritualists will most likely quote from the National Association's Declaration of Principles: "We affirm that the Precept of Prophecy contained in the Bible is a Divine attribute proven through Mediumship."[9] What does this mean? Spiritualism does not rest on the Bible, but the Bible rests on spiritualistic experiences. B. F. Austin explains, "The Bible so far as it is inspired and true is based upon Mediumship and therefore both Christianity . . . and Spiritualism rest on the same basis. Spiritualism does not depend for its credentials and proofs upon any former revelation."[10] In so far as the Bible displays supernormal knowledge, that is alleged to come from mediums. But the Bible is not in its entirety inspired revelation from God. The real basis of Spiritualism is not the Bible, it is the experience of the individual Spiritualists. For example, Christians believe in life after death as taught in inspired Scripture. But Sir Oliver Lodge said, "I know that certain friends of mine who have died still exist, because I have talked with them!"

Unsatisfied with what stands written, Spiritualists crave secret information. "The underlying thought in all forms of divination is that by employing certain means men are able to obtain knowledge otherwise beyond their reach."[11] God has not deemed it wise to reveal everything. "The secret things belong unto the Lord our God: but those things which are revealed belong unto us and to our children forever, that we may do all the words of this law" (Deut. 29:29). Surely in the Bible we have more than we can fulfill. It is all inspired and profitable that the man of God may be perfect, thoroughly furnished unto all good works" (I Tim. 3:16-17).

What may be said to Spiritualists who remain unwilling to submit to Biblical teaching alone as inspired? For the sake of argument suppose the Spiritualists were right at this point. Suppose people were to obtain guidance now from spirits of the dead. Then to whom shall they go when contact cannot be made? For eighteen years Claude D. Noble tried to contact the spirits of Darrow and Thurston. According to a pact made when they were alive, the survivor would hold an object associated with the deceased on the anniversary of his death and his spirit would knock it out of the survivor's hand. That would break the barrier between life and death. But Noble says, "Nothing has ever happened." And rather than appoint a successor for the fruitless vigil, he adds, "I've been at this for 18 years and nothing has come of it. I think I'll let it die with me."[12] On what shall he base his confidence in life after death? If his life was to be governed by the highest teachings from the spirit world, by what standard has his religious faith and life been governed these 18 silent years?

When communications allegedly do come from the dead, it is a problem to determine whether the message is true or false. Its source could be a "naughty spirit" or *Poltergeist* bent upon deceiving. Such influential Spiritualists as William Crookes and Sir Conan Doyle admitted that there is no known test by which you can tell a bona fide spirit from a deceiver.[13] Furthermore in the afterlife spirits retaining a sense of humor may enjoy practical jokes at our expense! Of one instance, Sir Oliver Lodge said, "Silly spirits wanted to have a game."[14] They may even give bad counsel in fields outside the scope of their knowledge. A University of Michigan professor sued a Detroit medium for $16,000 because at her advice he lost his money in a bad investment. But she claimed in no way to be responsible since she merely put him in contact with Thomas Carlyle, the Scottish essayist and historian.[15]

Spiritualists admit not only that the spirits may deceive, play jokes, and blunder, but that a medium's purported spirit-message may not come from the spirits at all. In accounting for the failure of spirit messages regarding worldly affairs, B. F. Austin alludes to the sitter's very strong desire and will (a frequent circumstance among those consulting mediums) and admits:

> The medium in a sensitive condition is more largely dominated by vibrations of the sitter than by the vibrations of the spirit world and the sitter gets back a reflex of his own mind and will. Sometimes the mortal vibrations of a circle are stronger than those from the spirit realm. A sitter under such conditions gets back the message he has brought.[16]

To take spirit-communiques as the sole source of serious religious commitments, some test must be devised by which to know whether or not they are falsehoods, jokes, or mere self-projections.

But suppose spirit-messages do come and convey truth, how much is really learned? "Take all the spiritualistic messages ever received at their face value," concludes G. W. Butterworth in *Spiritualism and Religion,*

> and they add nothing significant to human knowledge, no fresh scientific truth, no development of art, no pregnant saying. If all that survived were a shadow life, capable of retaining a feeble identity for a time, till like a cloud of smoke it vanished into space we should expect very much the same kind of messages that Spiritualism provides us with today.[17]

Is this a sufficient basis for an entire religion? Granted that the real person does survive the burial of his body, what shall we believe about God and the world, man and sin, Christ and salvation, the Holy Spirit and the Christian life, the Christian church and things to come in our troubled world? On some of today's most urgent religious problems Spiritualism's best contributions have nothing to say.

And just how certain is the Spiritualist's case for life after death? Has immortality been scientifically proved? Spiritualists who claim it has want their theories to be received as a science. What then is the verdict of competent psychical research? Henry Sidgwick, founder of the Society for Psychical Research, related his conclusions to William James, who wrote:

> Like all founders, Sidgwick hoped for a certain promptitude of results: and I heard him say, the year before his death, that if anyone had told him at the outset that after twenty years he would be in the same identical state of doubt and balance that he started with, he would have deemed the prophecy incredible. It appeared impossible that that amount of handling evidence should bring so little finality of decision.

And what was the considered judgment of the noted American psychologist, William James? He continues:

> My own experience has been similar to Sidgwick's. For twenty-five years I have been in touch with the literature of psychical research, and have been acquainted with numerous "researchers." I have also spent a good many hours (though far fewer than I ought to have spent) in witnessing (or trying to witness) phenomena. Yet I am theoretically no "further" than I was at the beginning; and I confess that at times I have been tempted to believe that the Creator has

eternally intended this department of nature to remain *baffling*, to prompt our curiosities and hopes and suspicions all in equal measure, so that, although ghosts and clairvoyances, and raps and messages from spirits, are always seeming to exist and can never be fully explained away, they also can never be susceptible of full corroboration.[18]

More recent studies may confirm the occurrence of remarkable phenomena, but not the hypothesis that they are produced by spirits. Mrs. Eileen J. Garrett, for years a highly successful medium, has abandoned the spirit hypothesis in favor of a "magnetic field" into which our natural powers can reach. What are now regarded the supernormal perception of the few, she expects to become the gradually accepted powers of the many.[19] At Duke University J. B. Rhine's carefully controlled experiments, with thousands of instances statistically eliminating possibilities of fraud and chance, have, in the judgment of men like Dr. Shaefer, Professor of Physics at the University of Heidelberg, "established the reality of these phenomena as far as telepathy and clairvoyance are concerned.[20] And this is the conclusion of Reginald Omez, who writes the volume on *Psychical Phenomena* for the *Twentieth Century Encyclopedia of Catholicism*. Philosopher Antony Flew, in *A New Approach to Psychical Research*, joins the psychologist Thouless in maintaining that "evidence for the reality of the phenomena is now so overwhelming that scepticism can only be justified by ignorance of the experimental results."[21] None of these scholars, however, accepts the Spiritualist hypothesis.

Commitment to Spiritualistic phenomena as the authoritative source and test of truth remains scientifically unjustified, philosophically tenuous, and religiously meager. How tragic to confine oneself to such ambiguous phenomena when Jesus Christ came to give life and life abundantly (Jn. 10:10). He came not to destroy the law and the prophets but to fulfill them (Mt. 5:17-18). Christians, having found abundant life through the written Word (Jn. 20:31), will share their Biblically founded assurance so that Spiritualists may know that they have eternal life (I Jn. 5:13).

It is not enough to accept the Bible as the primary source and final test of truth; it must be soundly interpreted. Christian Scientists accept the Bible as interpreted by Mary Baker Eddy's *Science and Health with Key to the Scriptures*. Mormons accept the Bible as interpreted by Joseph Smith's *Book of Mormon, Doctrines and Covenants,* and *Pearl of Great Price.* Similarly Spiritualists claim that "Modern Spiritualism furnishes the KEY to the Bible."[22] In all three cults the alleged Biblical ideas are extremely different. The one Bible cannot teach flat contradictions.

If anyone seriously wants to know what the Bible teaches, he may discover the author's meaning by studying his entire work in terms of his life, culture, language, style, and purpose. To introduce into any piece of literature "key" ideas unknown to the author is to destroy the intended meaning. At this point every writer who expects a fair hearing must practice the golden rule with other writers. If he alters the meaning of a sentence or paragraph, can he ethically claim the original author's support for the idea? According to the Bible itself people may handle it deceitfully (II Cor. 4:2) and twist it to their own destruction (II Pet. 3:16). Christians are concerned that they themselves and their Spiritualist friends avoid that grave danger.

When Spiritualists assert that their views coincide with primitive Christianity they alter the meanings of Bible writers. Admitting this, D. Mona Berry writes, "By a slight change of name, 'medium' for 'prophet,' 'clairvoyant' for 'discernment of spirits,' 'psychic phenomena' for 'miracles,' 'spirit lights' for 'tongues of fire,' the close affinity of the two systems becomes apparent to all sincere investigators and students."[23] Reminiscent of Mary Baker Eddy's glossary of terms, this "slight change of name" makes the Bible endorse what its writers emphatically opposed! The prophets received their messages, not from spirits of the dead, but from God. Spirits were discerned (I Cor. 12:10) not by clairvoyant apprehension, but by their teaching about Jesus Christ (I Jn. 4:1-3). Biblical miracles, unlike Spiritualistic phenomena, took place in nature and in broad daylight. They served not to entertain or comfort a mere individual but to establish God's redemptive program. And Pentecost was hardly "the greatest Seance in history"[24]—not one voice from departed dead was heard. Rather the Holy Spirit came, with attendant indications like fire and wind, as Jesus promised. Never in the New Testament are Christians engrossed in communing with spirits of their dead. After a thorough examination of alleged spiritualism in the Bible, G. W. Butterworth eloquently says,

When Stephen was stoned and James the brother of John was beheaded, how many disciples must there not have been whose hearts yearned for a word from these brave young men whom they had known and loved? Yet the record is silent concerning them. The early Church, like an army, pursues its way. It knows that some must fall, and their loss is an occasion for mingled sorrow and pride. But it cannot spare time to linger in the thought of them. . . . No doubt their names were recalled in the services of the local churches in which the martyrs were known. Every Christian would be taught that there was a "communion of saints" and that the veil which separated life from death was a thin one. But it was God who mattered. If living and departed were alike in communion with him, they were not far from each other. There the problem must be confidently left "until the day break, and the shadows flee away."[25]

Nevertheless Joseph P. Whitwell says that the NSAC's Declaration of Principles means "belief and acceptance of the truths which are contained in the Bible."[26] Apparently he refers to the "truths" Spiritualists read into the Bible. As George Lawton found, "Spiritualists argue the existence of a spirit world from mediumistic messages and discover mediumistic powers whenever a description of a spiritual world is found. They spiritualize at will preceding philosophies."[27]

In 1907 the Progressive Spiritual Church withdrew from the National Spiritualist Association of Churches, insisting that its members accept a confession of faith based not upon the N.S.A.'s Declaration of Principles but upon the authority of the Holy Bible.[28] However, authorities, even in written form, become insignificant in comparison with their intensely individual experience. "What need has the believer of the verbal testimony of others who are reporting on events which transpired thousands of years previously, what need has he of written authority when he has the testimony of his own eyes and ears!"[29] Spiritualists put the fallible word of departed human spirits above the infallible Word of God's Holy Spirit. How much better to acknowledge the possibility of misinformation in spirit messages and to accept the Scripture as the only inerrant test of truth. Genuine Christian experience never contradicts plain Bible teaching.

Summing up, if for our religious authority we take spirit messages, the spirits may fail to communicate. If they do communicate, we cannot tell whether the message is a lie, a blunder, a joke, or a reflex of our own minds. Because the content of spirit messages is so limited many of our most urgent questions will go unanswered. Even the "proof" for life after death remains a disputed theory. Spiritualism reads into Scripture ideas not held by its authors and denies, in practice at least, that the Bible teaches God's inspired truth.

The Priority of the Gospel

A second question focuses attention on the Bible's central message. Christians may ask Spiritualists: "Is your main business the preaching of the gospel?" What answer may be anticipated?

There may be uncertainty about the nature of the gospel. If so, have them read I Corinthians 15:3,4, where Paul sets forth the gospel he preached. Christ (the anointed one of God the Father) died for our sins, was buried and the third day rose again according to the Scriptures. Anticipated by God's Old Testament people, enacted by Jesus Christ and proclaimed by all his New Testament followers and the church to this day, the gospel is the core of Christianity. Its declaration should be the Spiritualists' major mission.

However, we search Spiritualist literature in vain for emphasis on the gospel. It is not found in the N.S.A.'s Declaration of Principles.[30] Rather, stress falls upon infinite Intelligence, the golden rule, and endless possibility of self-reformation. No urgent call to decision for Christ in this life determines one's destiny. Neither is the gospel featured in Joseph P. Whitwell's interpretation of the Principles.[31] Rather, he teaches, since all men manifest infinite Intelligence all are children of God. They need no rebirth by the Holy Spirit. By personal striving they make heaven for themselves. Spiritualist writings tell us what man through communication with the departed can do for himself, but not what God has graciously done for man through the incarnation, death, and resurrection of Christ. Like Paul's Jewish brethren, Spiritualists "have a zeal for God, but not according to knowledge. For they being ignorant of God's righteousness, have not submitted themselves unto the righteousness of (which comes from) God" (Rom. 10:2-3). So, like Paul, our "heart's desire and prayer" for Spiritualists is that they might be saved (Rom. 10:1).

What then is the main business of Spiritualism? In the broadest sense Spiritualists would present to the world "the newer and fuller gospel of the Harmonial Philosophy."[32] As such Spiritualism purports to "explain the enigmas and riddles of life. It brings all realms of nature under law and asserts that man's whole duty in life is to find out the laws of nature and conform to them."[33] Unquestionably the major source of this rationalism is spirit-messages. And what is the true mission of spirit-messages? B. F. Austin gives four answers to that question:

> First to convince men of the continuity of human life. Secondly to spiritualize our thoughts, affections and lives by instruction and guidance. Thirdly to bring us Consolation in the sorrows and bereavements of life. Fourthly, to enable us to reach through Mediumship exalted and powerful spiritual helpers in the great crises of life.[34]

The preoccupation with spirit messages is based upon the assumption that after death life continues without the body in the same vicinity. No impassable barrier nor immeasurable distance separates the dead from the living. Only the denseness of the physical body with its interests keeps us from observing the spirit world. Our receptors are not properly attuned to pick up the signals of psychic energy. But just as we know there are sound and light waves above and below our sensory perceptibility, so there are psychic forces. A medium has developed the ability to disengage himself from the usual conscious activities and go into a trance. In that state the medium has varying degrees of sensitivity to communications from the spirit world.

Christians may not differ with the Spiritualist description of the next life, but Christians who govern their lives by Scripture decidedly oppose the Spiritualist's attempt to communicate with the dead. According to Jesus' description in Luke 16, the souls of the unsaved rich man and the saved beggar were both separated by an impassable barrier from the living. The rich man who desperately desired to warn his living brothers of future torment, did not hope for any spirit communication with them. The only possibility of communication seemed to be through a resurected body. Even communication with the resurrected dead, Jesus said, would not make his relatives believe.

Knowing the human heart, our Lord said, "If they hear not Moses and the prophets, neither will they be persuaded though one rose from the dead" (Lk. 16:31). The dead cannot communicate with the living and it would be useless if they could.

How then does the Bible account for spiritualistic phenomena which are not fraudulent or psychologically explained? While people cannot contact spirits of the dead, they can contact evil spirits, or demons. The demons are not spirits of dead people, but fallen angels who, in allegiance with Satan, war against God (Eph. 6:12). A girl who made her masters rich by divination at ancient Philippi was possessed by an unclean spirit (Acts 16:16-18). Their income was cut off, however, when in the name of the Lord Jesus Christ Paul and Silas cast the demon out of her. The ministers of Satan employ superhuman knowledge and power for deceitful purposes (Rev. 9:20-21; 16:13-14). No one committed to Christ and righteousness can offer himself to the sinister purposes of the devil (I Cor. 10:21). Any Spiritualist who desires the highest teaching from the world beyond will avoid any practice which might associate him with the father of lies who was a murderer from the beginning (Jn. 8:44).

Whoever knowingly persists in practices subject to satanic control cuts himself off from God and His blessing. Such apostasy in Israel was punished by death. "The soul that turneth after such as have familiar spirits ('controls'), and after wizards, to go a whoring after them, I will even set my face against that soul, and will cut him off from among his people. . . he shall surely be put to death; they shall stone him with stones" (Lev. 20:6,27; Ex. 22:18). God's people could not endanger themselves by association with those who joined forces with the wicked one. "Regard not them that have familiar spirits, neither seek after wizards, to be defiled by them: I am the Lord our God" (Lev. 19:31. No man can serve two masters. The potential for evil in spiritualistic phenomena led to such abominations in Canaan that God had to destroy its seven nations. If Israel yielded to the same temptations, she too would be driven out (Dt. 18:9-14). God is no respecter of persons. In all righteousness He must judge any who knowingly join the devil's conspiracy. So Manasseh, king of Judah, in spite of his position was put to death (II Kings 21:6). Similarly Israel's first king, Saul, who sought the witch of Endor, lost his throne and his life (I Chron. 10:13-14).

In contrast, whoever would receive the blessings Israel enjoyed must, like Josiah, put away every trace of spiritism. We plead with Spiritualists today as Isaiah did long ago, instead of seeking "wizards that peep and mutter should not a people seek unto their God? . . . To the law and to the testimony: if they speak not according to this word, it is because there is no light in them" (Isa. 8:19-20). "Sorcery" is not highly "spiritual"; it is a product of sinful "flesh" (Gal. 5:20). Having forsaken the Biblically revealed gospel of God's grace, sorcerers remain forever "outside" the holy city, Jerusalem (Rev. 22:15).

According to the Bible, then, Spiritualism's main business is nothing short of devilish business. Spiritualists fail to proclaim the gospel to the ends of the earth. In place of our Lord's great commission they put the consulting of spirits. However comforting the temporary results may be, they cannot usurp the place of redemptive truth. Since Satan disguises himself as an angel of light it is not strange that his servants also disguise themselves as servants of righteousness (II Cor. 11:14-15). The apostle Paul long ago warned that there is no other gospel, only perversions of Christ's gospel. Furthermore, he wrote by the Holy Spirit's inspiration, "if we, or an angel from heaven," should preach to you a message contrary to that gospel, "let him be accursed" (Gal. 1:8-9). One who displaces the gospel with spirit messages cannot escape that plain teaching of God's Word. How urgent, then, is the Spiritualist's need to turn from his perverted gospel to the one true gospel.

Christ

In order to help a Spiritualist find firm faith in God, a Christian directs discussion to Jesus Christ. Jesus said, "I am the way, the truth and the life: no man cometh unto the Father but by me" (Jn. 16:6). And the New Testament further asserts that what we think about Christ is crucial. "Whosoever transgresseth, and abideth not in the doctrine of Christ, hath not God. He that abideth in the doctrine of Christ, he hath both the Father and the Son" (II Jn. 9). A Christian concerned for Spiritualists will ask, "Do you believe that Jesus is the Christ, the eternal Word of the Father who became flesh?" (Jn. 1:1,14). Of the eternal Christ manifest in human form John wrote, "as many as received him, to them gave he power to become the sons of God, even to them that believe on his name" (1:12).

What will a Spiritualist be likely to say about Jesus Christ? A clear expression of the Spiritualist belief appears in B. F. Austin's answers to three specific questions.

> Do Spiritualists deny the existence of the historic Jesus? No. The vast body of Spiritualists, including all their representative writers, accept Jesus as an historical character. They do not deny his miracles, though they hold it is impossible to make certain to human minds the happenings of two thousand years ago. Spiritualists as a body venerate the name and character of Jesus and regard him as the world's great Teacher and Exemplar.

> Do Spiritualists believe in the divinity of Jesus? Most assuredly. They believe in the divinity of all men. Every man is divine in that he is a child of God, and inherits a spiritual (divine) nature. Just as a man develops his intellectual and spiritual nature and expresses it in life, he is "God manifest in the flesh." Since Jesus attained to and manifested in a very unusual degree the divine attributes of spirit no spiritualist would question his divinity.

> Does Spiritualism recognize Jesus as one person of the Trinity, co-equal with the Father, and divine in a sense in which divinity is unattainable by other men? No. Spiritualism accepts him as one of many Savior Christs, who at different times have come into the world to lighten its darkness and show by precept and example the way of life to men. It recognizes him as a world Savior but not as "the only name" given under heaven by which men can be saved.[35]

Spiritualists should be fully aware that they deny the plain teaching of Scripture: "Neither is there salvation in any other: for there is none other name under heaven given among men, whereby we must be saved" (Acts 4:12). Jesus is not the only Savior, according to Spiritualists, because He is not uniquely the son of God. Jesus differs from other men only in degree, but not in kind, they say. And they may even put this teaching into the mouth of Christ. For example, in a mimeographed letter to clergymen Samuel Jacoby claims to have heard by clairaudience Jesus saying to him:

> I, Jesus of Nazareth, now offer these living declarations as a solution to the world's manifold difficulties - which the clergy are self-mandated to eradicate - will you so help.

Give to the people the truth that will make them free - to relieve them of the suspense in which you now hold them - burdening them with a soul bondage of a false concept of me - Jesus of Nazareth - as the God of all creation and created things.

I am not the King of Kings nor the Lord of Lords, as has been put upon me by some of your primitive minded men of the old theological school . . . . we were simple Jewish folks - living an honorable life when gossips began to talk that I was the Messiah . . . Why call me the Lord Jesus Christ, I am not the Lord of Creation, or your God as many of you believe to this day - dismiss these foolish things from your minds - erase them from your books of record.

All of you, my brothers, have the Christ Spirit to find within the latent powers of the Godhead of which you are endowed as I was an am today.

We are called the holy family, but we are no more holy than thou, my brother, nor any of our brethren, only in so much that we are humble servants one to another.[36]

In his own handwriting Samuel Jacoby added:

These trancendent declarations ware prepared by the Father's anointed Son Jesus of Nazareth: the Master Teacher: Who now comes to the world's clergy to remove the abominations of the virus of your theological garbage substituted for the golden rule emphasized by the Master Teacher during his great mission to remove the darkness in the people's mind - for ages - and still today on this entire planet - Why?

The style attributed to Jesus seems remarkably similar to the style of Samuel Jacoby! And the ideas of Jacoby also are quite obviously ascribed to none other than Jesus Christ.

If a message from the spirit world supports the orthodox doctrine of Christ's deity, as one from a Julia did, Spiritualists have a ready escape from the contradiction. They say that a spirit at first tends to think in terms of his old faith. In time a spirit like Julia will realize that Christ is no more a divinity than any other man, but is a great person and teacher.[37] The whole structure of dependence on continued spirit messages falls if "God has in these last days spoken unto us in his Son" (Heb. 1:1) and if the inspired Scripture is sufficient to make the man of God thoroughly furnished to every good work (II Tim. 3:16-17). So Spiritualists will never be able to give Christ or the Bible the preeminent place they hold in Christianity. Spiritualism is not "clarified Christianity" as Rev. Ford asserted; it is blasphemously anti-Christian.[38]

The doctrinal test by which to discern the spirits requires an unqualified confession that Jesus of Nazareth, the Christ (Messiah) is of God (in a way other men are not) (I Jn. 4:1-3). One who does not believe that Jesus Christ has come in the flesh is "a deceiver and an anti-christ" (II Jn. 7). Spiritualists should understand the seriousness of their denial of Christ's deity.

In claiming to be the Son of God, Jesus made it clear to the Jews that He was claiming more than to be a member of the human race (a son of God as all men are by creation). The Jews sought to kill Him because He said that "God was his Father, making himself equal with God" (Jn. 5:18). Upon another occasion Jesus said, "Before Abraham was, I am." And the Jews again tried to stone him for blasphemy. They did the same when he said, "I and my Father are one" (Jn. 10:30). If Jesus taught of Himself what Spiritualists teach, His life would never have been threatened. That He claimed to be far more than a teacher or medium is clear when the Jews told Pilate, "We have a law, and by our law he ought to die, because he made himself the Son of God" (Jn. 19:7). To hold as Spiritualists do that Jesus was not essentially one with the Father is to say that Jesus was a liar or a lunatic. He could not have been, like the founders of other world religions, a great interpreter of truth to his age, if the astounding claims He made for Himself were untrue. So great were these claims that one can only conclude He was Himself a deceiver or seriously deluded. Distinguishing Himself from all others, Jesus said, "Ye are from beneath; I am from above: ye are of this world; I am not of this world" (Jn. 8:23). And Jesus Himself explained the consequences of denying this fact: "if ye believe not that I am he, ye shall die in your sins" (Jn. 8:24).

On the other hand, Jesus promised, "He who believes in Me, as the Scripture said, 'From his innermost being shall flow rivers of living water.' But this He spoke of the Spirit, whom those who believed in Him were to receive; for the Spirit was not yet given, because Jesus was not yet glorified (Jn. 38-39). The higher, richer life which Spiritualists properly seek may be found, not in attempted conversation with human spirits, but by faith in Jesus Christ and the consequent reception of the Holy Spirit. Jesus came that we might have life, and that we might have it abundantly (Jn. 10:10). His promise that believers could do even greater works than He had done (Jn. 14:12) was to be fufilled through prayer in Christ's name and through the help of the Holy Spirit who would remain with them forever (Jn. 14:13-16). Very much aware of the sorrow accompanying a loved one's loss, Jesus promised, "I will not leave you as orphans; I will come to you . . . the Helper, the Holy Spirit, whom the Father will send in My name, He will teach you all things, and bring to your remembrance all that I said to you. Peace I leave with you; My peace I give to you; not as the world gives, do I give to you. Let not your heart be troubled, nor let it be fearful" (Jn. 14:18-27).

Faith in Jesus Christ as the eternal Son of God is not for genuine Christians simply a piece of dead dogmatism. By faith in Christ a person begins a life of communion with God's Spirit. The Holy Spirit assures believers of eternal life and leads throughout this life. "For all who are being led by the Spirit of God, these are the sons of God. . . . The Spirit Himself bears witness with our spirit that we are children of God, and if children, heirs also, heirs of God and fellow heirs with Christ" (Rom. 8:14-17). Through faith in Christ and fellowship with the Holy Spirit Christians receive all the values Spiritualists hope to find in psychic phenomena: certainty of life after death, more spiritual thought, consolation and help in the crises of life. But these are not conditioned upon the uncertainties of seances. They are based upon God's unfailing promises (objectively) and upon the inner communion of the Holy Spirit (subjectively).

Spiritualists might ask the Holy Spirit's illumination as they study other evidence in Scripture for Christ's deity. At His birth Jesus was called Immanuel which means God with us (Mt. 1:23). His miracles were not limited to healings; He raised the dead and controlled the forces of nature. When by a word He calmed the perilous storm, men marveled saying, "What kind of a man is this, that even the winds and the sea obey him" (Mt. 8:27)? Unschooled as He was, His teaching is unexcelled. Although at any time he could have called legions of angels or disappeared, Jesus willingly endured the cross for the sake of others. He died. Three days later he came forth from the grave demonstrating to the world that he had conquered sin and death. Thomas, unbelieving in spite of others' reports, finally saw the evidence for himself and exclaimed, "My Lord and my God" (Jn. 20:28)!

Indeed the eternal Word of God (Jn. 1:1) had become flesh and dwelt among us (Jn. 1:14,18). He who existed in the form of God did not regard equality with God a thing to be grasped, but emptied Himself, taking the form of a bondservant, being made in the likeness of men (Phil. 2:6-7). Jesus Christ was the very radiance of God's glory and the exact representation of God's nature (Heb. 1:3). Higher than any angel, Christ's throne (power) is eternal (Heb. 1:8) and immutable (Heb. 1:10-12). The creator of everything that had a beginning (Jn. 1:3) whether in heaven or earth, visible or invisible (Col. 1:16), Jesus Christ sustains everything in existence to this day (Col. 1:17). Furthermore He heads the Church which He purchased with His own blood (Col. 1:18; Acts 20:28). At present His authority in heaven and earth provides the resource for discipling the world (Mt. 28:18-20). He is building His church and the gates of hell cannot prevail against it (Mt. 16:18). But the time will come when He shall again be revealed from heaven, but this time in flaming fire taking vengeance on those who do not know God and obey the gospel (II Thess. 17:-10). As King of Kings and Lord of Lords He shall finally destroy the powers of evil and establish righteousness forever more (Rev. 19:11 - 22:21).

To believe in Christ simply as a great man, different only in degree from other men, is an affront indeed. "For in him all the fulness of deity dwells in bodily form" (Col. 2:9).

Redemption

As it is all-important to believe that Jesus Christ was God manifest in the flesh, it is equally essential to believe that He died for the sins of the world. Christians concerned about the welfare of Spiritualists will ask them, "Do you believe that Christ's shed blood is the only basis for the forgiveness of your sins?"

A Spiritualist's answer may very well begin by attacking the notion of sin. All men are said to be children of God; a spark of divinity dwells in all.[39] Unthinkable then is the idea that men are born with a sinful nature. Furthermore evolutionary science is thought to have disproved the Biblical teaching on man's sin. Writing in *The National Spiritualist*, Frank D. Warren says,

> The orthodox belief is that the human race began with Adam and Eve. But man did not descend from Adam and Eve but ascended through the natural evolutionary process from lower orders of animal life; and the Infinite Intelligence of Nature has decreed that man shall continue to ascend - the world without end.
>
> Science has proven the Garden of Eden story to be a myth; and orthodox religion is, therefore based upon a myth. The faulty logic is simply staggering. How can a mere belief in atonement through the blood of Jesus save man from the "original sin" of Adam and Eve in the Garden of Eden - when there was no Garden of Eden, and no Adam and Eve, and no "original sin?"[40]

Again Spiritualists must choose their ultimate authority. If they follow the general teaching of their movement, they must deny the Bible's plain teaching. However, Christians, like their Lord, acknowledge that God created Adam and Eve at the beginning (Mt. 19:4). Man is the product not of a gradual moral evolution, but of a righteous Creator. Nevertheless, as Genesis 3 teaches, man sinned. "Therefore just as through one man sin entered into the world and death through sin, so death spread to all men, because all sinned" (Rom. 5:12).

While the Bible insists that God created man in His image, it never minimizes the pervasiveness of fallen man's sin. By nature a child of wrath (Eph. 2:3) man is dead in his trespasses and sins (Eph. 2:1). His mind is blinded to spiritual truth (Eph. 4:18), his desires are evil (Eph. 2:3) and his will is enslaved to sin (Rom. 6: 16-17). Try as he will, he cannot liberate himself (Rom. 7:14-25). Although his conduct frequently appears good to human observation, the best of men comes short of God's perfect standard. Has anyone always kept the golden rule? "There is none righteous, not even one" (Rom. 3:10-23). Man's moral disease is incurable, apart from the atonement of Jesus Christ.

Because Spiritualists fail to admit the pervasiveness of sin they think man is capable of improving himself without any atoning provision of divine love. Asked if Spiritualists recognize any special value or efficacy in the death of Christ for man's salvation, B. F. Austin frankly answered,

No. Spiritualism sees in the death of Jesus an illustration of the martyr spirit, of that unselfish and heroic devotion to humanity which ever characterized the life of Jesus, but no special atoning value in his sufferings and death. The world has had uncounted illustrations of men who have died for the truth. All such deaths have a moral value and influence, but not in a sense of a ransom price for the souls of others, as taught by the so-called orthodox churches.[41]

Spiritualists deny not only that Jesus' death was a ransom, but also that it had any substitutionary value as a penalty for others' sins. In 1908, on the sixtieth anniversary of modern Spiritualism, Professor Hiram Corson of Cornell University said,

The literature of Spiritualism . . . is destined to transform, if not, perhaps in time, do away with, theology . . . and to make THE LIFE OF THE SPIRIT the all in all in religion, as it was the all in all with the founder of Christianity. Jesus taught Salvation comes from WITHIN, not from without. There could be no such thing, in the nature of things, as a vicarious atonement for the sins of the world. Man can be AT ONE with the Universal Spirit only through his own spiritual vitality. That alone is Salvation.[42]

The correspondence from Samuel Jacoby makes Jesus to mouth the typical Spiritualist position. "I have also declared to this instrument to say unto you for me, Jesus of Nazareth - that no man is saved by my blood - just because I was nailed to a cross."[43] Jesus goes on to say, according to Jacoby, that he cannot understand why the same honor was not bestowed on Socrates, who drank the hemlock so nobly.

To the Spiritualist, as to many others, the death of a substitute and the justification of a sinner seems unjust. As Converse E. Nickerson put it, "Man must make his own heaven if he will merit such a celestial happiness; were God to deal otherwise with His offspring it would not be justice to either man or God."[44] If Christians are to help Spiritualists accept the gospel they must, like the apostle Paul, explain how God can at the same time be just and the justifier of one who has faith in Jesus (Rom. 3:26). Christians must be ready to answer Arthur Conan Doyle who wrote, "One can see no justice in a vicarious sacrifice, nor in the God who could be placated by such means. Above all, many cannot understand such expressions as the 'redemption from sin,' 'cleansed by the blood of the lamb,' and so forth."[45]

Several issues are involved in the Christian doctrine of redemption. In the first place people rightly emphasize God's absolute
justice. Because of divine justice man's sin must receive its deserved
penalty. What a man sows he will reap. But he has sowed the seeds
of his own death! " The wages of sin is death" (Rom. 6:23). "The
soul that sinneth, it shall die" (Ezek. 18:20). The death of which
the Bible writers speak is not only the separation of the spirit from
the body (James 2:26), but also the separation of the spirit from
God. In the latter sense, often called spiritual death, people are
"separate from Christ, excluded from the commonwealth of Israel,
and strangers to the covenants of promise, having no hope and without God in the world" (Eph. 2:12). They are at enmity with God,
far off from God and strangers to God. Although they owe their very
life and breath to God, morally and spiritually they are not children
of God, but children of the devil (Jn. 6:44). Apart from the intervention of Christ on their behalf they shall remain separated from
God, or spiritually dead, forever.

God would be perfectly just if He allowed all men to reap
exactly what they have sowed in eternal death. But God, against
whom man has rebelled, is no impersonal principle or law, but a
loving being full of mercy and grace. Although we justly deserved
His wrath, He showers upon us His goodness. He satisfies His justice
and provides for pardon in the death of Jesus Christ. It is not that
He sends some third party unrelated to the case. Rather Jesus, who
as we saw was one with the Father, willingly took the place of the
guilty sinner. The offended Judge pronounces the full penalty in
satisfaction of perfect justice. He then steps down from the tribunal,
puts his arm around the shoulder of the condemned, and pays his
complete penalty. At Calvary He suffered not only an excruciating
physical death, but an indescribable separation from the Father —
spiritual death. Although without sin Himself, He bore the awful
consequences of others' sins (II Cor. 5:21).

United to Christ by faith, sinners meet the full demand of divine
justice. And it cannot be exacted a second time. By faith a sinner
forms a partnership with Christ. Then before the bar of divine justice the sinner no longer stands alone and condemned. Christ and the
believer stand together as one. "In Christ" the believer is declared
perfectly righteous and receives the gift of eternal life. Believing in
Christ he becomes morally and spiritually a child of God (Jn. 1:12).

As a member of the divine family he is a joint-heir with Jesus Christ of all the riches of divine glory (Rom. 8:17). Legally adopted into God's family, the believer's sonship depends, not upon what he does, but upon what Christ did. The Christian lives for God, not out of fear, but out of gratitude. Lovingly he does his best to honor the One who ransomed him from the slave market of sin.

The death of Jesus Christ, then, is far more than an example of selfless devotion. It is at the same time the satisfaction of divine justice and gift of divine grace. By the offering of Christ God remains just and justifies those who believe in Christ (Rom. 3:24-26). No longer spiritually dead while they live, believers enjoy spiritual life. Through the blood of Christ's cross they are reconciled to God and at peace with Him. In loving acceptance and joyful communion they fellowship with God for time and eternity. Far from denying the efficacy of His death, as Jacoby alleged, Jesus regarded it the major purpose for His incarnate life. What Christ really said was, "the Son of Man did not come to be served, but to serve, and to give His life a ransom for many" (Mk. 10:45).

Some very religious Jews in New Testament times thought they could earn their own way to heaven without Christ's atonement for their sin. The urgent warning of the book of Hebrews to them still applies to Spiritualists:

> Anyone who has set aside the Law of Moses dies without mercy on the testimony of two or three witnesses. How much severer the punishment do you think he will deserve who has trampled under foot the Son of God, and has regarded as unclean the blood of the covenant by which he was sanctified, and has insulted the Spirit of grace? For we know Him who said, "Vengeance is mine, I will repay." And again, "The Lord will judge His people." It is a terrifying thing to fall into the hands of a living God. (Heb. 10:28-31).

How much better to be able to say with Paul, "having been justified by his blood, we shall be saved from the wrath of God through him" (Rom. 5:9). All who will may enjoy the reassurance of the Scripture which says, "Therefore having been justified by faith, we have peace with God through our Lord Jesus Christ" (Rom. 5:1). The Christian's prayer to God for Spiritualists is that they might know that peace!

Christ's Resurrection

Another integral part of the gospel the Christian shares with his fellow-men affirms that, having died for our sins, the third day Jesus rose from the grave. The Bible says, "if you confess with your mouth Jesus as Lord, and believe in your heart that God raised him from the dead, you shall be saved" (Rom. 10:9). Because the Scriptures make belief in Christ's resurrection a condition of salvation, Christians ask Spiritualists: "Do you believe that Jesus rose from the dead?"

In answering this question Spiritualists may employ terms with meanings quite strange to the Christian context of thought. If they affirm belief in Christ's resurrection, they probably mean that His spirit materialized before sitters at seances. Interpreted as some sort of confirmation of spiritualistic phenomena, they may accept the idea. As such it would be an event repeatable according to laws of the spirit world. But if Christ's resurrection was a once-for-all physical miracle accomplished in the world of ordinary observation by the free and gracious purpose of almighty God, difference will become apparent.

Spiritualists suggest that the appearances of Christ after His death were materializations, the disappearance of His body, apportism, and the lifting of the stone, levitation. All of this, according to the Easter service in the Spiritualist Manual, was "governed by Natural Law." And it is inferred that psychic phenomena today are produced by the same law. So we may be able to do even greater things.[46] Like all spiritualist phenomena, the resurrection of Christ was intended to prove simply that personal identity continues after death.

> What would be the purpose of this demonstration if it had no bearing upon the lives of all of us? Only something mysterious, and undefinable to believe in? The phenomena of nature is [sic!] a mystery until we understand it, but only in unbiased earnest seeking for an explanation shall we find the answer. . . . It is incumbent upon all of us to tarry in the city of Jerusalem. In other words, the seat of knowledge - our churches, classrooms and seances to become endued with power from on high, since all power resides in knowledge and understanding, when the stone of the sepulchre will be rolled away only to find that our departed loved ones are right in our midst - living entities eager to reveal themselves to us.[47]

And Spiritualists like to say that their evidence for life after death is "a million fold stronger than the evidence the world possesses of the truth of historical Christianity" (that is, for the resurrection).[48] Christians, then, must be prepared to discuss the nature of Christ's resurrection, its significance, and the evidence in support of it.

Was the resurrection of Christ an instance of materialization or a unique miracle in the redemptive plan of God? In materialization a spirit allegedly assumes or causes other things to assume a visible form. Ectoplasm (a "supernormal protoplasmic substance") emanates from the body of the medium and produces physical effects. Alleged photographs of such materializations show fogginess around the edges of an "umbilical cord" to the mouth of the medium.[49] An apport is the alleged supernormal movement of an object, and levitation refers to the raising of objects from the ground by supposed supernormal means. All of this is thought to happen in accord with regular psychic laws.

The Spiritualist's hypothesis, ingenious as it may be, fails to account for the varied data of Christ's resurrection. To begin with, the resurrection appearances of Christ were totally unexpected and spontaneous. They were not sought for nor contrived by any preparations in a seance room. Butterworth, after patient analysis, concludes, "There is no genuine parallel between these stories of various and spontaneous appearances, indoors and out of doors, and the carefully prepared phenomena, held in darkened rooms, of modern Spiritualism."[50] The appearances occurred to men and women, to individuals alone and to groups of up to eleven, and on one occasion five hundred at once. Sometimes Jesus talked with them, sometimes He walked with them for miles, sometimes He started a fire, cooked fish and ate with them. His appearance was not foggy in the least. Some at first thought he was a gardener or an ordinary stranger walking along the same road. No medium was required and He was not limited by any ectoplasmic "umbilical cord." As abruptly as the appearances began they ceased. No ghostlike apparition could have transformed the despairing disciples into courageously sincere witnesses to the risen Christ. When the frightened disciples in a locked room at first thought they had seen a spirit, Jesus Himself said, "Why are you troubled, and why do doubts arise in your hearts? See my hands and my feet, that it is I myself; touch me and see, for a spirit does not have flesh and bones as you see that I have"

(Lk. 24:38-39). He then asked if they had anything to eat. They handed Him a piece of broiled fish and He ate it in their sight.

The evidence for Christ's physical resurrection is abundant and varied. That a Spiritualist should claim there are but two eyewitnesses to the resurrection shows utter disregard for evidence. B. F. Austin ignores some 498 others in order to make the exaggerated claim that evidence for Spiritualism is "a million fold stronger!" A quick reading of I Corinthians 15:1-9 apart from the concluding chapters of each Gospel is sufficient to display the irresponsibility of such allegations. But it is not merely a question of the amount of evidence, it is also a matter of the quality of evidence. The Biblical records have for the last two hundred years been subject to the most severe types of literary and historical criticism. Because the various hypotheses based on laws of nature failed to account for aspects of the data, recent scholars have tended to abandon the attempt to give rationalistic explanations of the narrative as it stands.[51] Spiritualists might well follow the experts in this regard.

Furthermore, from the Biblical point of view, the purpose of the resurrection includes far more than certification of a spirit-life after death. Among other things, Christ's resurrection proves to all men that He is the Son of God (Rom. 1:4), and the world's appointed Judge (Acts 17:30-31). It certifies that everyone who believes on Him has received the forgiveness of sins (Acts 10:43) and justification (Rom. 4:25). The risen Christ is exalted above every other creature to head the church and righteously rule the universe (Eph. 1:20-22). Not only the future resurrection of all men, but their entire salvation from sin is secured by Christ's return to life.

Christians should alert Spiritualists to the tragedy of rejecting the risen Christ: "If Christ has not been raised then your faith is vain, and you are still in your sins" (I Cor. 15:14,17). But Christ has been raised! May Spiritualists trust the One who actually can deliver them from sin as well as the grave!

Personal Trust

The gospel calls for belief in the doctrines of Christ's deity, death, and resurrection, and it calls for more. It challenges all men personally to trust the living Lord. Christians are concerned, then, that Spiritualists also experience this vital relationship. Why not frankly ask, "Are you personally trusting Jesus Christ as your Savior and Lord?"

When referring to faith Spiritualists often deplore a blind or superstitious belief. They also tend to minimize the importance of faith in the sense of religious beliefs. The faith in which they are concerned is the faith that "moves mountains." That kind of faith "is the positive assurance of power, energy and omniscience of God's Eternal Spirit, operating through man in our mundane sphere."[52] Although the faith that moves mountains is said to have "small, if any relation to religious beliefs,"[53] it seems to be joined to one — the belief in life after death. No philosophy is complete without a demonstration of unending life.[54] In this regard reason is called the glorious diadem which God provided to distinguish man from the beasts."[55] Furthermore, "without some certain knowledge of God, how can we worship Him?"[56] This certain knowledge seems largely limited to man's personal mortality. But somehow as a result of this one "demonstrated" fact "Spiritualism puts a new and much broader interpretation on many dogmas taught by the leading religious systems."[57] It is sometimes difficult to see how this "more rational" understanding necessarily follows from Spiritualistic phenomena. Why, for example, is God conceived of in an impersonal pantheistic way?

Christians may point out that they too deplore blind faith or superstitious gullibility. It therefore becomes evident that mountain-moving faith has a closer connection to soundly established religious beliefs than Spiritualists want to admit. From the Christian standpoint it seems narrow-minded indeed to accept evidence of a psychic sort only. Would not a more rational approach openmindedly consider evidence from any source whatsoever? Indications of God's existence and concern for man in time and eternity may be seen in experiences of conversion, answered prayer, communion with God, and fellowship with others in Christ. From the realm of history come "signs" like the origin, dispersion, preservation, and reestablishment of the Jewish people. There is the prophetic preparation for Christ's coming and its marvelous fulfillment. Christ's miracles, in nature as well as human life, culminate in His bodily resurrection and attest His deity. The origin of the Christian church, and the change in the day of worship require an explanation. Add the striking phenomena connected with the Bible and the data converge to support belief in the triune God of the Bible and His redemptive plan stretching through time into eternity. Spiritualists are urged to make as thorough a study of Christian evidences and apologetics as they wish others to make of psychic phenomena.

When a Spiritualist is invited to become a Christian he is not asked to abandon intelligent thought in favor of unfounded faith. The relationship of faith to evidence in Christianity is not totally different from their relationships in other fields. In explaining the given data relevant to a problem, several hypotheses may be considered. The rational man accepts the hypothesis which consistently explains the greatest amount of evidence with the fewest difficulties. But in accepting as true a certain explanation, he exercises faith. Another scientist or physician may diagnose the case differently and exercise his prerogative of choosing another explanation. He may have a different faith. The data remains the same; the interpretations differ. So with psychic phenomena. No one denies what men have actually experienced; but some explanations of the phenomena differ from others. And so it is with Christianity. The experiences of Christians for centuries are given; many believe they can be consistently accounted for only on the assumption that the God of the Bible lives and acts in the way the Scriptures teach He does. Many Spiritualists may not have given this hypothesis a fair hearing. They may never have thoroughly studied the Bible for themselves to see whether the facts may support this conclusion. As people who pride themselves on openness to truth and scientific reasoning, they will want to make this examination. They know too well the irrationality of those who dismiss out of hand their own position. Christianity does not stifle investigation; it welcomes it.

While the evidence for faith may be examined, the object of faith remains unseen. Christians believe in the invisible God and trust His redemptive love. No man has seen God at any time, but "the only begotten" of the Father has made Him known to man (Jn. 1:18). Now Jesus no longer walks the earth. The visible linguistic signs of the Bible now disclose the object of Christian faith. Through taking God at His inspired Word, Christians have found fellowship with Christ. And He has sent the Holy Spirit to dwell in their bodies as in a holy temple. Spiritualists who desire a person to person, rather than a person to creed, relationship, may find it in genuine Christian experience. The experience of faith is not simply a belief in the after life; it is continuous fellowship with the eternal Father, the risen Christ, and the Holy Spirit.

Christian faith is urgent indeed. The decisions of this life settle our eternal destiny. Nowhere in the teaching of Christ or the Bible is there any hope of endless reformation. Any responsible person who passes from this life in unbelief has not the slightest hint of hope. "It is appointed unto man once to die, and after that the judgment" (Heb. 9:27). Since a Spiritualist's eternal destiny is settled in this short life, Christians urge him to believe, and to believe now.

Grace Alone

No permanent happiness or peace may be enjoyed unless a person is right with God. Our relationship to God is ultimately our greatest concern. The question is not how we appear to ourselves, or how we compare with others. Sooner or later we shall face the question of how we appear in God's sight. We dare not simply assume that if we try to be good and do our best that this will meet divine standards. To guide us in our relationship to Him God has given us His Word. In the Bible we learn that God is satisfied with nothing short of perfect righteousness — absolute Christlikeness. By this norm every man has fallen short. All stand condemned by strict justice.

However, apart from anything they deserve, God has arranged to give Christ's perfect righteousness. Those who receive this gift enjoy a proper relationship to Him. They are considered by the Father as righteous as His only begotten Son. Christians stress what the Scripture underlines: "a man is justified by faith apart from works of the law" (Rom. 3:28). That is why Christians ask Spiritualists, "Do you depend upon some acts of your own for your salvation, or is your trust in the grace of God alone?"

Concertedly Spiritualists say, we earn our own way. "We affirm the moral responsibility of the individual that he makes his own happiness or unhappiness as he obeys or disobeys Nature's physical and spiritual laws."[58] The interpretation of this seventh article in the National Spiritualist Association's Declaration of Principles follows:

> Man himself is responsible for the welfare of the world in which
> he lives; for its welfare or its misery, for its happiness or unhappiness
> and if he is to obtain Heaven upon Earth, he must learn to make that
> heaven, for himself and for others. Individually, man is responsible
> for his own spiritual growth and welfare. Sins and wrong-doing must
> be outgrown and overcome. Virtue and love of good must take
> their place. Spiritual growth and advancement must be attained by
> aspiration and personal striving. Vicarious atonement has no place
> in the philosophy of Spiritualism. Each one must carry his own cross
> to Calvary's Heights in the overcoming of wrong-doing and replacing
> them with the right.[59]

Spiritualists fail to mention what concerns Christians the most —
a person's standing before God. And they plainly disavow any dependence whatsoever upon anything God has done for sinful man.

A number of assumptions are involved. First, Spiritualists
teach that man has limitless possibilities. A child is viewed as "a
repository of infinite possibilities and not born in sin."[60] All the child
needs is training and an avenue of expression. Nature, figuratively
speaking, says, "Go out into the world. Make something out of
yourself!"[61]

In the second place, Spiritualists assume that knowledge can
produce character. "As man thinks God-like thoughts and comes
into deific conjunction, he also gains an increasing command of
spiritual powers and prerogatives."[62] E. W. Sprague goes so far as to
say, "Right thinking is man's true savior." He explains,

> It very soon establishes his self-reliance, and self-reliance, coupled with
> right thinking will develop man's moral nature to the highest point
> and prepare him to enter into spiritual unfoldment of those higher
> gifts and faculties that place him in communion with spirits in the
> spiritual realms.[63]

According to the third assumption, progress is "absolutely
certain."[64] God's gracious help is not needed. Even the most de-
graded personalities in time attain to the greatest heights.[65] It is
pointed out, however, that it is easier to begin progression in the
earth life. But in various spheres or levels progress persists without
end.

Each of these assumptions fails to fit the facts of Scripture
and human experience. A child is born in sin (Ps. 51:5). His
potentialities are great indeed, but not infinitely great. His sinful

nature taints the best of his achievements. Unworthy motives are mixed with wholesome ones. Even prayer, fasting, and almsgiving may be totally unacceptable to God. Like the Pharisees of old, he may adorn the tombs of the prophets, but in God's sight be corrupt (Mt. 23:14-15,23,29). The finest training produces only an educated sinner. Potentially man's discoveries of nuclear power may be used for destructive as well as peaceful purposes. Human possibility is severely curtailed by human depravity.

For the same reason knowledge does not automatically produce character. We all know better than we do. Man is more than a reasoning machine. His appetites and drives often cause him to act in a way quite irrational. And this is as true with the educated as the uneducated. Our finest cultures produce educated criminals. Some are incorrigibly evil. The Bible realistically acknowledges that they remain so eternally. When Jesus said, "You shall know the truth and the truth shall make you free" (Jn. 8:32), He immediately explained, "If therefore the Son shall make you free, you shall be free indeed" (Jn. 8:36). Truth about this world or the world to come does not regenerate. Man's character is basically changed by faith in the sinless Christ who said, "I am the way, the truth and the life" (Jn. 14:6).

And nowhere in Scripture is support found for the notion of absolutely certain progress. The certainty, apart from divine grace, is defection from God's will. Lucifer, the highest of created beings, thinking he would be like the most High became Satan. Adam and Eve with the finest of surroundings chose to gain knowledge of evil as well as good. Cain slew Abel. Wickedness engulfed the world of Noah, the cities of Sodom and Gomorrah, the land of Canaan, and Israel itself in spite of all God's prophets could do. Christ found the people of his day to be in dire need. The disciples were far from perfect and the early church was plagued with problems. The Spiritualists' attempts to build their own heaven, like those of the tower builders at Babel, end in confusion. What is certain is not progress but despair.

Faith, the antidote to despair, simply accepts God's gracious gift of righteousness. The gift from above, of course, is free. No payments remain; Christ paid it all. Human works are not the price of righteousness with God, but the product of righteousness with God. The ransomed lovingly live for their liberator. So the faith that justified is "faith that works by love" (Gal. 5:6). In the Christian's life good works are the fruit of the Holy Spirit.

The Spiritualist's effort to fulfill moral law fails, because of a deficiency not in the golden rule, but in sinful human nature, the "flesh." The Bible explains, "What the Law could not do weak as it was through the flesh, God did: sending his own Son in the likeness of sinful flesh and as an offering for sin, he condemned sin in the flesh, in order that the requirements of the Law might be fulfilled in us, who do not walk according to the flesh, but according to the Spirit" (Rom. 8:3-4). The person who depends on his own "flesh" for making heaven on earth is destined for disappointment. But the Scripture says, "Whoever believes in him shall not be disappointed" (Rom. 10:11).

Summing up, Spiritualism can in no sense be called Christianity. On all seven tests its stance is anti-Christian. Spiritualism does not accept the Bible as the final standard of faith and practice. It gives priority, not to the preaching of the gospel, but to spirit messages. It denies the deity of Christ, His substitutionary atonement and resurrection from the dead. No personal trust in the living Lord Jesus Christ is advocated and the hope of salvation rests not in divine grace but human attainment. Anyone who thinks that Spiritualism is Christian labors under a delusion — a delusion which may in fact be Satanically inspired. But God can deliver a soul from the grasp of Satan himself!

> The Lord's bond-servant must not be quarrelsome, but be kind to all, able to teach, patient when wronged, with gentleness correcting those who are in opposition, if perhaps God may grant them repentance leading to the knowledge of the truth, and they may come to their senses and escape from the snare of the devil, having been held captive by him to do his will (II Tim. 2:24-26).

A dramatic example of deliverance from demonic control was reported in *Christian Life,* January, 1952. In the inquiry room Evangelist W. Douglas Roe invited a girl of twelve and a middle-aged woman to accept Christ as their Savior from sin.

> Suddenly the young girl began to cry, "I can't accept Jesus Christ as my Savior! . . . I can't! . . . I can't! At this the older woman broke in, "I shouldn't have come here . . . I know I shouldn't."

She wrung her hands. "My spirit will be displeased . . . . I can't
see . . . There are balls of fire in front of my eyes!"

Then she explained she was a medium and that her spirit was
displeased with her presence at a gospel meeting. Rev. Roe understood the problem, found out the name of the spirit, and asked God's
help. Then he took the woman by the wrist and said, "Red Blanket,
I charge you in the name of the Lord Jesus Christ, and through the
power of His shed blood, to leave this woman and this room now!"
At this the woman relaxed and said, "He is fading from my sight.
For the first time I can see you, Mr. Roe." During the next two days
while believers prayed he explained the gospel to her.

> And on the closing night of the meetings, she was the first one to come
> down the aisle as we sang "I've wandered far away from God, Lord,
> I'm coming home." Her action seemed to release the power of the Holy
> Spirit upon the meeting. Before we had finished singing, seventy-five
> persons had come forward. And in that little church a real revival had
> broken out as the powers of hell were overcome by the blood of the
> Lord Jesus Christ.

Christians pray that other Spiritualists may be able to say with her,
"I know there is power in the name of Christ. For through his name
I have cast the spirits out of my home. And through His cleansing
blood, I now receive Him as my Savior and Lord."

FOOTNOTES

1. Palmer Emerson, "Can a Bad Individual Be at the Same Time a Good Spiritualist," *Centennial Book of Modern Spiritualism* (Chicago: The National Spiritualist Association of United States of America, 1948), p. 124.
2. Reginal Omez, *Psychical Phenomena*, translated by Renee Haynes, *Twentieth Century Encyclopedia of Catholicism*, Vol. 36 (New York: Hawthorne Books, 1958), p. 14.
3. Palmer Emerson, *op. cit.*, pp. 8-10.
4. *Time*, October 18, 1954, p. 62.
5. Robert P. Evans, "Normandy: Stronghold for Sorcerers," *Greater Europe Mission News Bulletin*, April, 1953, pp. 4-8.
6. Reginald Omez, *op. cit.*, p. 136.
7. Maurice Barbanell, *This Is Spiritualism* (London: Herbert Kenkins, 1959), p. 157.
8. *Ibid.*, p. 62.
9. *The National Spiritualist*, February, 1954, p. 2.
10. B. F. Austin, *The A. B. C. of Spiritualism* (Milwaukee: National Spiritualist Association Churches, n.d.), question 11.
11. T. Witton Davies, "Divination," *International Standard Bible Encyclopedia* II (Grand Rapids: Eerdmans Publishing Company, 1949), p. 861.
12. *The Endicott* (N.Y.) *Daily Bulletin*, April 4, 1957, p. 5.
13. See J. K. Van Baalen, *The Chaos of Cults* (Grand Rapids: Eerdmans Publishing Company, 1960, third revision), p. 43.
14. Oliver Lodge, *Raymond* (London: Methuen and Co., 1916), p. 194.
15. *The Binghamton* (N.Y.) *Press*, January 21, 1955, p. 8.
16. B. F. Austin, *op. cit.*, question 45.
17. G. W. Butterworth, *Spiritualism and Religion* (London: Society for Promoting Christian Knowledge, 1944), p. 142.
18. William James, *Memories and Studies* (New York: Longmans Green and Company, 1911), p. 174.
19. Eileen J. Garrett, *My Life: as a Search for the Meaning of Mediumship.* See G. W. Butterworth, *op. cit.*, pp. 161-62, 170-71, 182, and J. Stafford Wright, *Man in the Process of Time* (Grand Rapids: Wm. B. Eerdmans Publishing Company, 1956), p. 110.
20. Reginald Omez, *op. cit.*, pp. 30-33, 115-16.
21. Antony Flew, *A New Approach to Psychical Research* (London: Watts & Co., 1953), p. 136.
22. D. Mona Berry, "Comparisons," in *What Is Spiritualism?* ed. Emil C. Reichel (Milwaukee: National Spiritualist Association of Churches, n.d.), p. 39.
23. *Ibid.*, p. 38.
24. B. F. Austin, *op. cit.*, question 23.
25. G. W. Butterworth, *op. cit.*, pp. 101-102.
26. *Spiritualist Manual* (Milwaukee: NASC, 1955), p. 36.

27. George Lawton, *The Drama of Life After Death* (New York: Henry Holt & Co., 1932), p. 560.
28. *Ibid.*, p. 154.   29. *Ibid.*, p. 138.
30. *Spiritualist Manual*, p. 34.
31. *Ibid.*, pp. 35-36.
32. B. F. Austin, *op. cit.*, question 31.
33. *Ibid.*, question 65.   34. *Ibid.*, question 40.
35. *Ibid.*, questions 15, 16, 17.
36. Samuel Jacoby, in a mimeographed letter to Gordon R. Lewis, Pastor, People's Baptist Church, New Castle, Delaware, July 7, 1951.
37. George Lawton, *op. cit.*, p. 66.
38. *Ibid.*, p. 227.
39. *Centennial Book*, p. 24.
40. Frank D. Warren, "False Gods of Tradition," *The National Spiritualist*, April, 1954, p. 4.
41. B. F. Austin, *op. cit.*, question 19.
42. *Centennial Book*, p. 50.
43. Samuel Jacoby, *op. cit.*
44. Converse E. Nickerson, *Modern Spiritualism* (Milwaukee: National Spiritualist Association of Churches, 1959), p. 20.
45. Arthur Conan Doyle, *The New Revelation* (New York: George H. Doran Company, 1918), p. 55.
46. *Spiritualist Manual*, p. 69.
47. Meta H. Baker, "Teachers Department," *The National Spiritualist* Vol. 36, No. 357, April, 1954, p. 5.
48. B. F. Austin, *op. cit.*, question 83.
49. Maurice Barbanell, *op. cit.*, see photographs pp. 48, 88, 144, 176.
50. G. W. Butterworth, *op. cit.*, p. 92.
51. J. A. T. Robinson, "Resurrection in the N.T.," *The Interpreters Dictionary of the Bible IV* (New York: Abingdon Press, 1962), p. 47.
52. Robert J. MacDonald, "Faith and Works," in *What Is Spiritualism?* p. 34.
53. *Ibid.*
54. B. F. Austin, *op. cit.*, question 77.
55. Converse E. Nickerson, *op. cit.*, p. 34.
56. *Ibid.*
57. D. Mona Berry, *op. cit.*, p. 37.
58. *Spiritualist Manual*, p. 34.
59. Joseph P. Whitewell, *op. cit.*, pp. 35-36.
60. *Ibid.*, p. 76.
61. Thomas Grimshaw, *op. cit.*, p. 139.
62. Henry Wood, *op. cit.*, p. 143.
63. *Ibid.*, p. 145.   64. *Ibid.*, p. 148.   65. *Ibid.*, p. 189.
66. V. Douglas Roe. "I Clashed with the Spirit World," *Christian Life*, January, 1952, pp. 21, 64, 66.

FOR FURTHER STUDY

G. W. BUTTERWORTH, *Spiritualism and Religion* (London: Society for Promoting Christian Knowledge, 1944). A scholarly criticism of Spiritualism and its interpretations of Scripture in terms of Spiritualistic phenomena.

GEORGE LAWTON, *The Drama of Life After Death: A Study of Spiritualist Religion* (New York: Henry Holt and Company, 1932). A thorough description of Spiritualist beliefs and practices.

REGINALD OMEZ, *Psychical Phenomena, The Twentieth Century Encyclopedia of Catholicism* Vol. 36 (New York: Hawthorn Books, 1958). A survey of the history, subject matter and methods of psychical research with an evaluation by a Roman Catholic scholar.

J. STAFFORD WRIGHT, *Man in the Process of Time* (Grand Rapids: Wm. B. Eerdmans Publishing Company, 1956), p. 91-137. An evangelical's assessment of Spiritualism.

SUGGESTIONS FOR TEACHERS

Good teaching is marked by clarity of purpose. Review the content of this study and attempt to synthesize it in your own mind. This material may be divided into two sections for two teaching sessions. Put into a few words a statement of objectives for classroom presentation. *Confronting the Cults* differs from some other works on the subject in that its purpose is not primarily negative — refuting false doctrine, but positive — winning cultists to Christ.

1. Use the lead questions throughout the series to form the major divisions of the teaching sessions. Illustrate the way these questions keep discussion centered on the gospel by moving quickly back to them from irrelevant issues.

2. Anticipate replies Christians may expect to these questions from Spiritualists. Evaluate the Spiritualist position and give specific guidance in answering erroneous beliefs.

3. Build confidence for effective personal witness by helping your group to formulate possible approaches and answers. Use simple role playing situations to involve the group in learning the major doctrines of Spiritualism. After the material has been studied allow several people to take the position of the cultist in confronting the believer. Let others assume the role of a believer. Simulate a conversation. Try various ways of presenting truth in the face of error.

4. Ask members of the class to give their personal testimony of salvation by grace as they would to Spiritualists.

SAMPLE LESSON PLAN

SESSION 1

Aim

To guide the class to a knowledge of Spiritualist teaching on religious authority and the gospel's importance.

To help the class develop skills of witnessing to those who accept spirit messages as a major source of religious truth.

Outline

A. Authority
    Question: "Do Spiritualists base their teachings on revelations other than the Bible?"

B. The Gospel's Priority
    Question: "Is the main business of Spiritualism the proclamation of the gospel? What is Spiritualism's major emphasis and what does the Bible say about it?"

Conclusion

Sum up the Spiritualist position and the best ways to help Spiritualists see The unique importance of the Bible and the gospel.

SESSION 2

Aim

To guide the class to a knowledge of Spiritualist teaching on the person of Christ, His death and resurrection and the need for personal trust in Christ and His grace alone.

Approach

Review briefly the previous lesson and set an attitude favorable to helping Spiritualists, not embarrassing them.

Outline

A. The Person of Christ
    Question: "Do Spiritualists believe that Jesus is the Christ, the eternal Word who became flesh?"

B. Redemption
    Question: "Do Spiritualists believe that Jesus died for their sins?"

C. The Resurrection of Jesus Christ
   Question: "Do Spiritualists believe that Jesus Christ arose from the
   dead?"

D. Personal Faith
   Question: "Do Spiritualists personally trust Jesus Christ as redeemer
   and Lord?"
   Question: "Do Spiritualists depend on some achievements of their own
   to provide justification or is it only by God's grace?"

Conclusion

Sum up the Scriptural teaching on these subjects and challenge the class
to confront Spiritualists with the gospel.